TEACHING AND LEARNING FOR THE TWENTY-FIRST CENTURY

EDUCATIONAL GOALS, POLICIES, AND CURRICULA FROM SIX NATIONS

Fernando M. Reimers
Connie K. Chung

EDITORS

Harvard Education Press
Cambridge, Massachusetts

Library of Congress Control Number 2015955160

Paperback ISBN 978-1-61250-922-8
Library Edition ISBN 978-1-61250-923-5

Published by Harvard Education Press,
an imprint of the Harvard Education Publishing Group

Harvard Education Press
8 Story Street
Cambridge, MA 02138

Cover Design: Ciano Design
The typefaces used in this book are Adobe Garamond Pro, Glober, Helvetica Neue, and Solano Gothic MVB

We dedicate this book to the memory of Soraya Salti (1970–2015) and to educators like her around the world, who embody the radiant hope and promise of education in the twenty-first century, in which teachers and students have the means to create the kind of future they want for themselves, their countries, and their world.

CONTENTS

A Comparative Study of the Purposes of Education in the Twenty-First Century

Fernando M. Reimers and Connie K. Chung

As many scholars and observers have noted recently, we live in a "very turbulent moment—whether we are talking about technology, global politics, airline travel, world financial markets, climate change . . . Everywhere we turn, we are confronted with VUCA—volatility, uncertainty, complexity, and ambiguity."[1] The field of education has not been immune to this turbulence, with rapid changes taking place both inside and outside traditional educational systems: the advent of customized, worldwide, online learning, for example, seems to make the boundaries of school buildings and even nation-states permeable; the idea of competency certification in education introduces new possibilities into a system largely driven by automatic academic promotion based on age; and the need to "learn to learn" and the demand to provide an education relevant to students' lives are more pressing than ever in the face of rapid change around the globe.

Education is increasingly perceived as important by the public. A recent global survey of attitudes administered in forty-four countries identified having a good education as the most important factor for getting ahead in life, on a par with working hard and significantly more important than knowing the right people, being lucky, or belonging to a wealthy family. Furthermore, a good education is considered very important to getting ahead in life by a greater percentage of the population in developing and emerging economies than in advanced economies. The percentage of the population who said having a good education was very important to getting ahead in life is 62 percent in the United States, 85 percent in Chile, 67 percent in Mexico, 60 percent in India, and 27 percent in China.[2]

Paradoxically, even as the perception of the importance of a quality education is growing, confidence in schools is dwindling. In the United States, for example, opinion surveys of representative samples of the population document a decline in the percentage of those who express "a great deal" of confidence in public schools, from 30 percent in 1973 to 12 percent in 2015. Today, there is considerably more confidence in the military (42 percent), business (34 percent), the police (25 percent), or organized religion (25 percent), than in schools.[3]

Ensuring that education is relevant to the demands that students will face over the course of their lives—such as the demand to live long and healthy lives, to contribute positively as active members of their communities, to participate economically and politically in institutions that are often local as well as global, and to relate to the environment in ways that are sustainable—is an adaptive challenge. This task requires reconciling multiple perspectives in defining the goals of education in response to different perceptions of what problems and opportunities merit the attention of schools, which are, after all, a relatively recent institutional invention, particularly in their aspiration to teach all children. This task is different from the technical challenge of seeking ways to improve the functioning of schools to help them better achieve their intended goals, once a certain consensus has been achieved about what those are. The adaptive challenge is one that educators and societies engage with from time to time, more episodically than the technical challenge of seeking continuous improvement in the effectiveness of schools. Clayton Christensen and his colleagues at the Harvard Business School have characterized the tension between these technical and adaptive challenges as that between sustaining innovation and disruptive innovation.[4]

Setting goals, reflected in narratives that provide direction and animate individual and collaborative effort, is central to any organized human endeavor. In part at least, the aspiration to achieve these goals is the reason organizations exist. The same is true for educational institutions, whether individual schools, school districts or local education jurisdictions, or state and national systems. In education, the question of defining goals typically concerns the definition of who should learn what.

For example, in the aftermath of World War II, nations made the effort to create a series of global institutions to ensure peace and stability, including the right of education as one of the necessary elements of such a strategy. The inclusion of the right to education in the Universal Declaration of Human Rights, drafted following the war with the aim of ensuring global security, sparked a global movement to achieve the goal of educating all children. This movement produced a remarkable transformation in educational opportunity, changing the world from one where most children did not have the opportunity to set foot in a school in 1945, to one where most children now enroll in school and have access to at least a basic education, with the majority transitioning to secondary education.[5]

This global movement sought to provide ALL students with the opportunity to gain a fundamental education. Not surprisingly, what should be included in a fundamental education has been, and remains, very much the subject of debate. This debate includes questions such as how much emphasis should be given to knowledge acquisition, relative to social and personal development. It also includes questions about the level at which knowledge should be mastered and skills developed. Literacy, for example, a fundamental skill that is one of the goals of basic education globally, can be developed at many different levels. Mathematical literacy, similarly, can include very different levels of content. In a seminal contribution to guiding how such goals can be formulated, Benjamin Bloom proposed a taxonomy of learning objectives that organized them in a hierarchy of cognitive complexity. He argued that learning objectives could be classified as cognitive, affective, and psychomotor, and that each of those in turn could be organized in a hierarchy. The cognitive domain, for example, ranged from knowing facts, at the low end of cognitive complexity, to analyzing or evaluating them, and finally to using them in creative ways.[6]

How these learning goals are taught and met is the purview of curriculum. As an instrument to organize and achieve such goals, the curriculum can vary widely. Across the world there are differences as to which levels of government attempt to influence curriculum, and at what level of specificity those influences are applied. In the United States, for example, states, districts, teachers, and the schools where they work traditionally had the autonomy to develop educational goals, including developing a specific scope and sequence and the lesson plans to translate those into actual classroom activities that create learning opportunities. In recent decades some national governments have taken on a greater role in defining goals, specifying a minimum set of standards to be taught and providing broad direction about the minimum level at which those standards should be taught. In the United States these are called education standards, and it is expected that specific curricula will still be developed by teachers, or groups of teachers, in ways that are aligned with those standards. In contrast, there are countries, such as Mexico, where a national curriculum has a much greater level of specificity, often to the level of prescribing specific lessons. In these cases, national textbooks and teacher guides are often the instruments that translate that curriculum into expected instructional routines.

These patterns in how various levels of education governance participate in the definition of curriculum can change over time. Colombia, for example, abandoned a highly prescribed national curriculum as part of a series of reforms in the 1990s, in favor of more general standards such as those used in the United States. Conversely, the United States has moved in the direction of adopting national standards for some subjects. As we conducted the research for this book, we found that the six countries we studied—Singapore, China, Chile, Mexico, India, and the United States—varied in the degree to which governments prescribed learning goals and curricula. Accordingly, in our discussion we will use the term "curriculum frameworks" or "standards" to refer to learning objectives and goals, and the term "curriculum" to refer to specific scope and sequences.

EDUCATION IN THE TWENTY-FIRST CENTURY

The approach of the year 2000 caused a number of governments, development organizations, and other groups to examine the relevance of education given the social, economic, and political changes expected in the new century. Analyses of the US labor market, for example, show that over the last fifty years the number of jobs that require routine manual activities, and even routine cognitive tasks, has drastically declined, whereas jobs requiring nonroutine analytic and interpersonal tasks have increased.[7]

Over the last two decades there has been significant conceptual work and advocacy aimed at broadening the goals of education to better prepare students for the demands of the present millennium. UNESCO, for instance, which was created at the establishment of the United Nations in 1947 to support the right of education for the purpose of contributing to peace, published a milestone document in 1972. The Faure Report, also known as *Learning to Be*, argued for the necessity of lifelong education to develop capacities for effective functioning and participation in society, and for a society committed to supporting lifelong learning. In the last decade of the twentieth century, UNESCO commissioned Jacques Delors, former president of the European Commission, to head the preparation of a report outlining a framework for education in the twenty-first century.[8] The Delors Report, titled *Learning: The Treasure Within*, was the result of a major global consultation that took place over several years in the 1990s, and argued that the four pillars of education should be to learn to know, to do, to be, and to live together.[9]

At the start of the twenty-first century, the Organization for Economic Cooperation and Development (OECD) undertook two related initiatives. One was an expert consultation on key competencies necessary for functioning in OECD member states—the Definition and Selection of

Competencies (DeSeCo) program.[10] The second initiative was a periodic exercise assessing the knowledge and skills of fifteen-year-olds in the areas of literacy, math, and sciences—the Program for International Student Assessment (PISA).

Other supranational efforts to redefine the competencies that schools should develop in the twenty-first century include the Assessment and Teaching of 21st Century Skills (ATC21S), sponsored by major technology companies Cisco, Intel, and Microsoft, an initiative focused on developing new assessment systems aligned with twenty-first-century skills; and enGauge, a framework of literacy in the digital age published in 2003 by the North Central Regional Educational Laboratory and the Metiri Group, an education consulting group. The enGauge report describes how technology is transforming work, and argues that it should also transform education by providing opportunities for students to develop technology literacy. The report outlines four broad twenty-first-century competencies, each encompassing multiple specific domains:[11]

Digital literacy
> Basic, scientific, economic, and technological literacies
> Visual and information literacies
> Multicultural literacy and global awareness

Inventive thinking
> Adaptability, managing complexity, and self-direction
> Curiosity, creativity, and risk taking
> Higher order thinking and sound reasoning

Effective communication
> Teaming, collaboration, and interpersonal skills
> Personal, social, and civic responsibility
> Interactive communication

High productivity
> Prioritizing, planning, and managing for results
> Effective use of real-world tools
> Ability to produce relevant, high-quality products

More recently, a unit of the World Economic Forum produced a report examining skill gaps in various countries. They synthesized various literatures on twenty-first-century skills as follows:[12]

Foundational literacies
    Literacy
    Numeracy
    Scientific literacy
    ICT literacy
    Financial literacy
    Cultural and Civic Literacy

Competencies
    Critical thinking, problem solving
    Creativity
    Communication
    Collaboration

Character qualities
    Curiosity
    Initiative
    Persistence
    Adaptability
    Leadership
    Social and cultural awareness

In many of these documents, the competencies that were included in the list of "twenty-first-century skills" were in part determined by how framers perceived the "twenty-first century" and the major challenges and opportunities they saw associated with it. For example, the enGauge framework included the following "real-life" examples they saw taking place in the future:

- *The Workplace*: Farmers are checking soil moisture from their hand-held computers, and factory workers are guiding robots.
- *Education*: Teachers are serving as facilitators, exploring with their students the vast world of ideas and information.

- *Health Care*: More efficient systems are linking together county, state, and federal facilities, accelerating the study, diagnosis, and treatment of diseases through networked applications and medical databases.
- *Public Safety*: Officials are gaining access to instantaneous emergency-response information and interoperation of critical equipment regardless of jurisdiction.
- *Government*: Free and universal access to information is increasing for all citizens, whose informed opinions are in turn shaping policy and fostering greater global democracy.
- *Ethics*: Ethical issues are no longer just about right and wrong but also about informed choices between two rights—such as doing all we can to save lives and allowing people to die with dignity.[13]

These "goals for the twenty-first century" are also bound by the particular emphasis or the agendas of the organizations sponsoring them. For example, the recent report of the World Economic Forum referenced above identified competencies based on expectations for work to meet industry demands. The Program of International Student Assessment, developed by the OECD, also used normative criteria drawn from an analysis of life and work demands to define competencies. Literacy in PISA, for example, is understood as the level of literacy necessary "to function in a knowledge-based economy and in a democratic society." Such normative criteria are helpful as benchmarks against which to examine the intended goals in national education systems. For example, the distribution of levels of student achievement in student assessments based on a national curriculum is typically very different from the distribution of those levels in the PISA studies. One interpretation of such difference is that the national curricula have different "ambitions" than those reflected in PISA. The testing of problem-solving competencies in PISA is in part a response to the outcry that the assessment instrument needs to be more complex.

However, as educational leaders have focused on developing more complex learning goals—increasing in cognitive complexity and in multidimensionality that includes cognitive as well as social and emotional complexity—one could expect that the development of curriculum should draw not only on identification of demands for work and life, but also on a scientifically based understanding of how individuals develop over time in those multiple dimensions, and about the nature of the interrelationships in the development of these various dimensions. The great contribution of Swiss educator Henry Pestalozzi in the 1800s was precisely to point out that children were not little adults, but that development proceeded in "stages" and that teaching could be most effective if it were adapted to the particular stage of the learner, and hence that children should be taught differently than adults.[14] This insight was perfected by Swiss psychologist Jean Piaget, whose theory of cognitive development was based on documenting the features of the type of cognitive processing that characterized different stages, and the nature of progression from one stage to another. Piaget's theory caused a major paradigm shift in psychology, unleashing the cognitive revolution. The developments emerging from this revolution, most notably in the last three decades, were consequential for the design of curriculum. Howard Gardner, for example, a major contributor to cognitive psychology, in his challenge to a unified theory of intelligence with a multidimensional view of human development, sparked a series of educational developments toward greater personalization and differentiation of instruction in ways that helped cultivate different forms of intelligence, and not just one.[15]

In spite of the obvious need for a theoretical underpinning to the design of curriculum, most conversations about "twenty-first-century education" to date have failed to draw a connection between the proposed twenty-first-century competencies and any psychological theories of how those competencies are developed, in particular in relationship to one another, as a unified developmental process. A recent effort in the direction of bridging this gap is a report of the National Research Council in the United States, an organization established in its original form by President Abraham Lincoln to help inform issues of public concern with scientific evidence. The National Research Council convened an expert group led by Margaret Hilton and James Pellegrino to produce a report on twenty-first-century skills. Titled *Education for Life and Work: Developing*

Transferable Knowledge and Skills in the 21st Century, this report synthesized psychological and social science research evidence on skills that have demonstrated short- or long-term consequences for individuals.[16] The report draws on other literature to identify those competencies, and then synthesizes psychological evidence on what is known about how they develop and about their outcomes for individuals. The report summarizes those skills in the following framework:

1. **Cognitive Competencies**

   1.1 *Cognitive Processes and Strategies*
   Critical thinking; problem solving; analysis; reasoning and argumentation; interpretation; decision making; adaptive learning; executive function

   1.2 *Knowledge*
   Information literacy, including research using evidence and recognizing bias in sources; information and communication technology literacy; oral and written communication; active listening

   1.3 *Creativity*
   Creativity and innovation

2. **Intrapersonal Competencies**

   2.1 *Intellectual Openness*
   Flexibility; adaptability; artistic and cultural appreciation; personal and social responsibility; cultural awareness and competence; appreciation for diversity; adaptability; continuous learning; intellectual interest and curiosity

   2.2 *Work Ethic/Conscientiousness*
   Initiative; self-direction; responsibility; perseverance; grit; productivity; type 1 self-regulation (metacognitive skills, including forethought, performance, and self-reflection); professionalism/ethics; integrity; citizenship; career orientation

2.3 *Positive Core Self-Evaluation*
Type 2 self-regulation (self-monitoring, self-evaluation, self-reinforcement); physical and psychological health

3. Interpersonal Competencies

3.1 *Teamwork and Collaboration*
Communication; collaboration; teamwork; cooperation; coordination; interpersonal skills; empathy/perspective taking; trust; service orientation; conflict resolution; negotiation

3.2 *Leadership*
Leadership; responsibility; assertive communication; self-presentation; social influence with others

Because it is the most systematic and comprehensive review of scientifically based research on twenty-first-century skills, we draw on this NRC taxonomy in this book, and use this categorization to examine national curricular frameworks in the various countries we study. In some ways, these competencies identified as being necessary for the twenty-first century—for example, critical analysis, innovation, creativity, scientific thinking, self-knowledge and self-management, and the interpersonal, social, and perspective-taking skills to work in teams—are not new, and perhaps were needed as early as our primitive ancestors first devised ways to live and work together. However, what has been identified as being unique to our times is the fact that these skills are necessary not just for the elite few but are for everyone. Indeed, these competencies are increasingly important not just for individual and national economic well-being but also for promoting vibrant civic spheres, solving pressing issues, and nurturing effective collaborative organizations—all necessary in the turbulent times of the new century.

One reason to engage in the systematic examination of the intended goals for education is that over the last several decades, many nations around the world have embraced educational strategies that include the assessment of student knowledge and skills. Those include assessments of student knowledge based on national curricula, as well as participation in comparative studies of assessment. Measurement of what students know and of what they learn in school is helpful, but unless what is measured aligns with what schools are trying to teach, and unless those results are interpreted in the context of the goals schools are trying to achieve, measurement can distort those goals. This unintended detrimental effect of assessment is reflected in the expression "what gets measured is what gets taught." As assessment results play a greater role in the national discussions about education, it is especially important that conversations be framed in terms of what education goals are driving schools. Test results should not drive goals, nor should they substitute for them.

Educational opportunity is created when students and teachers engage in purposeful learning activities that help students develop in various ways. This requires clear goals, the skills to translate those goals into sound curriculum and pedagogy, and the leadership of teachers and school administrators to focus their work in supporting the creation of those opportunities. In a nutshell, educational opportunity requires an effective system to support learning, including supportive organizations, resources, and sound policies.

THE GLOBAL EDUCATION INNOVATION INITIATIVE AND LEARNING IN THE TWENTY-FIRST CENTURY

In this context, we notice two important gaps in how education systems create opportunities for students to learn what they need to be self-authoring in the twenty-first century. One is that teacher education programs and education leadership preparation programs in many of the world's developed and emerging economies are not only based on theories of the past, but are delivered in outmoded ways such as rote classroom instruction. The other is that we lack a unified theory of how the various twenty-first-century competencies relate to one another to inform the design of curriculum and pedagogy to promote their development.

We convened the Global Education Innovation Initiative at the Harvard Graduate School of Education, with partners from around the world, because we believe that the ability of leadership to support the development of students' twenty-first-century competencies is one of the key levers to improving student learning. We made this effort, believing that the innovation gap in education leadership preparation is dire, and that a knowledge gap hinders educational practice and policy worldwide, as no trusted source exists of which leadership approaches are most effective. We believe we risk a huge lost opportunity to build leadership for the education systems that serve the majority of the world's children, if we do not marshal the resources at our disposal to research and practice effective education suited for the challenges and opportunities of this century. In particular, we are seeking answers to the question of what it takes to lead schools and education systems to lasting improvement in terms of helping students develop the competencies they will need in the latter half of the twenty-first century.

The discussion about how to prepare students for citizenship and economic participation in the new century must address the need to acquire key competencies and to learn skills beyond the basics, such as digital, civic, self-knowledge, and interpersonal competencies. While discussions about educational priorities and policies are not new, there has been little research into the mechanisms by which these objectives are enacted into policy and prioritized to help develop and support relevant competencies in students; we know even less about how these processes and skills may be influenced by social, political, and other system contexts.

In this book we wanted to examine how instructional priorities are represented in national curricular frameworks, and how these frameworks reflect the competencies that students need to thrive in the twenty-first century, as identified by research. In the following chapters, researchers and practitioners from Chile, China, India, Mexico, Singapore, and the United States discuss these questions and the findings from their respective studies in this area. This book seeks to address the knowledge gaps described above by adding to the body of international comparative research on educational policy and curriculum studies.

We chose the countries for this study in part because four of them (China, India, Mexico, and the United States) have large education systems enrolling large student populations. Together, the education systems in these four countries include about 40 percent of the total world student population. In addition, we selected these countries, including Chile and Singapore, because we know that they have each made education an important development priority over a sustained period of time. In selecting countries in this way we thought we would be able to learn about how nations where education is a social priority frame their educational goals, and to identify what they do to help educators translate those goals into actual opportunities to learn. The countries include countries at various levels of economic development, in various regions of the world, reflecting diverse educational traditions. By necessity, we included countries in which we were able to identify institutions interested in joining the research consortium that forms the Global Education Innovation Initiative. Like the selection of countries in any cross-national study, this one reflects intentionality and practicality, design and opportunity. Not all countries we had hoped to include in the study are included, nor has our intent been to have a group of countries that is representative of the world.

Table I.1 summarizes a few selected indicators for the countries included in the study. The countries clearly vary in terms of the number of students served but are similar in that they reflect relatively high levels of access to primary and secondary education. In addition, there are obvious differences in level of economic development, as reflected in income per capita.

Table I.1 shows that there are important differences among the countries we are comparing, which should be kept in mind when we analyze the results of the study. One noticeable difference is the size of the education system. The relatively small system of Singapore, for instance, and the very high levels of per capita income, represent a rather different context than those experienced by the significantly larger system of India, with much lower levels of per capita income. Other differences among these countries, which will not be part of our analysis in this book, concern the expectations adults have for children, schools, and the ways in which they support school learning and education more generally.

Using data from the 2015 World Values Survey, a cross-national study of values, Table I.2 shows how the countries included in this study vary

TABLE I.1 Student enrollment numbers* in Chile, China, India, Mexico, Singapore, and United States, relative to the world

| | TOTAL STUDENTS ENROLLED | | PERCENTAGE OF STUDENTS ENROLLED | | | | | GNP Per Capita (PPP) |
| | | | Net Enrollment | | Gross Enrollment** | | | |
	Primary	Secondary	Primary	Secondary	Primary	Secondary		
Chile	1,472,348	1,571,374	92%	87%	100%	99%		21,942
China	98,870,818	94,324,415	n.a.	n.a.	126%	92%		11,907
India	139,869,904	119,148,200	93%	n.a.	114%	71%		3,813
Mexico	14,837,204	12,467,278	96%	68%	105%	88%		16,370
Singapore	294,602	232,003	n.a.	n.a.	n.a.	n.a.		78,763
United States	24,417,653	24,095,459	91%	87%	98%	94%		53,042
Sum	279,762,529	251,838,729						
World	712,994,323	567,831,226						
Percentage	39%	44%						

*Figures are for 2013 or nearest available year.

**Gross enrollment counts students of all ages, including students whose age exceeds the official age group. Thus, if there is late enrollment, early enrollment, or repetition, the total enrollment can exceed the population of the age group that officially corresponds to the level of education, leading to ratios greater than 100 percent. (https://data-helpdesk.worldbank.org/knowledgebase/articles/114955-how-can-gross-school-enrollment-ratios-be-over-100)

Source: http://data.worldbank.org/

TABLE I.2 Important child qualities (percentage of respondents who mentioned each quality)

	Chile	China	India	Mexico	Singapore	United States
Independence	49	70	63	39	72	54
Hard work	31	75	63	38	61	66
Feeling of responsibility	77	66	66	75	70	65
Imagination	22	17	51	24	19	31
Tolerance and respect for other people	82	52	62	78	54	72
Thrift, saving money and things	36	51	58	35	47	32
Determination, perseverance	54	26	65	27	44	36
Religious faith	28	1	61	35	26	43
Unselfishness	43	29	55	43	26	33
Obedience	46	8	57	55	38	28
Self-expression	36	11	40	19	14	18

Calculated using data from World Values Survey (2010–2014).

in terms of expectations that people have for the education of children. Adults were asked to identify important qualities that should be cultivated among children, and Table I.2 shows the percentage of adults who mentioned each of the qualities listed. In China and Singapore, for example, a much greater percentage of the population values independence, followed by India and the United States. That percentage is lower in Chile and Mexico. Hard work from children is highly valued in China, India, Singapore, and the United States, but less so in Chile and Mexico. Responsibility is highly valued in all countries. Imagination is not valued by most people, but it is most highly valued in India, and least valued in China, Singapore, Chile, and Mexico. Tolerance and respect for others is valued by most people, but less so in China, India, and Singapore. Self-expression is not highly valued by most people, but more so in India, and significantly less so in China, Singapore, Mexico, and the United States.

The qualities that adults consider important in children are reflected in the views parents, as well as teachers and school administrators, have about what should be taught in schools. A recent survey in the United States of parental views on the qualities that are most important to teach children underscores responsibility and hard work, but assigns relatively less priority to curiosity, obedience, tolerance, persistence, empathy, or creativity.[17] Consistent with these findings, when asked what skills are most important for children to get ahead in the world today, Americans emphasize communication (90%), reading (86%), math (79%), teamwork (77%), writing (75%), and logic (74%), while placing lesser emphasis on science (58%). Significantly fewer people emphasize athletics (25%), music (24%), or art (23%).[18]

These differences in parental expectations are likely to influence the way in which families engage with schools, their degree of satisfaction with and support for schools and schoolwork, as well as the additional activities they arrange for their children to supplement what schools do in cultivating qualities parents consider important. A survey examining the perceptions of the pressure parents place on students, conducted in twenty-one countries, shows important differences. Americans are the most likely to say that parents do not put enough pressure on their children (64%), whereas Chinese are the most likely to say that parents put too much pressure on them (68%). In Mexico 42 percent of those surveyed think that parents don't put enough pressure on students, with 20 percent saying they put too much, while in India the numbers are 24 percent and 44 percent respectively.[19] These cultural differences in parental expectations are likely to influence the curriculum priorities in various countries.

RESEARCH METHODS: THE CASE FOR LEARNING FROM COMPARISONS

The notion that we might learn valuable knowledge from comparing education systems is quite old. Before public education systems existed, travelers would transport stories of how people were educated from one country to another. The modern aspiration to educate all children created a new urgency for this kind of exchange of ideas, and it was in the period following the French Revolution that Marc-Antoine Jullien proposed the systematic study and exchange of comparative education practices. Jullien devoted some time to studying the educational model developed by Pestalozzi in Switzerland. Aware that other educators had developed alternative education methodologies, he led the systematic exchange of documentation and discussion over those practices. He also proposed a systematic survey of how education was organized in various localities, identifying who was being educated, in what kind of institutions, who was doing the teaching, and what was being taught. It was Jullien's hope that the examination of such comparative evidence would help those making decisions about how to expand education.

Many public education systems were assisted in their creation by this kind of comparative knowledge base. In the United States, for example, John Quincy Adams, the sixth president of the United States, while serving as Minister to Prussia, devoted some time to studying the educational institutions of that region, which he discussed in a travel book written for his contemporaries in the new country, *Letters on Silesia*. Later, Horace Mann, the proponent of public education in Massachusetts, also devoted time to study the public education system in Prussia and France, as a way to inform debate in the United States about how to build a universal system of education.

In South America, Simón Bolívar, one of the leaders of the independence movement, visited Joseph Lancaster in London to learn about the educational approach Lancaster had developed to educate large groups of children, at low cost, with a limited number of highly skilled teachers aided by student-monitors. Bolívar persuaded Lancaster to travel to Caracas in the early years following independence, where he helped established the first teacher training school. The Society for Promoting the Lancasterian System for the Education of the Poor engaged in the active dissemination of knowledge about how to organize the Lancasterian method of instruction across several countries.

The field of comparative education was formally established in the United States with the founding of Teachers College at Columbia University, in the early twentieth century. It was there that the International Institute (now known as the International and Comparative Education

Program)—the first center for comparative studies in education—was created in hopes that the knowledge developed in this center would help inform how to prepare teachers at a time when educational expansion would provide opportunity to children from social backgrounds that had previously been denied it. John Dewey was one of the best-known American educators associated with this center, and through his travels as well as his teaching of students from many different countries, Dewey actively engaged in the cross-national dissemination of ideas about educational purposes and practices. Dewey's work is of particular significance to this book because his idea that what we teach is how we teach, and his writings on the nature of education for democratic life, underscore the central importance of the purposes of education and how those purposes are intertwined with pedagogical practices and curriculum.

In recent years, the most public discussions based on international comparisons draw on the results of international studies of educational achievement, either those conducted by the International Association for Educational Achievement, such as the Progress in International Reading Literacy Study (PIRLS) or the Trends in International Mathematics and Science Study (TIMSS), or more recently the PISA studies conducted by the OECD. These studies have been able to draw on a wide range of variation of educational outcomes and practices, and to learn from the world as a laboratory. They represent an extension, to the cross-national level, of the school effectiveness studies that examine what results are achieved by students—typically in the domains of literacy, mathematics, and science, with a few studies focusing on civics—and then relating those results to teaching practices, characteristics of teachers and schools, and structural characteristics of education systems, such as the degree of school autonomy. The knowledge generated by these studies is immensely valuable, as is the knowledge generated by school effectiveness research more generally, in helping us understand what factors are associated with variation in learning outcomes.

But these studies omit the investigation of policy intent; they are not studies of the effectiveness in implementing a particular curriculum, nor analyses of what is intended in the curriculum. Because education is an intentional enterprise, much can be gained by an explicit investigation of the intended purposes of education, including what a curriculum is attempting to teach students and how the intended learning can be achieved. Furthermore, understanding the process of education as the result of explicit attempts to modify the goals of education—in other words, the responses of education institutions to adaptive leadership—should complement the vast knowledge that exists about ways to improve the effectiveness of schools, such as the process of sustaining innovation or technical improvement of schools. Tackling these questions is the goal of the Global Education Innovation Initiative, and of this book.

In this study, we undertook to examine policy and curriculum frameworks, as well as to interview key policy makers, in order to identify how diverse education systems have described the skills that public education systems should help students gain in the twenty-first century. We focused this study on countries that had a relatively sizable number of children, as well as on countries in which education was a clear priority on the government policy agenda, on the assumption that these two factors would create the condition for more intentional attention to the work of education institutions. In countries where a large percentage of the population is in school, it is self-evident that what schools do can have a fairly immediate impact in shaping the character of the society, in ways that schools in countries with lower percentages of students cannot. In addition, large numbers of students are associated with large numbers of teachers and institutions, making schools a very visible and important face of the state—often the largest employer in the country, often also the state institution to which most people have access. Chile and Singapore do not necessarily fit this criteria in terms of the number of students in school, but Chile is a setting in which a democratic transition placed education at the center of the government reform agenda and, in Singapore's case, there has been ongoing priority accorded to education since the nation's founding.

Major data sources for the book include the following: document analysis (as of policy documents, curricular frameworks, white papers, and official government reports); literature review of relevant research articles and books; and interviews with policy makers, national and local educational stakeholders, and experts.

PLAN OF THE BOOK

Chapter 1, "Singapore's Systemic Approach to Teaching and Learning Twenty-First-Century Competencies," examines the systemic efforts that Singapore has taken to prepare students for the realities of the twenty-first-century global workplace and society. Specifically, it focuses on the key policies, initiatives, and strategies implemented across major sectors of the education system to develop students' twenty-first-century competencies. It also highlights the close collaborations between policy makers, schools, and the National Institute of Education that help to achieve these educational initiatives and goals. The chapter ends by discussing future challenges for Singapore.

Chapter 2, "Thinking Big, Acting Small: Lessons from Twenty-First-Century Curriculum Reform in China," explicates the policies and strategies adopted to advance contemporary education in China, including continuous experimentations and innovations to change the content and ways to deliver education. China's curriculum to teach twenty-first-century competencies, intended and implemented, is contingent upon historical context and policy reforms implemented on a larger scope. Hence the chapter takes a dual perspective: historical and systemic. First, it reviews historical contexts that had an impact on shaping education for the twenty-first century in China; second, it examines how the concept of education for the current century has taken shape in the policy reforms and landscape of curriculum as a result of the reforms—specifically changes in the strategy, content, and ways to deliver education. The chapter concludes with five lessons of twenty-first-century curriculum reform for potential replication, namely, evidence-based, participatory policy making; provision of professional support for teaching; learning from the world; experimentation; and balancing between centralization and decentralization, emphasizing both unity and diversity.

Chapter 3, "Strong Content, Weak Tools: Twenty-First-Century Competencies in the Chilean Educational Reform," considers the place the twenty-first-century competencies approach has occupied within Chilean primary and secondary education since these skills were incorporated into the national curricula, in the context of a broader educational reform implemented since the mid 1990s. The chapter analyzes the interplay between the relevance assigned to these new competencies, and the goals and emphases of educational policies and programs oriented to implement them in the actual educational system. The study contributes to critically discussing the priorities of the Chilean educational policies in the last two decades; also, by expanding the concept of quality education, it paves the way for further studies on the relevance of twenty-first-century competencies to both educational policies and school effectiveness research.

Chapter 4, "Curriculum Reform and Twenty-First-Century Skills in Mexico: Are Standards and Teacher Training Materials Aligned?," analyzes how twenty-first-century skills were defined and conceptualized in the new curriculum in Mexico, and discusses the degree of alignment among standards, learning goals, and teacher training materials. In a similar trend to other countries, Mexico recently introduced in its national curriculum a definition of twenty-first-century skills. However, an open debate remains about how these skills were defined, and how this inclusion may result in changes in instructional practices and student learning.

Chapter 5, "Twenty-First-Century Competencies, the Indian National Curriculum Framework, and the History of Education in India," looks at the evolution in the educational policies in the changed social and political scenario in recent years, including a short case study of a nongovernmental organization that initiated practices which influenced the current curricular goals. The chapter summarizes the history of education in India and the richness that has evolved, and also examines the links between the twenty-first-century competencies and the existing curricular aspirations, showing how these skills do or do not appear in the existing framework.

Chapter 6, "Mapping the Landscape of Teaching and Learning for the Twenty-First Century in Massachusetts in the Context of US Educational Reform," examines the key policies and strategies implemented to develop students' twenty-first-century competencies, including an analysis of the Common Core standards as they were adopted in Massachusetts, vis-à-vis a summary report commissioned by the National Research Council about twenty-first-century competencies. The chapter ends by discussing current and future opportunities and challenges.

Finally, "Theorizing Twenty-First-Century Education," the conclusion, summarizes how curricular frameworks have changed in the countries examined in the study and how those changes incorporate cognitive, social, and intrapersonal domains of competency. The chapter engages with the paradox that even as the goals for education are expanding, support for schools and educators is dwindling. This chapter proposes that at the heart of this paradox lies the failure of the strategies followed to implement twenty-first-century education to be based on a sound theory.

In sum, with this book, we want to engage stakeholders in education in a global conversation about the purposes of education for the current century, which, in our mind, includes preparing students with the competencies, the agency, and the desire to address the larger issues that face all of us.

The need for such an education was most recently echoed in a report of a commission of the US Department of Education:

> A world-class education consists not solely of mastery of core subjects, but also of training in critical thinking and problem-solving, as well as in 21st-century concerns like global awareness and financial literacy. Such high levels of education are key to self-reliance and economic security in a world where education matters more than ever for the success of societies as well as individuals.
>
> But American schools must do more than ensure our future economic prosperity; they must foster the nation's civic culture and sense of common purpose, and create the unified nation that e pluribus unum celebrates. So much depends on fulfilling this mission: the shared ideals that enable our governmental system to hold together even in the face of fractious political disagreements; the strength of our diversity; the domestic tranquility that our Constitution

promises; and the ability to maintain the influence—as example and power—that America has long projected in the world. We neglect those expectations at our peril.[20]

Understanding how leaders of national education systems around the world conceive of the goals of education in the twenty-first century is an essential step to understanding whether the relatively recent global goal of educating all children can indeed provide all students the necessary competencies to shape their future.

Singapore's Systemic Approach to Teaching and Learning Twenty-First-Century Competencies

Oon-Seng Tan and Ee-Ling Low

National Institute of Education, Nanyang Technological University, Singapore

The twenty-first century has brought with it globalization and rapid technological advancements. With these rapid changes, governments need to consider how schools can prepare their students for the future and think about the type of fundamental skills and competencies necessary for them to function competitively when they enter the workforce. While academic qualifications remain important, they do not guarantee that workers will be able to adapt to the rapidly changing demands in the global workplace. Therefore, educators are increasingly being pressed to incorporate competencies required for success in the current century within their education system.

The focus on preparing students for twenty-first-century competencies is no different in Singapore.[1] There is a clear attempt to articulate a coherent and systemic response to today's educational challenges and opportunities that has resulted in the mapping of education outcomes to twenty-first-century workforce skills and competencies via a holistic review of the education system. Internationally, several councils and associations have been established to catalogue the essential competencies for the new century, including the National Research Council (NRC) and the Assessment and Teaching of 21st Century Skills project (ATC21S). The ATC21S developed a framework that analyzed each of ten important twenty-first-century skills using the Knowledge, Skills, Attitudes, Values, and Ethics (KSAVE) structure, which was put together after collating studies from various organizations and countries.[2] The NRC used three domains—cognitive, intrapersonal, and interpersonal competencies—that are required for one to succeed in the current century, albeit with reference to the American market.[3] The basis of the educational review was formed by environmental scans and analysis of future trends and inputs from other educational stakeholders such as government agencies, schools, universities, parents, voluntary welfare organizations, and unions,[4] along with additional source documents from the European Union, the OECD, and countries such as the United States, Japan, Australia, Scotland, and others as references.[5] The result of this comprehensive review ascertaining the demands of a twenty-first-century landscape was the development of a 21st Century Competencies (21CC) framework that articulates a set of desired student outcomes of a twenty-first-century learner. The student outcomes are underpinned by core values and supported by social and emotional learning skills. Through this articulated 21CC framework, schools are guided to initiate changes to their curricula, pedagogies, and assessments, as described in greater detail below.

This chapter attempts to achieve three goals. First, it is a descriptive study and meta-analysis of the policies and initiatives in the Singapore education system introduced for the purpose of twenty-first-century competencies. Major data sources include an extensive literature review of relevant materials, the framework developed by the Ministry of Education (MOE) for desired student outcomes and twenty-first-century competencies, the Teacher Education Model for the 21st Century developed by the National Institute of Education (NIE), and official government reports and other web-based materials. Second, factors enabling successful implementation of such policies will be discussed. Finally, this chapter will discuss real-ground challenges encountered by the stakeholders across the education system in the implementation process and will offer a critical perspective of the future challenges that lie ahead. Data backing up the critical perspectives offered was collected via focus group discussions and e-mail or interviews with key educational stakeholders.

HISTORICAL BACKGROUND TO SINGAPORE AND ITS EDUCATION SYSTEM

Singapore is an island city-state that lies south of West Malaysia, only 137 kilometers (85 miles) north of the equator, with a land area of no more than 650 square kilometers (250 square miles). Singapore is strategically located at the crossroads between the Far East and West, making it one of the busiest sea and air hubs in the world, a convenient seaport of call, and an equally convenient transit location for travelers from the Southern to the Northern Hemisphere and from the Far East to Europe and North America.

Singapore was founded by the British in 1819 and achieved independence in 1965. As reflected in the latest Population in Brief 2014 publication released by the National Population and Talent Division in June 2014, Singapore's population numbered 5.47 million, comprising 3.87 million Singapore residents (of which 3.34 million are Singapore citizens and 0.53 million have permanent residency) and 1.60 million non-residents who do not live in Singapore. In terms of ethnic makeup of its citizen population, the Chinese form the majority of the population at 76.2 percent, followed by Malays at 15 percent, Indians at 7.4 percent, and others (mainly Eurasians) at 1.4 percent. Due to the diverse nature of its population makeup, the key purpose of education is for nation building and must be understood against the background of a multiethnic, multilingual, and multicultural community.

Singapore is economically prosperous, with a GDP per capita of US$56,319, one of the highest in Asia.[6] Singapore places great emphasis on education and spent about 3 percent of its GDP or SGD$11.7 billion (about US$8.86 billion) in 2014 on schools. The literacy rate of Singaporeans aged fifteen years and above, according to the 2010 Census of Population, is 95.9 percent, with 79.9 percent literate in English; those who are literate in two or more languages stands at 70.5 percent.

Singapore is relatively small as a nation both in terms of land size and population numbers. There are 360 schools in Singapore and about 33,000 education officers. The small size certainly helps in ability of the system to react nimbly to shifts in policy goals and initiatives and to implement these quickly and coherently systemwide.

In recent years, Singapore's education system has received worldwide attention because of its consistently high performance in cross-national tests of student achievement. In the most recent release of the results of the Trends in International Mathematics and Science Study (TIMSS) and Progress in International Reading Literacy Study (PIRLS)—held in 2011 and jointly conducted by the International Association for the Evaluation of Educational Achievement (IEA) and the TIMSS and PIRLS Center at the Lynch School of Education at Boston College—Singapore emerged top in fourth grade for both mathematics and science achievement, while at the eighth grade Singapore was top for science and second for mathematics achievement. In the 2012 Program for International Student Assessment (PISA) results, of the sixty-five participating education systems in the paper-based assessment component, Singapore was ranked top five in mathematics, reading, and science literacy skills. Undoubtedly, Singapore's focus on the importance of academic achievement in the earlier years of nation building contributed greatly to this performance. However, contrary to popular belief, the policy initiatives and goals of education in the Singapore system have not been guided by the quest to excel in these internationally benchmarked tests of student achievement; rather, the educational system has been dynamic in its response to shifts in national and global contexts, and has had to be adaptive in aligning its goals over the years to the changing opportunities and challenges that the nation faced as a whole. The next section documents some of the key movers of change and how these have shaped the educational philosophy, policy formulation, and implementation strategies for the system as a whole.

Key Phases of Education and Rationale

Singapore's education system has undergone several changes in philosophies and objectives over the past few decades, which can be characterized as four distinct phases: survival-driven, efficiency-driven, ability-driven, and values-driven. What is important to point out is that each of these phases was motivated by different needs faced by a newly independent nation and the sociopolitical development of the nation.[7] Changes in policy were therefore also triggered by the changing needs of a developing nation, and in each case the government took the lead to introduce the policy initiatives.

Survival-driven phase (1965–1978)

This phase was motivated by the need for the newly independent nation to survive economically, hence the name "survival-driven." After gaining independence in 1965 Singapore had to build its economy from scratch, and education became one of the most critical keys to ensuring that the economy was built for future sustainability. There were high levels of unemployment among its mostly unskilled population. Without any natural resources, education became the key to the growth and economic development of the nation. Consequently, the goal of education then was economic survival and to educate the general population quickly in order to build a strong labor force for the country.[8] The focus of the curriculum at the time was on basic skills of literacy and mathematics essential for work, and the main objective was to get a considerable proportion of the population to complete high school. In the 1960s to 1970s the number of schools built increased rapidly, creating an urgency to train a whole cadre of teachers for the newly built schools. The infrastructure of the teacher education campus was upgraded, and opportunities were provided for the faculty to upgrade their academic qualifications. This signaled the importance of teacher preparation and education.

During this phase education for all was provided at the primary level, but the "one-size-fits-all" education model did not take into consideration the different ability levels of students, and a substantial number of students who failed to pass the Primary Six Leaving Examination (PSLE)[9] left the system and did not further their studies. To reduce the high number of dropouts in the system, an education review committee was established, and their recommendations led to the introduction of the efficiency-driven phase.

Efficiency-driven phase (1979 –1996)

In 1979 an education review committee highlighted two main concerns of the education system: first, the high dropout rate where students who did not meet expected standards left the system prematurely, and second, the low standards of English literacy among students. The efficiency-driven phase was kick-started to address these two concerns. In 1980 a new education system was officially introduced in an attempt to reduce the number of school dropouts. Three differentiated streams were introduced in the primary and secondary schools to cater to students of differing abilities as opposed to a streamless, one-size-fits-all system. Here, the focus shifted from providing education for all to improving the quality of education provided. In other words, the shift was from providing quantity in terms of educational opportunities to a greater number of students to one of quality in raising educational standards for all students. Correspondingly, curriculum and assessment were standardized in schools to reduce performance variation and improve the quality of education to produce a workforce needed for the manufacturing industry, where more than half of its output was in electronics.[10] This phase continued until there was a need to move toward maximizing the potential of each individual in the system in order to prepare Singaporeans for the realities of the global workplace and economy.

Ability-driven phase (1997–2011)

From 1997, Singapore moved into the era of ability-driven education in order to prepare a workforce that was ready for the challenges of a globalized market. Through interactions with industry professionals there was the realization that a set of competencies beyond the academic domain were desperately required for an increasingly interdependent twenty-first-century workplace and society. As mentioned earlier, Singapore is a country with no natural resources other than its excellent geographical location and human potential. Its survival has thus always depended on its usefulness to major economic and political powers and its ability to innovate and stay relevant in the global market.[11] Therefore, through the ability-driven phase, the educational focus was on the development of every child to maximize his or her full potential through an education system tailored to to that purpose.

To help achieve this new goal the Thinking Schools, Learning Nation (TSLN) program was launched in 1997. Quality in schools became highlighted as a key to ensuring student success. Educational developments were geared toward responding to the economic and social needs of the people, and these needs were determined through local and international environmental scans, study trips, and focus group discussions. To support the TSLN vision, the Ministry of Education set up the Primary/Secondary/Junior College Education Review and Implementation committees (PERI/SERI/JERI) to study ways to improve the education system across different levels.[12] Their recommendations for improvement were implemented from 2010 onwards and will be described in greater detail throughout this chapter.

Values-driven, student-centric phase (2011–present)

The values-driven, student-centric phase was first announced in 2011 as a clear signal that holistic education of individuals was essential to survive in the twenty-first-century workplace and society. In his speech at the MOE Work Plan Seminar, Mr. Heng Swee Keat, minister for education, explained that values and character development had to be placed at the core of the education system because parents and educators alike have called for schools to develop students holistically in response to changing demands of a global work environment.[13] In particular, for a multiracial, multicultural society like Singapore, shared values allow its citizens to appreciate diversity and maintain cohesion and harmony. The goals of this phase are "every school a good school," "every student an engaged learner," "every teacher a caring educator," and "every parent a supportive partner." This values-driven phase goes hand-in-hand with the ability-driven phase, where schools not only teach academic and life skills but also help instill values and build character in students. In addition, this phase saw the removal of school rankings that were deemed as promoting academic competitiveness among schools and an obsession with test scores among parents. Schools also started to reach out to parents and the community to involve them and partner with them in the holistic development of their children. The four educational phases and what triggered them are depicted graphically in figure 1.1.

FIGURE 1.1   The four phases of education in Singapore (1965–present)

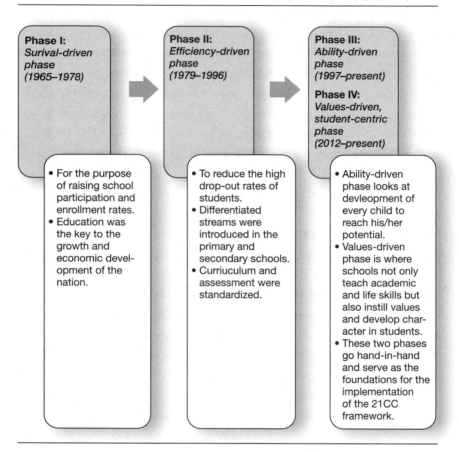

During the values-driven, student-centric phase, clear desired goals and outcomes of schooling and education are spelled out. The goal of the Singaporean education system is to nurture every child, regardless of his or her ability or achievement level. The ecology of educational reform is seen as resting on a set of shared values. The system has created more opportunities for students to move horizontally between academic streams at the secondary level[14] and beyond—to create more flexibility in the system and to recognize "late bloomers" who may not realize their academic potential in their early years of formal schooling. Another feature of the education system is the attention and resources it devotes to low progress learners. For many years, vocational education in Singapore was seen by almost everyone as an academic dead end, the place where students who had failed in the school system ended up. There was an urgent need to change this perception and to emphasize the commitment that every child will receive equal opportunities. To do this, students at Singapore's vocational Institute of Technical Education (ITE) were provided with world-class training, infrastructure, and resources. They built first-rate facilities supplied with the latest equipment, and a highly qualified professional faculty was employed to teach these students. A strong web of connections to industry and companies was built so that graduates from the ITE would have access not just to job opportunities, attachments, and internships but also to pathways for higher education.[15] Today, the resources devoted to vocational and technical training are immense, and the vocational and technical system forms a significant element of the Singapore educational story. This focus on "levelling up," so that the lowest progress learners get very high quality education and vocational training to prepare them adequately for their future, exemplifies the commitment to the educational philosophy of nurturing every child to maximize his or her potential.

As seen from this section detailing the different educational phases and policies accompanying them, it is clear that the Singapore education system may be characterized by nimble and responsive policy making that is geared toward fixing any potential kinks within the system and ensuring that the educational goals change with the changing local and global educational landscape. Challenges faced by the system will be discussed in the final section of this chapter.

SYSTEMIC COHERENCE ACROSS KEY STAKEHOLDERS IN EDUCATION

Systemic coherence and goal alignment across different stakeholders are also apparent when observing the Singapore education system. With the overall direction set by the MOE, the consistent alignment of policies and practices between the national education initiatives, the nation's teacher education institute (the NIE), and the clusters of school principals and teachers is necessary to implement and sustain continual efforts at improving and teaching 21CC at the school level. There is a well-balanced "autonomy versus standardization" framework in guiding key educational stakeholders in their practices. Each plays a distinct yet harmonizing role in achieving the desired outcomes of education. Having recognized that the quality of teachers determines the quality of education, a strong strategic partnership is needed between the key stakeholders.[16] The collective collaboration establishes long-term and sustained cooperation. Such a partnership aims to provide the necessary collaborative framework of shared values and goals that are aligned to a unified outcome. It gives support as beginning teachers transition from campus to schools, while enhancing the continued learning and professional development pathways available to the teaching workforce.

At NIE, the design and delivery of curriculum is done collaboratively with the key stakeholders across the education system, from the policy makers to the schools. This Singapore Teacher Education partnership model is known as the PPP (Policies-Practices-Preparation) model, as shown in figure 1.2.

FIGURE 1.2   The PPP partnership model for teacher education in Singapore

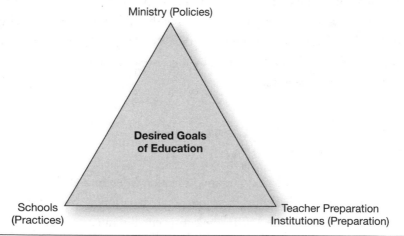

Source: Lee and Low, *Balancing between Theory and Practice* (2014)

This model is clearly explained in an e-mail interview by the immediate past director of the National Institute of Education, Professor Sing Kong Lee:

> At the heart of Singapore's educational success is the strong tripartite partnership which I call the Policies-Practice-Preparation model between the Ministry of Education (MOE), the National Institute of Education (NIE) and the schools. MOE as the lead educational agency provides leadership to articulate policies to establish the Goals of Education. Schools help translate the policies into appropriate practices so that students are educated through the National Curricula so that the Goals of Education are attained. NIE, as the nation's teacher education institute, helps translate the policies into relevant teacher preparation programs so that both the school leaders and teachers are equipped to deliver the goals of education in schools.[17]

The next few sections will document how this systemic coherence takes place in practice by providing extensive elucidation of the recent articulation of the 21CC framework and competencies, its subsequent translation in schools, and how teacher professional development and growth (both pre-service and in-service) are moving to meet the needs of delivering the twenty-first-century competencies systemwide.

Articulation and Translation of the 21CC Framework Systemwide

In 2009 the country's educational agenda was focused on developing twenty-first-century competencies in our learners to address the demands of the twenty-first-century workplace and society, as described earlier in this chapter. Discussions and interactions were carried out with key stakeholders and changes were introduced systemwide, starting at the primary school level, under the recommendations of the Primary Education Review and Implementation committee (PERI), and were then extended to the secondary and postsecondary levels.[18] The Curriculum 2015 (C2015) initiative was also started in light of the need to emphasize the holistic development. C2015 takes reference from Singapore's "intelligence nation" vision (iN2015) for Singapore to be totally connected as the world becomes increasingly linked. C2015 is a vision which emphasizes twenty-first-century skills and mind-sets, namely, the knowledge of world issues and current affairs; literacy in terms of numerical, linguistic, cultural, scientific, and technological skills; lifelong learning skills; and lastly, the ability to manage novel situations and communicate new ideas. Essentially, changes will be implemented in the curriculum, pedagogy, and assessment in order to fulfill the C2015 Student Outcomes.

With this push into adopting and teaching to gain twenty-first-century competencies, the ministry also articulated its Desired Outcomes of Education (DOE).[19] The DOE defines the aims of holistic education and spells out the values, skills, and attitudes that Singaporean students should attain at different stages of the education journey. The DOE states that a person schooled in the Singapore education system should have a good sense of self-awareness, a sound moral compass, and the necessary skills and knowledge to take on challenges of the future.[20] He or she is responsible to family, community, and nation, appreciates the beauty of the surrounding world, possesses a healthy mind and body, and has a zest for life. In sum, to cite from the DOE document, the learner emerging from the Singapore education system ought to be

- a confident person who has a strong sense of right and wrong, is adaptable and resilient, knows himself/herself, is discerning in judgment, thinks independently and critically, and communicates effectively;
- a self-directed learner who takes responsibility for his/her own learning, who questions, reflects, and perseveres in the pursuit of learning;
- an active contributor who is able to work effectively in teams, exercises initiative, takes calculated risks, is innovative, and strives for excellence; and
- a concerned citizen who is rooted to Singapore, has a strong civic consciousness, is informed, and takes an active role in bettering the lives of others around him/her.[21]

In line with these new guidelines, a review of primary education that was completed in 2009 charted the strategic directions for education for the next ten years.[22] The two broad recommendations are

- to balance the acquisition of knowledge with the development of skills and values through increased use of engaging and effective teaching methods, more holistic assessment, and a stronger emphasis on nonacademic aspects within the curriculum; and
- to invest more resources in schools in the areas of manpower, funding, and infrastructure.[23]

Based on this evolving view of the purposes of schools in this most recent phase of Singapore's education, a conceptual framework was developed to serve as a guide for teachers and school leaders to build twenty-first-century competencies among their students across the educational spectrum. Figure 1.3 illustrates the desired student outcomes and the twenty-first-century competencies.

The 21CC framework was used as a reference document with the ultimate goal of producing students who are confident persons, self-directed learners, concerned citizens, and active contributors—attributes deemed critical for survival in the twenty-first century. Social and emotional competencies, such as relationship management and social awareness, have been included in the framework as well.

At the core of the 21CC framework lie the values that are deemed to shape the individual. The competencies considered necessary for twenty-first-century survival are civic literacy, global awareness, cross-cultural skills, critical and inventive thinking, and information and communication skills.[24] Many of these competencies were already being taught in schools before the 21CC framework was implemented; however, the framework is in place so that schools will aim to strike a better balance between teaching of content knowledge and the acquisition of the necessary competencies and values for effectively functioning in a twenty-first-century environment. The following three sections briefly describe key components of the framework.

FIGURE 1.3 Desired student outcomes and 21CC

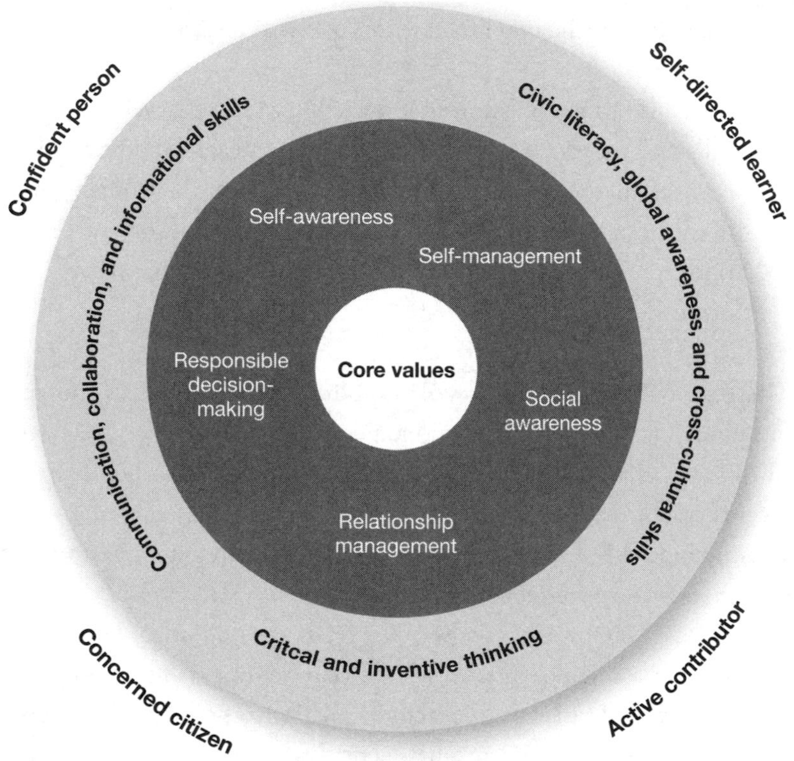

Source: http://www.moe.gov.sg/education/21cc/

Core values

Values are seen as being key in defining a person's character. They shape the beliefs, attitudes, and actions of a person, and are therefore selected to form the core of the 21CC framework.[25] The core values are derived from Singapore's shared values, family values, Singapore 21 Vision, and the National Education messages.[26] These values are articulated to stakeholders as shown in table 1.1.

Social and emotional competencies

The middle ring of the 21CC framework signifies the social and emotional competencies, which are skills necessary for students to recognize

TABLE 1.1 Core Values in the 21CC Framework

Respect	Responsibility	Integrity	Care	Resilience	Harmony
The child demonstrates respect when he believes in his own self-worth and the intrinsic worth of all people.	The child is responsible if he recognizes that he has a duty to himself, his family, community, nation and the world, and fulfills his responsibilities with love and commitment.	The child is a person of integrity if he upholds ethical principles and has the moral courage to stand up for what is right.	The child is caring if he acts with kindness and compassion, and contributes to the betterment of the community and the world.	The child is resilient if he has emotional strength and perseveres in the face of challenges. He manifests courage, optimism, adaptability and resourcefulness.	The child values harmony if he seeks inner happiness and promotes social cohesion. He appreciates the unity and diversity of a multicultural society.

Source: Ministry of Education, *Nurturing Our Young for the Future: Competencies for the 21st Century* (Singapore: Ministry of Education, 2010).

and manage their emotions, develop care and concern for others, make responsible decisions, establish positive relationships, and handle challenging situations effectively. These are explained in table 1.2.

Emerging twenty-first-century competencies

The outermost ring of the framework represents the emerging twenty-first-century competencies necessary for the globalized world today. Broadly, these are outlined in table 1.3.

Comparison of the 21CC Framework by the National Research Council

A comparison of the Singapore 21CC framework was made with the competency framework proposed by Hilton and Pellegrino of the NRC.[27] The Hilton and Pellegrino model aligns the various competencies that were identified into three domains of cognitive, intrapersonal, and interpersonal

TABLE 1.2   Social and Emotional Competencies in the 21CC Framework

Self-awareness	Self-management	Social awareness	Relationship management	Responsible decision making
The child has self-awareness if he understands his own emotions, strengths, inclinations, and weaknesses.	The child can manage himself effectively if he has the capacity to manage his own emotions. He should be self-motivated, exercise discipline, and display strong goal setting and organizational skills.	The child has social awareness if he has the ability to accurately discern different perspectives, recognize and appreciate diversity, and empathize with and respect others.	The child can manage relationships effectively if he has the ability to establish and maintain healthy and rewarding relationships through effective communication, and is able to work with others to resolve issues and provide assistance.	The child can make responsible decisions if he has the capacity to identify and analyze a situation competently. He should be able to reflect upon the implications of decisions made, based on personal, moral, and ethical considerations.

Source: Ministry of Education, *Nurturing Our Young for the Future: Competencies for the 21st Century* (Singapore: Ministry of Education, 2010).

TABLE 1.3 Emerging 21st Century Competencies in the 21CC Framework

Civic literacy, global awareness, and cross-cultural skills	Critical and inventive thinking	Communication, collaboration, and information skills
Society is becoming increasingly cosmopolitan and more Singaporeans live and work abroad. The young will therefore need a broader worldview and the ability to work with people from diverse cultural backgrounds, with different ideas and perspectives. At the same time, they should be informed about national issues, take pride in being Singaporean, and contribute actively to the community. Through these skills, the youth are expected to have an active community life, possess a strong national and cultural identity, and develop a sense of global awareness as well as sociocultural sensitivity.	To be future-ready, the young need to be able to think critically, assess options, and make sound decisions. They should have a desire to learn and explore, and should be prepared to think out of the box. They should not be afraid to make mistakes and face challenges that may at first appear daunting. They should learn to develop reasoning and decision-making skills, be curious and creative, carry out reflective thinking, and manage complexity and ambiguity.	With the Internet revolution, information is often literally just a click away. It is important that students know what questions to ask, how to sieve information and extract that which is relevant and useful. At the same time, they need to be discerning so that they can shield themselves from harm, while adopting ethical practices in cyberspace. Importantly, they should be able to communicate their ideas clearly and effectively. Skills to be inculcated in students include openness, ability to manage information and use it responsibly, and ability to communicate effectively.

Source: Ministry of Education, *Nurturing Our Young for the Future: Competencies for the 21st Century* (Singapore: Ministry of Education, 2010).

competence. Cognitive ability looks at factors such as fluid intelligence (reasoning, induction), crystallized intelligence (verbal comprehension, communication), and retrieval ability (creativity, ability to generate ideas). Intrapersonal competencies include openness, conscientiousness, and emotional stability, while interpersonal competencies explore the main factors of agreeableness and extroversion. Comparing the two frameworks, all the competencies in Singapore's 21CC framework can be categorized in the three domains of cognitive, intrapersonal, and interpersonal competencies, as as shown in table 1.4.

The skills represented in the middle ring of the Singapore 21CC framework—the social and emotional competencies of self-awareness,

TABLE 1.4   Competencies in Singapore's 21CC Framework Categorized in Cognitive, Intrapersonal, and Interpersonal Domains

Cognitive	Intrapersonal	Interpersonal
• Responsible decision making • Critical and inventive thinking • Information skills	• Self-awareness • Self-management • Social awareness • Civic literacy, global awareness, and cross-cultural skills • Core values	• Relationship management • Communication and collaboration

self-management, and social awareness—are almost all aligned to the intrapersonal competencies in the framework by Hilton and Pellegrino,[28] with the exception of relationship management, which fits nicely into the interpersonal domain. The Singapore competency of civic literacy, global awareness, and cross-cultural skills also fits into the intrapersonal domain and can be aligned to the Hilton and Pellegrino notion of openness, cultural awareness, and appreciation for diversity. The competencies of responsible decision making, critical and inventive thinking, and information skills in the Singapore 21CC framework fall neatly under the Hilton and Pellegrino domain of cognitive competencies, as they similarly look at cognitive processes and strategies, knowledge, and creativity. Communication and collaboration from the Singapore 21CC model is the other competency that falls under the Hilton and Pellegrino domain of interpersonal competencies, which looks at areas of communication and collaboration.

In short, competencies in the Singapore framework fit well in the three Hilton and Pellegrino domains of cognitive, intrapersonal, and interpersonal skills. On the other hand, there is less emphasis in the Singapore model in areas of positive core self-evaluation and leadership compared to their prominence in the Hilton and Pellegrino model. The caveat here is that the Singapore case study is not conducted in a way that can truly validate the model put forth by Hilton and Pellegrino. The following section provides a brief description of some of the observations that were made based on broad comparisons of the two frameworks.

Standards and benchmarks for 21CC

Following the introduction of the Framework for 21st Century Competencies and Student Outcomes in 2010, and as part of the systemic process of orienting its policies toward 21CC development, MOE embarked on a learning journey with five secondary schools between 2011 and 2013 to co-develop and trial whole-school approaches to 21CC development. During this process it conducted internal and external scans by scouring relevant local and international literature of existing practices in this area, and engaged in consultancy work with local and foreign academics.[29] To further support schools' efforts in this area, MOE also developed a set of standards and benchmarks to be used as a common point of reference for MOE and schools when planning for 21CC development. The standards are the twenty-first-century competencies—the outer ring of the framework as shown in figure 1.3—while the benchmarks further clarify and specify the standards, indicating developmentally appropriate targets for each stage: Primary 3 (Year 3) and Primary 6 (year 6), Secondary 2 (year 8) and Secondary 4/5 (years 10/11), and Junior College 2/Pre-University 3 (years 11 and 12). The benchmarks are pegged at levels that are achievable by the majority of students by the end of each stage. They do not impose a ceiling on students who are able to progress beyond the expected benchmark, but indicate the minimal competencies students should have acquired at the respective stages.

The standards and benchmarks outline what students should know and be able to do at each stage of their schooling journey, and provide a common point of reference for all teachers to plan and create learning experiences as well as gather evidence of learning when it comes to the emerging 21st Century Competencies.[30]

INITIATIVES IMPLEMENTED IN SCHOOLS

With the 21CC framework in place, schools need to equip students with the necessary knowledge, skills, and values for the new century. To incorporate the twenty-first-century competencies in the academic curriculum, schools have refined their pedagogy and assessment. For instance, many of the competencies and values depicted in the 21CC framework (e.g., civic literacy, critical thinking, cross-cultural and communication skills) are now explicitly taught in schools. To enable students to keep track of their own progress, schools are supported in the development of tools for holistic feedback and assessment. In addition, the quality of physical education, art, and music education was also strengthened. Schools have also employed co-curricular activities as a means of developing twenty-first-century competencies in students.[31] These initiatives are described in greater detail in the following sections.

Curriculum and Assessment

In order to enhance efforts at providing holistic education, the curriculum[32] and assessments were refined so as to make the teaching and learning of twenty-first-century competencies explicit through the medium of the academic content subjects. The 21CCs were envisaged to be seamlessly delivered through appropriate pedagogies and content. There are some 21CCs that are naturally inherent in the syllabus learning outcomes of certain subjects (such as civic literacy and global awareness in social studies), while others are naturally inherent in the pedagogies associated with other subjects (for instance, the scientific inquiry process in science nurtures critical thinking).

The quality of physical education, art, and music education was also strengthened as these subjects were considered to be integral to designing a holistic education experience for students. For instance, students at the upper secondary level are expected to be able to show their awareness of international trends in performing arts through their presentation of art works.[33] The infusion of values and twenty-first-century competencies enable students to develop physical robustness, enhance their creative and expressive capacities, and shape their personal, cultural, and social identity. Values and competencies are explicitly taught during character and citizenship education (CCE) lessons. CCE was formally introduced as a subject at all levels in all primary and secondary schools in 2014,[34] such that schools had to set aside curriculum time for it.[35] Before this, moral education was taught in schools but not formalized in such a manner, and schools were not obliged to conduct these lessons.

To create the space for critical thinking in the classroom, the content of all subjects was reduced by 30 percent. Testing and assessments were also redesigned to encompass critical thinking.[36] The purpose of the curriculum reduction was to free up space and time in the school curriculum to promote thinking and self-directed learning, as these are recognized as important skills required for the globalized economy.[37]

Examinations were revised to bring about a greater emphasis on twenty-first-century competencies. For example, thinking skills were incorporated through assessing students' skills in evaluating, synthesizing, decision making, and problem solving. Project work was implemented in every school, as it was deemed to help develop in students qualities such as curiosity, creativity, resourcefulness, and teamwork, which are highly valued and necessary for today's global world.[38] Project work is defined as "a learning experience which aims to provide students with the opportunity to synthesize knowledge from various areas of learning, and critically and creatively apply it to real-life situations. This process of fulfilling the project work components enhances students' knowledge and enables them to acquire skills like collaboration, communication, and independent learning, [and] prepares them for lifelong learning and the challenges ahead."[39]

Programme for Active Learning

The Programme for Active Learning (PAL) was introduced in primary schools to strengthen the emphasis on nonacademic programs with the objective of providing students with a more balanced and holistic primary education. The objectives of PAL are threefold: to provide students with broad exposure and experiences through fun and activities in sports and games as well as the performing and visual arts; to facilitate the all-round development of students; and to provide varied avenues for students to develop social and emotional competencies. PAL modules are experiential in nature and incorporate learning in a creative, fun, and enjoyable way. Additional manpower support was provided to schools to assist in planning, design, and implementation of PAL, as well as the financial support so that schools are able to engage instructors to conduct PAL modules, and to build areas conducive to learning for PAL. Students who have gone through the PAL are expected to exhibit confidence in what they do and express themselves effectively, to exhibit curiosity and a positive attitude toward learning, and to enjoy group experiences and teamwork.

National Education

National Education continues to be an important platform in the school curriculum, and it is another means of implementing the 21CC framework. The original objective of introducing National Education was to develop national cohesion, instill the drive for survival, and foster in students a sense of identity, pride, and self-respect that they have as Singaporeans.[40] It was also intended to strengthen the desire in students to contribute to a society and world that is larger than themselves.[41]

Co-curricular activities

Schools are also developing twenty-first-century competencies in students through a vast range of co-curricular activities (CCA), as these serve as natural platforms for the development of skills and values. Co-curricular activities have always existed in schools and are authentic platforms for the development of twenty-first-century competencies because they provide the perfect contexts for the learning and living of moral values, the acquisition and practice of soft skills, and the provision of a platform for social integration of children from different backgrounds and ethnic groups. However, CCAs were previously for learning of additional competencies in sports or arts and had no 21CC focus. To use CCAs as a platform for teaching twenty-first-century competencies, and to successfully infuse those competencies into CCAs, a three-pronged approach was undertaken.[42] First, there was a need to create the desired culture that supports student and teacher reflection and that encourages personal excellence. Second, school leaders were key movers needed to build a shared vision for CCA in their schools; the support structure for each CCA had to be increased, and more deliberate professional development and preparation for teachers helming CCAs had to be put in place. Third, opportunities for the infusion of twenty-first-century competencies in the CCA had to be identified, processes at the program level in CCA to develop twenty-first-century competencies had to be worked out, and guidance on the infusion of the competencies through the provision of program exemplars had to be given to schools.

Infrastructure and ICT

National education initiatives to create the infrastructure for school change had to be introduced.[43] One such initiative was the introduction of a comprehensive integration of ICT (information and communications technology) into curriculum and pedagogy in schools.[44] Singapore's first Masterplan for ICT in Education was launched in 1997, and it outlined a wide-ranging strategy for creating an IT-based teaching and learning environment in every school, so that all students will be IT-literate when they have completed their education.[45] Monetary resources for physical infrastructure and training of teachers had to be allocated from the national budget.[46]

The second ICT Masterplan for Education was started in 2003. Building on the foundation set from the first masterplan, the second plan aimed to strengthen the integration of ICT into the curriculum, and to lay the ground for the innovative use of ICT in schools. All schools were expected to achieve a baseline level of ICT use, and the MOE lent their support through the provision of resources and infrastructure. Schools were also given the autonomy to take full ownership of their schools' ICT implementation.

The third ICT Masterplan for Education was launched in 2009, and the acquisition of 21CC was explicitly stated as part of its objectives. The goal of this third masterplan was to ensure that students are able to carry out self-directed and collaborative learning through the effective use of ICT. Students were expected to learn to explore alternatives and make sound decisions, formulate questions and generate their own inquiries, plan and manage their time and workload effectively and efficiently, and reflect on their own learning, to name a few among many other twenty-first-century competencies integrated in the masterplan.[47] Through this masterplan, school leaders were expected to create the conditions in schools to harness ICT for enhancing teaching and learning. Teachers were expected to have the capacity to plan and deliver ICT-enriched learning experiences for students as well as nurture them to become responsible ICT users.

Along with the three ICT masterplans, an "Innovation and Enterprise" (I&E) initiative was started in 2004. It aimed to develop the spirit of innovation and enterprise through a systemwide approach.[48] Through the I&E initiative, schools were encouraged to experiment with new types of learning for their students and make decisions for themselves instead of sticking to a one-size-fits-all mold. [49]

One of the key initiatives of the IT masterplan was the establishment of six schools known as FutureSchools@Singapore. These schools were identified for the purpose of providing models for the integration of ICT into the curriculum and with the vision that their seamless and pervasive integration of ICT could be scaled up to other schools systemwide. Examples of these exemplary practices are digital modeling and games during math and science lessons, abstract concepts being taught via 3-D virtual worlds, and high-quality multimedia products used for developing language acquisition abilities and to enable a greater appreciation of the aesthetics.

Figure 1.4 gives an overview of the initiatives that were implemented in schools as part of the twenty-first-century competencies framework. The following case study demonstrates how these changes occurred in a particular school, the Kranji Secondary School, and how it went about implementing the initiatives articulated in the 21CC framework.

Case Study: Kranji Secondary School

Kranji Secondary School was founded in 1995 and is presently one of the top secondary schools in the western region of Singapore. The school has a total enrollment of 1,332 students and employs 86 teachers, 7 allied educators, and 15 support staff. The school started its 21CC journey in 2011 and used a phased approach for developing competencies in the academic curriculum by starting with the Secondary 1 classes and

FIGURE 1.4 School-based initiatives to support the 21CC framework

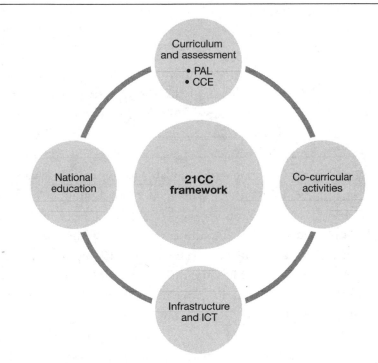

expanding by one level each subsequent year. A similar approach was used in the CCAs where the 21CC were introduced in all uniformed groups, one core sport, one performing arts group, and one club in phase one. The school did this by capitalizing on natural alignments with the total curriculum and leveraging on existing initiatives and programs, both academic and nonacademic, as well as focusing on service learning and student leadership in the CCAs.

To successfully implement the 21CC, the school also focused on the professional development of its teachers through increasing their familiarity with the 21CC framework, standards, and benchmarks; developing a shared understanding of 21CC; and enhancing teachers' competency in developing 21CC in curriculum planning. A core team was appointed and took the lead in carrying out a learning needs analysis, creating platforms for teachers to discuss 21CC matters, and sharing experiences and good practices.

In 2013, Kranji Secondary School was one of the few schools in Singapore to introduce the Thinking Curriculum. Under this initiative, students are exposed to Thinking Routines—simple protocols for exploring ideas and to make students' thinking visible to themselves and others so that they can improve it. For example, Thinking Routines are infused into project work for Secondary 2 students, who work on an interdisciplinary task that requires planning, teamwork, research, and critical thinking. Another example is getting Secondary 3 students to consider the challenges of living in a multiethnic society and using Thinking Routines to identify and focus on issues or problems. As the school heads into its fourth year of 21CC implementation, it will continue to revamp its Thinking Curriculum by creating a stronger link between explicit teaching and practice of Thinking Routines, using real-life applications on science and humanities, scaling up the use of Thinking Routines to all the upper secondary students, and injecting Thinking Routines into service learning.

In an e-mail interview with Miss Tan Hwee Pin, Principal of Kranji Secondary School, it was revealed that the school faces a couple of challenges in the implementation of 21CC. First, the school needs to consider how to better assess student outcomes in terms of critical and thinking processes. To overcome this, the school plans to identify a core group who will work on developing a range of assessments, both formative and summative, to measure student learning. This will be done in collaboration with other educational institutions that will provide an authentic learning context for students to apply their learning, thus creating a platform to assess students' thinking and help teachers better design lessons to bring about improved student outcomes in the areas of critical thinking and communication skills.

And second, it is a challenge to develop and multiply the competencies of teachers so they can design lessons with a sharper focus on twenty-first-century skills. The school has started to train a core group of teachers to be experts in the delivery of Thinking Routines and to provide guidance to other teachers in the use of 21CC rubrics with the purpose of identifying and understanding the opportunities that learning activities provide to build twenty-first-century skills in students. This core group of teachers will champion the professional development of their colleagues in this area, including conducting schoolwide workshops and mentoring the less experienced teachers. They will undertake studies using tools such as lesson study and action research to test emerging pedagogies to continually enhance the Thinking Curriculum. Given more resources, the use of Thinking Routines will be more pervasive when a whole-school approach is taken to make use of Thinking Routines in teaching and learning.

SUPPORTING TEACHER PROFESSIONAL DEVELOPMENT AND GROWTH FOR TWENTY-FIRST-CENTURY EDUCATION

With the Ministry of Education's articulation of the 21CC framework, the nation's teacher education institute undertook a total review of its teacher education programs using the framework as a guide and working in partnership with MOE and the schools.[50] This led to the articulation of the Graduand Teacher Competencies (GTCs) that outline the professional standards, benchmarks, and goals for graduands of the institute's teacher preparation programs. The GTCs are developed based on the annual teacher appraisal system, known as the Enhanced Performance Management System (EPMS), which spells out the expected teacher performance outcomes in terms of professional practice, leadership and management, and personal effectiveness. The GTCs indicate competencies that beginning teachers emerging from the teacher preparation program can be expected to possess, and these competencies are labeled as capacity-built (CB). Examples of such competencies are the following: adequate preparation to take on the core roles of nurturing the child and providing a high quality of learning of the child; strong subject mastery; and competencies related to the teaching and learning of the specific subject discipline, working with and respecting others, and attributes linked to personal effectiveness.

However, within a finite period available for teacher preparation, no pre-service program can be expected to fully equip teachers with all the competencies expected of a professional teacher. The teacher's professional development journey may therefore be viewed more appropriately as a continuum.[51] Additional competencies can be built and developed through continual professional development programs as the teacher progresses along his or her professional journey. The outcome of teacher education review is the articulation of the Teacher Education Model for the 21st Century, or TE21 for short, focusing on three key attributes of the twenty-first-century teaching professional: Values, Skills, and Knowledge.[52] TE21 presents recommendations that are intended to enhance the key elements of teacher education. Overall, there was an agreement of the broad principles necessary for pre-service and in-service training in the area of twenty-first-century competencies. Recommendations from the TE21 model guide the design and delivery of programs at the NIE and will be explained in detail in the following sections.

TE21: A Values-Driven Underpinning Philosophy

The TE21 model is firmly anchored on values. A three-pronged set of values—focusing on learner-centeredness, a strong sense of teacher identity, and contribution to the teaching fraternity—constitutes the values-centered philosophy underpinning the design and delivery of pre-service programs in Singapore.

Learner-centeredness: Belief that all students can learn

The first set of values puts the learner at the core of the teachers' work. In the Educational Psychology Core Courses, student teachers are introduced to key theoretical concepts about learners and learning and then asked to reflect on how these concepts can help teachers to facilitate and maximize learning at optimal levels for all students in diverse classrooms. Such reflections help student teachers to strengthen their beliefs that every child can learn despite the diversity of their profiles.[53]

Developing a strong sense of teacher identity

The second value paradigm is to enable teachers to develop a strong sense of professional teacher identity, since research evidence shows that those with a strong sense of teacher identity are likely to stay longer in the profession.[54] This identity may be manifested through teachers upholding the professionalism, integrity, and values of the teaching fraternity. A constant reminder about the ethos of the profession is documented in the Teachers' Pledge and creed which spells out the core mission of teachers as being able to bring out the best in their students.

Contribution to the profession and the community

The third value paradigm focuses on the professionalism of teachers in contributing back to the fraternity and the community at large. This is encouraged through the emphasis on group projects and collaborative learning in the pre-service teacher education courses so that the seeds of professional learning and sharing communities can be sown at pre-service and be brought into schools when graduands enter as beginning teachers.[55]

Key changes in the curriculum, pedagogies, assessment, physical infrastructure, as well as the addition of real-world learning have helped NIE to implement the TE21 model, as outlined in the following sections.

Curriculum changes

Coherent mapping of courses across the pre-service programs It is well acknowledged from research literature[56] that while the essential components necessary for preparing an excellent teacher may be present in a program, it is the coherence and the clear linkages built between the components that are the lynchpins ensuring the success of pre-service teacher preparation programs. For this reason, one of the first implementation strategies was to draw up a student teachers' learning journey and concept mindmap detailing exactly which component of training programs delivers a specific Graduand Teacher Competency or a specific value, skill, or knowledge domain outlined in the TE21 model.

Core mandatory programs focusing on values development In the twenty-first century, in addition to having a good disposition to lifelong learning, teachers need the skills and strategies to be more reflective, critical, and open-minded.[57] If teachers want to be effective in the classroom, they themselves must have participated in the processes and reflected on the values and dispositions of becoming a teacher.[58] One way of developing these value attributes in a pre-service teacher education program is to underpin a values-driven paradigm as part of its program.

The view about values development upheld by the teacher education institute is that values can be both caught and taught. Values can be taught through the formal curriculum as well as caught through experiential learning platforms such as service learning. For example, to ensure that values have a central focus in the teacher preparation programs, all student teachers are made to participate in two core mandatory programs: the Group Endeavors in Service Learning (GESL), a community-involvement experiential learning project, and the Meranti project (a personal and professional development two-day nonresidential workshop).

All student teachers participate in community projects of their choice in groups of twenty. They plan and implement the project with the help of a staff facilitator. In the process, they are sensitized to issues confronting our community, and they emerge confident of being able to facilitate community involvement projects in the future when they become qualified teachers.

The Meranti project (named after a tropical tree with extremely hard wood symbolizing resilience) helps student teachers to reflect upon their reasons for choosing teaching as a career and exposes them to a glimpse of their future roles as teachers through dialogue sessions with experienced teachers sharing real-life experiences. They also listen to academically "at-risk" students talking about the problems they face in learning and in schools in the twenty-first-century landscape.

Changes in pedagogies and assessment

The end goal of pre-service preparation is to produce thinking teachers who are effective instructors and facilitators of learning as well as good mediators and designers of learning environments. These are essential goals for anyone functioning in the twenty-first-century learning landscape where change is a constant and where information transfer is taking place at a breakneck pace. A few major pedagogical changes to achieve these goals are highlighted below.

Self-directed and real-world learning The major pedagogical change introduced has to do with the ownership of learning being transferred from the teacher (i.e., teacher educators) to the learner (i.e., student teachers). Three examples of practices used to build self-directed lifelong learners are:

- *Problem-based learning*: In the educational psychology courses, real-life school-based scenarios are used as discussion focal points. In this context, learners act as "active problem solvers" while teachers act as "mediating coaches."
- *Social context of education*: Student teachers are provided with a platform to organize student- led lessons where educational policies are discussed and reflected upon.
- *Real-world application*: Science courses are held on-site at junior colleges to encourage students to apply what they have learned to real lessons in schools.

Modeling the enabling power of technology Twenty-first-century teachers require new paradigms and competencies to prepare them to be mediators and designers of learning environments to engage their digitally native students. In this regard, the pre-service teacher education institute has recently developed its own Apple apps to enhance independent learning on the go, anytime and anywhere. One example is NIE mVideo that allows students to watch videos at their own pace, test their understanding on key concepts, and participate in online discussions. This app is designed with the flipped classroom in mind: content delivery is done outside the classroom while homework is done in the classroom.

The Assessment Competency Framework for twenty-first-century teaching and learning spells out a set of assessment literacy outcomes to be acquired by teachers from pre-service through to the professional teaching stage. Key processes that will enable both NIE educators and teachers to adopt innovative assessment practices *as*, *of*, and *for* learning are identified and scaled up across our programs (e.g., peer critique of lesson plans).

Transformation of physical infrastructure

In tandem with the pedagogical innovations, the physical infrastructure for teaching and learning must be transformed to support such innovations and skill acquisitions. To transfer the learning back to the students, the classrooms must be reconfigured. Accordingly, NIE has modified its classrooms, empowered by technology, to facilitate collaborative and interactive learning by students in groups.[59]

To implement the twenty-first-century competencies, teachers will be required to create an educational environment that is "increasingly flexible, customized, collaborative, and grounded by sound moral and social values."[60] They should also be able to respond to students who question more and who may learn better through self-discovery and an exchange of views with their peers as well as with their teachers as facilitators of their learning. The Deputy Director-General of Education (Professional Development) and Executive Director of the Academy of Singapore Teachers (AST), Mrs. Chua-Lim Yen Ching, shared her views below:

> The Ministry of Education works in close partnership with the National Institute of Education to design professional development programs that help our teachers develop and grow in their professional journeys. NIE also provides the research evidence-base to seed innovations in practice. The close practitioner-researcher nexus is important in order to ensure that research findings can be translated to improve practice that can ultimately help us to enhance student learning outcomes.

Improving the efficiency and equity of schooling depends on ensuring that teachers are highly skilled, well resourced, and motivated to perform at their best. Raising teaching performance is perhaps the policy direction most likely to lead to substantial gains in student learning.[61] Teacher education in Singapore attempts to engage education with its multifaceted challenges by a matrix of connectivity and alignment, allowing for a balance of autonomy and optimal monitoring and resourcing for their teachers. Teacher education builds on the national vision for Singapore to become a nation of thinking and committed citizens capable of contributing toward Singapore's continued growth and prosperity, and capable of becoming creative thinkers, lifelong learners, and leaders of change.

Educational initiatives are cascaded down to school leaders and teachers to ensure that all educators share the same vision and mission. A Philosophy for Educational Leadership for school leaders, an Ethos of the Teaching Profession related to teachers' professional practice, and the Desired Outcomes of Education (DOEs) together articulate the common purpose for educators.[62]

As many of the educational reforms require reflection, thinking, and creativity on the part of the teachers, schools also have to become learning organizations. Hence, there has been a push for the professionalization of school leaders and teachers, to get them involved as members of learning communities.[63] To achieve this, formal leadership training, such as the Leaders in Education Programme (LEP), was designed to equip leaders with requisite competencies and skills to manage schools as learning organizations.[64] For teachers, building their capacity to deliver the twenty-first-century competencies was crucial, and this would be achieved through pedagogical exemplars, training, and professional sharing.[65]

Academy of Singapore Teachers

In line with the need for training, the Ministry of Education established the Academy of Singapore Teachers (AST) to spearhead the professional development of Singapore teachers. It was envisioned to be the home of the teaching profession and a resource to help catalyze teacher capacity-building. Their mission is to build "a teacher-led culture of professional excellence centered on the holistic development of the child."[66]

A series of systemwide strategies were established to attain their vision. First, platforms for teacher-leaders to lead in professional learning were created via subject chapters, professional networks, professional focus groups, and professional learning communities. Second, strong organizational structures for professional learning were developed, among which are training entitlement for teachers; funding for MOE-organized courses; scheduled protected time for teachers to engage in lesson planning, reflection, and professional development activities; and an online portal providing one-stop access to learning, collaboration, and resources for all MOE staff. And third, to create a professional ethos, an MOE Heritage Centre was set up so that a slice of the past could be displayed to remind and inspire teachers, while awards and recognition for teachers were established to reward role models in education.

The Physical Education and Sports Teacher Academy (PESTA) and the Singapore Teachers' Academy for the Arts (STAR) were both set up in 2011. In the same year the English Language Institute of Singapore (ELIS) was set up to look at the professional development of English language teachers, while other centers catering to the professional development of Malay, Chinese, and Tamil language teachers were also established.

Teacher Growth Model

To support professional development planning, the Teacher Growth Model (TGM) was developed as a learning framework with desired teacher outcomes (see figure 1.5). The TGM Learning Continuum is organized according to five teacher outcomes: the Ethnical Educator; the Competent Professional; the Collaborative Learner; the Transformational Leader; and the Community Builder. Under each teacher outcome are the skills and competencies required for growth and development so that teachers can achieve the five teacher outcomes. Learning and development occurs in a variety of modes, such as courses, mentoring, e-learning, learning journeys, reflective practice, and research-based practice. Additionally, professional development courses are themed according to each desired teacher outcome so teachers can select the area that they would like most to be developed and sign up for courses themed under that outcome, for example, competent professional courses for those who want to hone their subject mastery competency.

FIGURE 1.5   Desired student outcomes and 21CC

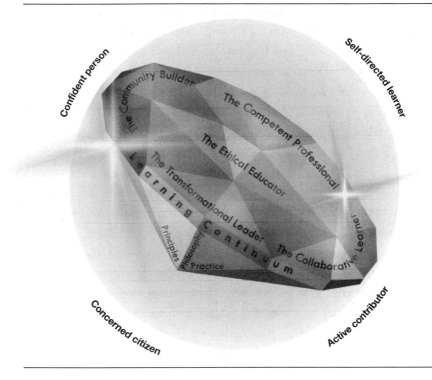

PROVIDING SYSTEMIC RESOURCES AND SUPPORT

To support these education reforms, the ministry has committed substantial structural and resource support. In addition to providing greater space for school-based flexibility in the curriculum by reducing content, there was also the freeing up of "an average of two hours per week for each teacher for professional planning and collaboration" by providing "one hour time-tabled time per week for teachers to reflect, discuss, and plan their lessons."[67]

An example of resource support provided by the MOE is the Flexible School Infrastructure (FlexSI) initiative where about S$40 million was set aside to allow schools to ensure that the school infrastructure was sufficiently flexible to support teaching approaches to better engage students in learning. Schools can modify their infrastructure, as by creating modular classrooms that can be opened up for larger group lectures or partitioned to become smaller areas for small-group discussions; developing an eco-street for the sciences; or building an outdoor amphitheater for the performing arts.[68] The infrastructural changes are to allow for interactive, experiential, independent, and hands-on learning.

Increasingly, primary schools are also being resourced with enhanced, new-generation infrastructure designed to support holistic education initiatives. Typical new features include "redesigned classrooms, outdoor learning spaces, and specialized rooms such as a band room, dance studio or performing arts studio and an outdoor running track."[69] The building of indoor sports halls and synthetic turf fields have also been undertaken to further enhance the infrastructure of the future.

Moving forward, both the teacher education institute and the Ministry of Education will further collaborate in resource development, by having teacher education faculty serve as consultants for MOE teams, leveraging on student teachers to produce resources for use in the classrooms, and tapping resources provided by teachers in milestone programs. In addition, the teacher education institute will also be a key partner in teacher professional development through the pre- and in-service training courses it provides, the postgraduate programs in more specialized fields, and the exploration of how e-learning can be harnessed in the classroom to improve the level of student engagement and thereby to improve student learning outcomes.

LESSONS LEARNED FROM THE SINGAPORE CASE STUDY

The push for the inclusion of twenty-first-century competences in Singapore's education system means new challenges and opportunities for schools. Singapore's experience in building an education system and national curricula to prepare students for a more globalized workplace and society has surfaced several lessons, some of which are highlighted below. These challenges have also been earlier articulated in a Ministry of Education document.[70]

First, the design of policy reforms must be clearly articulated and accompanied by serious implementation plans and the capacity to realize these plans. Singapore's key strength in educational reform lies not just in its ability to communicate its policy goals and intent but also in its adherence to a serious implementation plan that ensures that the initiatives are carried out with fidelity. Further, there is constant effort to seek ground-up views and feedback on policy issues that serve to initiate the next level of policy enhancements. A clear lesson from the Singapore case study is also that there needs to be a prioritization of resources and increased investments in areas of educational focus and emphasis so that the implementation can be scaled up systemically and best practices can be shared systemwide.

Another important point to raise is the importance of communication with consistency in the messaging of the initiatives, especially when some initiatives may take longer to implement and may span different governmental terms of office. A good way to include more twenty-first-century skills in schools is to get the buy-in of students, which was done retrospectively in Singapore's case. There is room for better communication and a higher degree of consultation with the students, which will allow them to share in and embrace the vision of change. Forums and dialogues between government officials and students would be a good way to interact with students—to hear and address their concerns to ensure more success in pushing through new policies and changes.[71]

Second, successful education systems tend to be open to new ideas and ways of innovation and are nimble in adapting to the changing educational landscape. In the case of Singapore, fresh ideas are very often sought deliberately by consulting senior professionals and administrators from both within the education sector and beyond. Looking beyond Singapore, it is also important to conduct environmental scans of other education systems internationally, both to learn from good practices as well as to adapt innovative ideas for the local context. Singapore does this by constantly organizing study trips to other education jurisdictions or participating in international platforms that generate such comparative case studies. An example of such an initiative is the Global Education Innovation Initiative

(GEII) helmed by Harvard University, the International Teacher Policy Study (ITPS) helmed by Stanford University, and the Asia Society initiative known as the Global Cities in Education Network (GCEN), all of which Singapore is a member of.

Third, the Singapore case study emphasizes the need to empower teachers and school leaders. Having a high-quality teaching workforce is paramount to the success of any education system. In the case of Singapore, teachers' roles have also changed in the different phases of educational development. For example, during the efficiency-driven phase, a teacher's main role was defined largely by her ability to transmit knowledge and values through a highly centralized curriculum. Although this core mission has not changed, it is clear that teachers are now given much more autonomy to design their own curriculum as long as they adhere to the DOE as a guide.

Fourth, the Singapore case study also shows that there are systemic structures in place to ensure that the policy initiatives can be shared systemwide. This is seen through the various zonal and cluster school systems where groups of school leaders meet perennially to share good practices and ideas about the implementation of latest educational initiatives.

IMPLEMENTATION OF 21CC IN SINGAPORE: ISSUES AND IMPLICATIONS

As with any systemwide implementation, there are real challenges and issues that have to be considered. Following are some of those raised by educators and practitioners in Singapore, either by e-mail or face-to-face interviews or expressed during a public symposium held in 2014.[72]

Competencies for the Future

Singapore educators were consistent in their expectation of a complex and uncertain twenty-first century. When asked about other skills that could possibly be included in the 21CC framework because they were essential in the current century, respondents mentioned the ability to handle ambiguity and uncertainty; knowledge in multiple disciplines rather than being constrained to one domain; knowing how to learn; and having a sense of social justice. The group of educators were also articulate about the need to inculcate in students an awareness of world events, cultures, and diversity, and to frame the 21CC contents to be more global in scope rather than individualistic. The schools might want to consider some of these as part of their twenty-first-century skills training for their students, bearing in mind the importance of giving students the space to explore and to allow ideas to flow. In a constantly changing landscape, the MOE 21CC framework cannot remain static but has to evolve with changing needs and time. Schools must be prepared to adapt, revise, and improvise.

Readiness of Teachers

Secondly, what should schools do to ensure that their teachers are ready for teaching twenty-first-century competencies and are equipped with the knowledge and competency to be role models for their students? Educators at the symposium were concerned about whether all teachers were sufficiently prepared to carry out this kind of intervention in the classroom, and whether schools needed to do more to improve teachers' competencies to another level.

Dimmock and Goh found that classroom pedagogy in Singapore was still focused principally on the organized and structured teaching of subject-based curriculum knowledge, largely shaped by national high-stakes assessment.[73] Some educators at the symposium pointed out that for teachers who are reliant on mentors and role modeling, there will be uncertainty on their part because they have not seen how twenty-first-century skills are to be taught. At the moment there is no consistent pedagogy across schools for teaching the new, higher-level, complex set of twenty-first-century competencies.[74] Moreover, teachers who have been educated too long ago in a teacher-dominated pedagogy may not currently have the necessary skills to meet the challenges posed to them in the future. Professional development, training, and retraining will be important. In addition, teachers need to be given space to make mistakes or fail and not have every misstep affect their work appraisal. The same twenty-first-century competencies of innovation and creativity should be applied to teachers in their work. Teachers need to be leaders and owners of their practice.

Involvement of Parents and Community

Thirdly, what is the role of the community in the teaching of twenty-first-century skills in the schools? How can the schools work together with key stakeholders such as parents, industry, and other training institutions? This is an issue that has yet to be fully addressed by schools in Singapore—how to bring parents into the school community to play a positive role. Values education needs to start from the family and not the school. However, with the push for 21CC, are schools overstepping their role as educators? Are schools doing too much that they are infringing on the care and upbringing duties of the parents? Are there specific character traits or values that should stay in the family and those that should come under the purview of the schools, and if so, who determines them? Where is the boundary between the school and parents? These are questions that need to be addressed by MOE as "character and values education" and "21CC" increasingly become the buzzwords for the Singapore education system. It is important to keep in mind that the tripartite relationship between parents, school, and community is critical in building up a child; it cannot simply be an effort on the part of the school, nor should the school embark on the 21CC journey alone. However, parent engagement and involvement is not an easy task. Parents have differing expectations, and it will be difficult to manage these expectations and get parents to be in tandem with the school and get wholly on board with all the 21CC initiatives that are to be implemented.

Mind-Set Changes

There was a consensus at the public symposium that the mind-sets of parents needed to be changed. Singapore is a country where meritocracy is the norm and integral to its political and educational systems.[75] Underpinning the whole education system is the belief that education is the route to advancement and that hard work pays off—for all students, regardless of background and ability.[76] Such a society includes social stratification, with individuals rewarded in occupational positions that provide varying degrees of influence, compensation, and status. Singaporeans have been persuaded to believe that those in leadership positions or those who are successful in life have worked hard and qualified through their own achievements. A sustained meritocracy like this places the maximum emphasis on ability, effort, and achievement.[77] Those who have achieved merit through their own efforts are granted stature, privilege, and respect in society. Success by this definition is pretty much the universal aspiration of Singaporeans from the moment they start school. As a result, educators at the symposium pointed out that despite the shift towards 21CC, assessment milestones and national examinations remain uppermost in the minds of parents and students alike, and academic pursuit therefore is still their ultimate focus. Singapore's education system has traditionally been one that is obsessed with grades, and the large and booming tuition industry provides evidence for the expectations that parents have for their children to excel academically.[78] Therefore, the examination-oriented mind-set poses a challenge to schools that want to innovate, as school principals are ultimately still held accountable for their students' performance in the national examinations.[79]

It was suggested that only with a systemic shift of focus from academic concerns to an emphasis on life skills, and a change of mind-set throughout schools, parents, and community alike, can the twenty-first-century competencies finally be ingrained in students at all levels and ages. This will be a lengthy journey as systemwide changes also have to be implemented for parents to accept the shift of focus away from grades. The challenge is whether the twenty-first-century initiatives delve deeply enough below the surface level to change the basic philosophy and approach to education.[80]

Reaction of Students

In a study by Ng, some students expressed their dissatisfaction with the approach of change.[81] While the message from the government was one that was advocating a shift away from examination results and encouraging creativity, on the ground, school leaders and teachers were still obsessed with results. Hence, students felt that the message was not consistent with what was experienced. Trapped in such an academic system, students themselves had no choice but to focus on results and grades as the education system was still functioning in a result-oriented paradigm. Promotion to the next level in school was still dependent on grades, while university entrance was also based on grades. This unresolved conflict between twenty-first-century soft skills and the need to perform well academically has led to students in a constant state of flux, finding that they are unable to let go of the stressful chase for every single mark and fully embrace innovation and creativity.

Danger of Widening the Equity Gap

While schools have started to strengthen physical education, art, and music education and place more emphasis on co-curricular activities as measures to infuse twenty-first-century competencies, if left unchecked these initiatives might instead serve to further instantiate the ideology of inequality, ultimately widening the gap between top and low achievers.[82] Though the idea behind exposing students to the broad areas of sports and performing arts is to give all children the opportunity to discover and hone their skills in a variety of nonacademic pursuits, it is not clear that all students are equally placed to do well in these areas. Even if the MOE provided all schools with the same amounts of financial support for these nonacademic programs, upper- or middle-class Singaporean parents are likely to enroll their children in activities such as exclusive sports camps, tennis lessons, and dance classes that engage expensive and exceedingly qualified instructors in order to secure higher achievements for their children in these domains—achievements that can then be used to secure placements for them in elite schools or to increase their chances of winning prestigious scholarships. Ironically then, the exposure of all students to a wider range of activities that also count for merit can lead to a greater monopolization of success by more privileged groups.[83]

Challenges to Be Faced

There are also clear challenges in the implementation of the twenty-first-century competencies that must be overcome if the 21CC framework is to be considered a success. First, in order to successfully implement each educational reform or initiative with fidelity, there is a need for strong mutual respect between the educational professionals and the political powers that govern the country. Both the professionals and political powers must be committed to a long-term goal for education for sustainability. This vision must transcend the transience of political leadership. In the case of Singapore, political stability has played a key role in ensuring continuity in education policy. The same political party has been in power since independence, although minority opposition parties have been winning seats within the government in recent years.

Second, there needs to be commitment towards a collective vision. In the case of Singapore, the clearly articulated desired goals of education serve as a guide, but alignment toward these goals must mean that the individual's ideals might need to be compromised for the sake of the collective vision. This also speaks of the cultural context within Singapore which makes the realization of a collective vision plausible and possible.

Finally, for systemic coherence to occur, there must be time and effort spent conducting many in-depth conversations with key stakeholders in education across all levels. It is of paramount importance that the Ministry of Education take into consideration not just the expert views provided by educational professionals and researchers or future employers of the products of our education system, but also the voices of parents, the community, and the students themselves. This requires much time and effort dedicated to focus-group discussions so that there is not just buy-in of education policies but that new education initiatives can also be seeded from ground up.

In the final analysis, Singapore's meteoric rise in its economy in a matter of a few decades was made possible through its educational success, which helped to build the human resources the economy needed. This success is a result of careful and deliberate judicious policy planning and formulation at every step of the way, and of fidelity in the implementation of each of these policy initiatives. The fidelity of implementation is made possible through systemic coherence and goal alignment, which in turn is achieved through the quintessential cultural and political context of

Singapore. This case study has also highlighted the real challenges already faced and the implications of such challenges for the future. The challenges underlie the important message that continued educational and economic success can only be sustained if Singapore continues to learn not just from its own journey but from other education systems around the world.

Thinking Big, Acting Small: Lessons from Twenty-First-Century Curriculum Reform in China

Yan Wang
National Institute of Education Sciences, China

This chapter explains how China's education reforms have attempted to prepare students for the twenty-first century, including a discussion of the context for these reforms, the efforts to promote a national conversation about twenty-first-century competencies, the resulting changes to the curricular landscape, and the strategies and challenges involved in the advancement of such competencies. A concluding section discusses the recent reforms to address the challenges and proposes that the approach of "thinking big, acting small" captures the lessons of China's current education reform.

INTRODUCTION

China is one of the largest developing countries in the world. Located in the eastern part of the Asian continent, on the western Pacific rim, it covers an area of 9.6 million square kilometers,[1] with a total population of 1.36 billion.[2] China is economically developing, and its GDP per capita reached 42,000 RMB Yuan in 2013, as a result of rapid economic growth for three decades—an impressive achievement. The great size of the country and its population in relation to its economic development level have made the achievement of widely accessible, quality education a formidable challenge.

In China there are twenty-three provinces, five autonomous regions, four municipalities directly under the central government, and two special administrative regions. Moreover, fifty-six different ethnic groups live within its borders, with the Han people accounting for more than 90 percent of the total population, and the remaining fifty-five groups referred to as "ethnic minorities." Each province, region, municipality, and ethnic group is distinct in its cultural tradition and economic development. Such variety and diversity have further contributed to the complexity of advancing education reform toward the goal of access, quality, and equity.

China is also one of the countries that have experienced the most rapid change on a large scale in the field of education. In slightly over fifty years it has established its education system from scratch, achieved a universally accessible nine-year basic education, essentially eradicated youth and adult illiteracy, and attained a 30 percent gross enrollment rate to higher education.[3] As a result, China now boasts the largest education system in the world. Statistics shows that there are 255,400 primary schools enrolling 98.6 million students, and 81,662 secondary schools enrolling 94.2 million students in 2013. The number of higher education institutions amounts to 2,442, with an enrollment of approximately 25.6 million students.[4] Similar to many countries, however, many challenges persist: while some areas, particularly in rural and poverty-stricken regions, are still relying on multi-grade teaching with inadequate facilities and teaching force, other areas, particularly in urban and developed regions, boast schools with facilities and teachers whose quality is comparable to those in top-performing developed nations.

Looking back at the past three decades, China has impressed the world not only by expanding access to education to many more students, but also by increasing the quality of that education, as attested by Shanghai's ranking at the top of the 2009 PISA results. Such progress is largely attributable to its persistent endeavors to reform its education system to be responsive to political, social, and economic development. These endeavors have continued into the twenty-first century, characterized by experimentations and innovations to change the strategy, content, and ways of delivering education. Among other policy initiatives, the curriculum reform that commenced at the turn of the century changed the purposes, content, and approaches to teaching and learning in China's schools. Further reforms were soon to follow, especially in teacher professional development and in the creation of demonstration and innovation schools.

CONTEXT OF EDUCATION REFORM FOR TWENTY-FIRST-CENTURY COMPETENCIES

The education system in China—shaped by thousands of years of history and influenced as well by contemporary political and economic reforms—operates differently from education systems in other countries. Therefore it is necessary to discuss the context for the current education reforms and the purposes of schooling in China before delving into a more explicit discussion about education for the twenty-first century.

Inherited Education Culture

As one of the world's most ancient civilizations, China has a recorded history of nearly four thousand years. Chinese peoples' perception of education, the value they place on education, and how education is conceptualized and delivered have been largely influenced by a strong and well-established culture of education, rooted in its rich and long history.

For over 1,300 years, education in China was essentially the self-motivated pursuit of learning in preparation for the royal court examination (*keju*), which was organized around a range of classics, such as the "Four Books" and "Five Classics," for the meritocratic purpose of screening and selecting talents for official service.[5] Confucius's statements, such as "Excellence in education leads to officialdom," illustrate the historical value education holds in China's culture. Common people, especially those with low socioeconomic status, used to possess few channels for social mobility other than education. Through success in royal court examinations, however, they could be appointed as officials that enjoyed high social status, changing not only their own destiny but also that of their whole family. This meritocratic tradition of selecting and cultivating talent has largely influenced the emphasis placed on today's education assessment system. While recent reforms have enabled students to enter university by alternative paths, China's high-stakes college entrance examination is the main determiner of a majority of students' college placements and further determiner of students' prospects for work and life.[6]

Changing Purposes of Schooling

Without knowing about the historical shifts in the purposes of schooling that have taken place in China, it would be hard to understand the most recent education reform oriented toward the twenty-first century. A range of educational purposes have been observed in the process of education development in China, encompassing political, economic, and social goals, yet each phase in history has featured a distinct priority in the education development agenda.

Ideological orientation (1949–1976)

Upon the foundation of the People's Republic of China, the main mission of education was defined as to "upgrade people's intellectual level and cultivate talents for national construction, to eliminate feudalist, comprador, fascist ideology, and develop the ideology of serving the people" in a fundamental Common Program, which prioritized ideological orientation for the purpose of nation building. The guideline of education was further said to be "serving the workers and peasants and serving the production and construction."[7] The priority of ideological orientation was illustrated in the argument by Mao Zedong in 1957: "Education must serve the politics of the proletariat and must combine with productive labor so that those being educated develop morally, intellectually, and physically, and become workers with socialist consciousness and culture."[8] "Moral, intellectual, and physical development" became the overarching socialist education guidelines. With moral development standing on top of the list, not only did schools offer courses on ethics and morals, but students were also encouraged to engage in various political campaigns and community activities, even to the neglect of intellectual and physical development. Political identity became a criterion for screening talents.[9] This orientation was highlighted to the extreme in the anti-intellectualism and deliberate degeneration of academic education during the devastating Cultural Revolution.

Manpower matching (1977–1998)

After the ten-year hiatus in national development brought about by the Cultural Revolution, China aspired to catch up with the rest of the world. The nation was steered from political struggle to economic reconstruction by means of economic reform, opening up under the leadership of the late Comrade Deng Xiaoping since 1978. Education was seen as a crucial means to buttress China's economic and social progress. As Deng Xiaoping stated in a 1985 speech, "Our nation, the power of our nation, and the potential of economic development depend more and more on the quality of laborers and the number and quality of intellectuals." This rationale was highlighted in the ground-breaking Decision on Educational Structural Reform issued in 1984, a complementary document to support the policy on economic reform: "Education must serve socialist construction, which in turn must rely on education. Our massive socialist modernization program requires us not only to give full rein to the skilled people now available and to future enhance their capabilities, but also to train, on a large scale, people with new types of skills who are dedicated to the socialist cause and social progress into the 1990s and the early days of the next century." Deng Xiaoping's directive "to train talent, and to train hundreds of millions of quality labor force suitable for modernization construction and millions of specialized talents for all walks of life,"[10] illustrates the priority that was placed on using education to develop China's human resources at the time.

In the meantime the college entrance examination was reinstituted for selecting and screening talents into higher education. It unshackled people's enthusiasm for education and enabled everybody to compete, by their performance on the examination, for the opportunity to enter universities (rather than being selected by political identity and recommendations by other people). Though officially the expected competencies for the new generation were redefined as "The Four Have's"—that is, citizens should have lofty ideals, integrity, knowledge, and a strong sense of discipline[11]—only knowledge could be measured by the college entrance examination, hence knowledge acquisition dominated teaching and learning for quite a while.

Holistic development (1999–present)

Starting from the late 1990s, while economic growth was still high on the government's agenda, social harmony became another priority in a context of cultural diversification as a result of economic reform and opening up to the world. In the education arena, the pursuit of social cohesion has been translated into the cultivation of ethics and values as well as "soft" skills such as "learn to be" and "learn to learn." Therefore, the state shifted from a strong, politically oriented, and narrow manpower-development conception of education to a broader perspective that puts emphasis on holistic development of Chinese citizens. In the same vein, the foci of curriculum and pedagogy shifted from the "two basics"—basic knowledge and basic skills—to a tridimensional goal encompassing "knowledge and ability, process and method, and emotion, attitude, and values." In effect, this shift introduced the more exhaustive list of twenty-first-century competencies into the Chinese education system.

Education Reform for Access and Equity

The initiative of twenty-first-century competencies was built on the foundation of universal access to basic education. Since the early 1980s the Chinese government has devoted substantial efforts to expanding access to education. The government legislated compulsory education in 1986 that obliged all parents to send their school-aged children to schools for a nine-year basic education—six years of primary and three of lower secondary education. Meanwhile, the responsibilities of providing education—in particular school governance and finance—were decentralized to local (county and township) governments. When the financial capacity of local government was not commensurate to the needs of their schools, community resources were mobilized for school sponsorship, including charging tuition and miscellaneous fees to fill the funding gap. This approach gained the schools in economically developed areas a much stronger financial base. Similarly, historically prestigious schools attracted more students and charged more fees, thus acquiring a better financial base for experimentation and innovation. As a result, access to schooling was expanded, although performance in various regions, areas, and even schools was unequal.

Twenty years later, when the country's financial reserves became much stronger, the government committed to funding compulsory education with public budgets. The resulting 2006 Amendment of Compulsory Education Law mandated nine-year basic education to be compulsory and free of charge and that the responsibilities of financing primary and lower secondary education should be shared among central, provincial, and local governments, which set their per-student expenditure now lower than the threshold (minimum) per-student expenditure decided by the central government. County/district governments are charged with the responsibility of funding, while provincial governments are required to allocate resources to lower-achieving areas. Thus primary and lower secondary education is provided to all school-aged children with no tuition or fees; they are also provided with free textbooks, and subsidies to disadvantaged students from centrally earmarked funds. In this way, a foundational universal access to nine-year basic education was achieved. Meanwhile, it became possible for the educationally developed areas to lead the education reform by cutting-edge experimentation and innovation, including curriculum and pedagogy reform relating to twenty-first-century competencies.

POLICY SHIFT TO ADVANCE TWENTY-FIRST-CENTURY COMPETENCIES

The shift toward twenty-first-century competencies in China has not happened overnight. China's move toward reforming its education system to meet the demands of the current century started from an ethos of "Orientation Toward Modernization, World, and Future" articulated by Deng Xiaoping in the early 1980s; went through a three-decade-long reflection and debate about quality-oriented education (as opposed to examination-oriented education); and resulted in a ground-breaking Basic Education Curriculum Reform.

Education Oriented Toward Modernization, World, and Future

The earliest notion related to education for the twenty-first century can be traced back to the late 1970s. It was realized that the system of education in China, a system largely copied from the Soviet Union, had not fit into the demand of the four modernizations,[12] nor was it suitable for the opening up of society following the end of the Cultural Revolution. Education reform reached a deadlock. In 1983 Deng Xiaoping, in his inscription at Jingshan School in Beijing, noted that education should be oriented toward modernization, the world, and the future. His statement was underpinned by three assumptions: first, education was regarded as a critical means of generating talents or skills for economic development; second, the education system should be opened up and renewed by drawing upon the experiences of other countries; and third, educators should take a forward-looking perspective to change the way of learning and teaching so as to foster the kind of knowledge and competencies that could meet the future needs of the nation. The inscription provoked the educators to rethink the approaches and strategies to reform and develop education. The China Education Society, at a national meeting themed on "three orientations," suggested that the following five relationships should be emphasized:

- The relationship between knowledge learning and intellectual development, including the cultivation of creativity
- The relationship between teaching well and learning well
- The relationship between education and production and labor
- The relationship between collective teaching and individual guidance, tailoring teaching to students' aptitude
- The relationship between curricular and extracurricular spheres, in school and out of school

Two years after the inscription, "three orientations" was written into the overarching policy document *Decision on Educational Structural Reform*, becoming the strategic guideline of education development and reform and being reiterated in major policy documents in the ensuing two decades. The China Education Society organized five more meetings, with the last one held in 1998, discussing how to implement "three orientations" and push education development into the twenty-first century, which had a far-reaching and profound influence on the education sector.[13]

Quality Education versus Examination-Driven Education

Once the college entrance examination was reinstituted after the Cultural Revolution in 1978, drilling for high scores in written examinations began to dominate in the classroom. Education in the 1980s was characterized by teaching to the test and learning by rote. The concept of quality education then emerged, as a corrective measure to deal with "examination-oriented" education. In Chinese, "quality," literarily, is a term close to "competency." Hence quality education was defined as a kind of education focusing on nurturing competencies (an earlier form of twenty-first-century competencies) rather than on imparting knowledge per se. The concept was originated from an editorial in the journal *Shanghai Education* in 1988 under the title "Quality Education Is the New Goal of Lower Secondary Education," and in 1990 "to push forward quality education in primary schools" became a local policy initiated by Jiangsu Province, a forerunner of education reform in China. Quality education was instituted as a national policy in the 1993 Outline of China's Education Reform and Development, which not only reiterated "three orientations" to accelerate education reform and development and further upgrade qualities of labors, but also emphasized a shift from "examination-oriented education" toward "quality-oriented education" that "fully encompasses the moral, intellectual, physical, and ideological development of all students, including the cultivation of their skills in literacy and science."[14] Among other things, the *Outline* highlighted students' practical skills and ability to be innovative. A series of national conferences were held to deliberate how to push forward "quality education."[15] In 1999, the *Decision on Deepening Education Reform and Fully Advancing Quality Education of the CCP and State Council* was promulgated at the third National Education Conference. In the *Decision*, quality education was redefined with a broader range of competencies, such as "entrepreneurship and practical ability, independent thinking and innovative awareness, scientific spirit and innovative thinking habits."[16]

Action Plan to Invigorate Education Oriented Toward the Twenty-First Century

The conversation about twenty-first-century education in China, in its formal sense, began from a survey initiated by the government in the late 1990s. Being aware of the challenges of the knowledge economy in the upcoming century, the government recognized education as a means to improve the nation's ability to innovate and enhance its competitiveness. The government sensed the urgency of updating the education system and started the reform by reassessing the strategy and priorities of education development. The survey involved over one hundred experts from various sectors as well as related government agencies and local education authorities. As a result, a blueprint for education reform titled Action Plan to Invigorate Education Oriented Toward the Twenty-first Century (*mianxiang 21 shiji jiaoyu zhenxing xingdong jihua*) was promulgated by the Ministry of Education, after endorsement by the State Council. The Action Plan mapped out developmental goals and programs to achieve the goals at the turn of the century in twelve areas. On top of the list of programs is the "cross-century quality education program."[17] The program highlighted the goal of "advancing quality education across the board and upgrading the citizens' quality and the innovative ability of the nation," and more importantly, to pursue "twenty-first-century basic education curriculum and textbooks" in schools, which became the prelude to the Basic Education Curriculum Reform.[18]

Basic Education Curriculum Reform

In the field of basic education, the Action Plan was translated into a policy titled the State Council's Decision on Reforming Basic Education. The reform started from a survey to assess the implemented curriculum from grades 1 to 12 from 1996 to 1997, and to check the relevance of the curriculum, content, pedagogy, homework, examinations, and assessment. The survey showed an overemphasis on instilling knowledge, with students learning mostly by rote memorization and mechanical drills. There was also a lack of consistency among various subjects, an imbalance in the distribution of courses, and a centralized curriculum that the administration could not fit with local realities. To address these issues, the Basic Education Curriculum Reform Outline was formulated and adopted.

As with many other policies, the formulation of the Outline followed five steps: conducting surveys, drafting, consulting, experimenting, and implementations and expansion.[19] It began with stakeholder surveys—including teachers, parents, researchers, local authorities, and communities—followed by the drafting of the document by a team of researchers, practitioners, and administrators. It then went through consultations with schools, teachers, and local governments to solicit their opinions on the relevance and feasibility of the policy. The trial policy was piloted in four provinces and amended on the basis of the resulting feedback. The finalized policy was implemented nationwide.

The Basic Education Curriculum Reform Outline is a typical example of the five-step policy-making process. The initial survey involved 16,000 students and over 2,000 teachers across nine provinces (regions) in primary and lower secondary schools, as well as 14,000 students and 2,000 teachers across eleven provinces in upper secondary schools. The curricula for both grades 1–9 and grades 10–12 were piloted before being extended nationwide. Tables 2.1 and 2.2 show how the curricula were rolled out stage by stage.

The 2001 Outline mapped out a range of guidelines for curriculum, pedagogy, and assessment for grades 1 through 12. In the same year, the basic education curriculum framework (scheme) as well as standards for twenty-two subjects were issued, followed by a regulation on compiling, reviewing, and selecting textbooks.[20] Soon after, the Upper Secondary Education Curriculum Scheme was issued in 2003, and standards for seventeen subjects were developed (including the standards for philosophy and

TABLE 2.1   Extension of China's compulsory education curriculum by stages

Year	% of students learning new curriculum
2001	0.5%–1%
2002	18%–20%
2003	40%–50%
2004	70%–80%

Source: Zhu Muju, 2007.

TABLE 2.2   Extension of China's upper secondary education curriculum by stages

Year	No. of participant provinces (regions)
2005	2
2006	7
2007	12
2012	Nationwide

Source: Zhu Muju, 2007.

politics issued in 2004). The reform profoundly changed education phi-losophy, content, and pedagogy for education from grades 1 through 12.

Core Competencies Initiative

The first decade of the current century has seen rapid economic growth accompanied by excessive material pursuit, the degradation of traditional culture, and ideological diversification. To address these issues, the social-ist core values were highlighted at the 18th Congress of the Communist Party convened in 2012. The core values comprise a set of moral princi-ples including prosperity, democracy, civility, harmony, freedom, equality, justice, the rule of law, patriotism, dedication, integrity, and friendship. In the same vein, the ultimate mission of education is defined as "cultivating morals and nurturing people, fostering socialist builders, and developing students morally, intellectually, physically, and esthetically."

In the meantime, China engaged in more dialogue and interaction with the world and began to learn more from other countries to inform policy making in the field of education. Inspired by the international trend of key competencies, the new ideology was translated into the core competencies initiative beginning in 2014. It attempted to fill the gap between educational goals and curriculum goals and to enhance the cultivation of general competencies as well as ethics and morals demanded by the twenty-first century, as illustrated in the following objectives:

1. Coordinating education at the primary, lower secondary, upper secondary, tertiary, and postgraduate levels, clarifying the educational goals at each stage and reinforcing coherence among learning of subjects at various stages.
2. Coordinating subjects such as moral education, Chinese language (reading, writing, and literature), history, physical education, arts, etc., enhancing the complementariness among various subjects and increasing students' abilities of comprehensively applying knowledge to solve real-world problems.
3. Coordinating curriculum standards, textbooks, teaching, assessments, and examinations; prioritizing the overarching role of curriculum standards, to push forward concerted reform of textbook compilation, teaching, evaluation, and examination.
4. Coordinating the forces of frontier teachers, administrators, pedagogical researchers, experts, scholars, and communities; giving play to their advantage and creating synergy in teaching, service, pedagogical guidance, research, and monitoring.
5. Coordinating classrooms, campus, social organizations, family, and society; reinforcing the linkages between classroom teaching, campus culture-building, and social activities; extensively utilizing social resources, design, and curricular and extracurricular activities for a favorable education environment.

The core competencies basically incorporate three dimensions—social participation, self-development, and cultural competencies—and so far ten indicators have been developed. The content of the core competencies has not been publicized yet. But it is fair to say that the initiative will reorient the school education to the challenges in the new century and bring about another wave of changes to the learning and teaching content and method in schools.

CHANGED CURRICULUM LANDSCAPE

The term "curriculum" in the context of China refers to the learning content to be delivered in school and to related pedagogy that is mostly embodied in textbooks. The curriculum landscape has gone through a drastic change since the adoption of the Basic Education Curriculum Reform in 2001. As noted above, the learning objective shifted from basic knowledge and basic skills (two basics) toward a broad range of "knowledge and ability, process and method, and emotion, attitude, and values" which are manifest in curriculum standards for all the subjects and are closer to cognitive, intrapersonal, and interpersonal competencies. The following section illustrates these changes in the curriculum standards of several subjects.

Twenty-First-Century Competencies in Curriculum Standards
Curriculum standards for mathematics
Typically, the educational goal of the subject of mathematics is to teach students knowledge and skills, mathematical thinking, problem solving, and emotions and attitude. In the same vein, the learning standards are structured around four aspects: the first two aspects are associated with cognitive competencies, the latter two are for interpersonal and intrapersonal competencies, as illustrated in table 2.3.

Curriculum standards for reading, writing, and literature
Similarly, the curriculum standards for reading, writing, and literature (Chinese language) are structured around knowledge and ability, process and method, and emotions, attitude, and values. The learning objectives

TABLE 2.3   General goals for grades 1–10 mathematics

Knowledge and skills	• Experience the processes of numeracy and algebra, calculation, and modeling; grasp the fundamental knowledge and basic skills on numeracy and algebra. • Experience the processes of collecting and processing data, analyzing issues with data, and obtaining information; grasp the fundamental knowledge and basic skills on statistics and probability. • Take part in integrated hands-on activities, accumulate mathematical activity experiences of solving simple questions by applying mathematical knowledge, skills, and methods.
Mathematical thinking	• Establish a sense of mathematics, awareness of symbols, and conception of space; develop ability of geometric perception and calculation, develop imaginative thinking and abstract thinking. • Learn to think independently, feel fundamental philosophy and way of thinking of mathematics.
Problem solving	• Learn to identify and raise questions from mathematical perspective, solve simple realistic issues by applying mathematical knowledge, and enhance application awareness and upgrade practical ability. • Learn to collaborate and communicate with others. • Form awareness of evaluation and reflection.
Emotions and attitudes	• Take part in mathematical activities actively and have curiosity for and readiness to learn mathematics. • Experience the joy of success in the learning process, foster perseverance to overcome difficulties and build up confidence. • Form learning habits such as conscientiousness and diligence, independent thinking, collaboration and sharing, reflection and questioning. • Foster scientific attitudes such as adherence to truth, correcting mistakes and being rigorous and practical.

Source: Ministry of Education, 2011.

for each grade are organized into five levels: literacy (recognizing and writing Chinese characters), reading, writing, oral communication, and integrated learning for four stages: stage1 (grades 1–2), stage 2 (grades 3–4), stage 3 (grades 5–6), and stage 4 (grades 7–9). While the first three levels are basically for cognitive competencies, that is, applying tools interactively, the latter two are mostly associated with interpersonal and intrapersonal competencies. The higher the grade, the more sophisticated the learning standards. For example, the standards for stage 3 that deal with writing include: a) understanding that writing is for self-expression and communication with others, and b) fostering habits of observing things in one's

surroundings, conscientiously enriching one's knowledge, cherishing individual particular feelings, and accumulating materials for writing. The
standards on the part of oral communication are specified as the following:

- to respect and understand others when communicating
- to participate in discussion and be unafraid of voicing one's
  own opinion
- to listen seriously and patiently, to capture key points and convey
  the message
- to express oneself clearly and appropriately
- after preparation, to make a simple presentation suitable to a
  specific audience and occasion
- to be aware of the beauty of language and avoid improper
  language[21]

Curriculum standards for science

At the lower secondary education level, the subject of science aims "to
maintain students' curiosity and longing for learning about natural phe-
nomena and to foster their attitudes of being in harmony with nature" as
well as "to nurture their scientific way of thinking and to be aware of individual and social problems and solve them with scientific knowledge,
approach, and attitude," among other things.[22] The learning goals incorporate four dimensions: a) exploration of science, b) knowledge and skills
of science, c) attitude, emotion, and value of science, and d) science, technology, society, and environment. Under the dimension of "exploration of
science," there are such integrated learning objectives as "expression and
communication," or more specifically, "to be good at collaborating with
peers, to be able to listen and respect different viewpoints and comments
and exchange opinions with others."[23]

Integrating and Streaming

The new curriculum is aimed at enabling students to engage in active
learning, to learn how to learn, and to acquire the ethics, knowledge, and
competencies demanded by the new era. It features more integration of

subjects for interdisciplinary learning, as a way to enhance students' "comprehensive application ability." To that end, a new course called Integrated Hands-on Activity (IHA), which integrates knowledge and skills of several subjects, has been incorporated into the curriculum framework (see exhibit 2.1). IHA is designed as a part of the compulsory curriculum at the compulsory education stage (primary and lower secondary education). The total instruction time for the nine years from primary through lower secondary is 9,522 teaching hours, with IHA accounting for 16–20 percent of that time, including labor and technology. (Table 2.4 shows a breakdown of instruction time by subject for the compulsory education stage.) In the meantime, a credit points system is applied in upper secondary education. A student is required to attain a minimum of 144 credit points before he or she graduates; the maximum number of points a student can earn throughout upper secondary education is 170, of which integrated hands-on activities account for 23 credit points.

On the other hand, the content was constructed in modules to facilitate streaming tailored to students with different interests and abilities. For example, the upper secondary level mathematics is composed of five compulsory modules and four elective series (modules); one additional

EXHIBIT 2.1

Additional subjects after the Basic Education Curriculum Reform

Grades 1–9/Compulsory Education Stage:
- Science
- Integrated Hands-on Activity/Course (information technology, research-based learning, community services, social practices)
- Art

Grades 10–12/Upper Secondary Education Stage:
- Integrated Hands-on Activity/Course (research-based learning, community services, social practices)
- Technology (general technology, information technology)
- Art
- Elective courses

Source: Ministry of Education, 2001.

TABLE 2.4   Subjects and instruction time in grades 1–9

Subject	Grade	% of total instruction time
Ethics and morals	Grade 1 and up	7–9%
History and geography	Grades 6–9	3–4%
Science	Grade 3 and up	7–9%
Reading, writing, and literature	Grades 1–9	20–22%
Mathematics	Grades 1–9	13–15%
Foreign languages	Grade 2 and up	6–8%
Physical education	Grades 1–9	10–11%
Arts	Grades 1–9	9–11%
IHA, local curriculum and school-based curriculum	Grades 1–9	16–20%

Note: Science for grade 3 and up includes physics, chemistry, and biology.
Source: Ministry of Education, 2001.

module for 2 points that takes up thirty-six teaching hours; series 1–2 (higher level) is designed for students who intend further study in the field of science and technology, while series 3–4 (lower level) is designed for those intending to study humanities and social sciences. The four elective series are basically part of school-based curriculum; that is, it is up to the school to decide which themes and content to teach for the four series (see table 2.5).

TABLE 2.5   Structure of mathematics curriculum at upper secondary level

Type	Content
Compulsory courses	• Module 1: Set, concept of function, and basic function I • Module 2: Preliminary solid geometry, preliminary plane analytic geometry • Module 3: Preliminary algorithms, statistics, probability • Module 4: Basic elementary function II, vectors on a plane, trigonometric identity transformation • Module 5: Solution of a triangle, sequence, inequality
Elective courses	• Series 1–2: Oriented toward technology and economics, etc. • Series 3–4: Oriented toward humanities and social sciences, etc.

Source: Ministry of Education, 2001.

IMPLEMENTATION OF TWENTY-FIRST-CENTURY COMPETENCIES

Undoubtedly the implementation of such a curriculum blueprint is challenging. The impact of the implementation is reinforced in some aspects by specific mechanisms of the education system, while it is undermined in other aspects.

Centralization and Decentralization

The curriculum framework is based on a governance structure that balances centralization and decentralization. The Ministry of Education is responsible for developing the national curriculum framework, deciding learning areas and subject categories, formulating national curriculum standards, and planning for curriculum implementation. Education authorities at provincial (autonomous regions or municipalities) levels map out their own plans for the implementation of the national curriculum and formulate the local curriculum on the basis of the national one in light of local circumstances and contexts. While implementing national and local curricula in the classrooms, schools are responsible for developing and selecting their own individual curriculum by taking into account local social and economic conditions, their own traditions and strengths, and their students' interests and needs.

The three-level curriculum structure thus encompasses national, local, and school-based curricula on the principle of "common basics, diversified options," with the national curriculum accounting for 80 percent and local and school-based curricula accounting for 20 percent of what students learn. The provincial governments are allowed to write and publish textbooks, and the choice of textbooks is delegated to district-county governments.[24] The discretion of which elective courses to offer is left to the schools. Such a structure allows substantial room for local innovation in developing twenty-first-century competencies.

Curriculum and Assessment

While the intended curriculum emphasizes twenty-first-century competencies, in the implemented curriculum cognitive skills are emphasized more due to the influence of the culminating college entrance examination. In China, the curriculum is largely implemented by means of textbooks; hence textbooks are more central to student learning than in many Western countries. Furthermore, at higher levels of education, the teachers also refer to examination specifications that could be different from the content of the textbooks.

Toward the end of K–12 education, examination specifications play an increasingly important role in the classroom, to the point where in practice they actually become the curriculum. The fact is that for over three decades most examinations, including the culminating college entrance exam, have remained paper-and-pen tests on a fixed number of subjects, and it is rather complicated to measure interpersonal and intrapersonal competencies on such tests. Hence the intended competencies mandated in the curriculum standards are often diluted in real-life teaching after being translated into textbooks and examination specifications. Over the past three decades, it has been emphasized that the college entrance examination should test more skills than knowledge, and indeed more skill- or ability-related items are now incorporated into the college entrance examination; yet, in general, the examination papers involve minimum measurement of interpersonal and intrapersonal competencies.

Experimentation and Innovation

In such circumstances, the extent to which cognitive, interpersonal, and intrapersonal competencies (especially the latter two) are taught largely becomes a decision made by local education authorities and even individual schools. The effectiveness of teaching and learning largely depends not only on their readiness to do so, but also on their capacity to impart the competencies. This has helped nurture a great deal of bottom-up experimentation and innovation. The reform of the college entrance examination has also created more opportunities that favor schools such as Shiyi School, recently designated as a National Pilot School for Deepening Basic Education Reform after ten years of school-based reform (see exhibit 2.2).

Nonetheless, diversification of teaching and learning is parallel with disparity among various regions. As mentioned above, those better-

EXHIBIT 2.2

Experimental reform of Shiyi School

Shiyi School, a flagship school of Education Structural Reform, is a typical example of bottom-up experimentation and innovation. Established as a public school in 1952, it acquired autonomy for governance and became a public-owned private-run school in 1992. Since then the school has engaged in continuous reforms to change its curriculum, pedagogy, and school administration. Over two decades, the school totally changed the traditional ways of teaching and learning. It has more flexible curriculum, applies a learning credit points system, and also involves students and parents in school governance. Instead of organizing students' learning in fixed classes on dozens of subjects, every student has his or her own personalized schedule. Overall it offers over a thousand courses from which 4,600 students can choose, including some courses tailored to students' special needs. The students form classes, clubs, and learning communities based on their interests and abilities. Many of the courses and activities in the school relate to emerging issues of the twenty-first century. The students have won laureates in various domestic and international competitions, and all are high achievers in college entrance examinations, with a big proportion recruited by overseas universities. In 2011 it was designated by the government as a national pilot school for Education Structural Reform due to its success in school governance reform. It has now become a model (exemplary school), in China and the school itself has started a nationwide debate on how to deliver education and govern schools.

resourced areas attract a stronger teaching force and boast more exposure to international experiences. They also tend to excel in realizing or even surpassing the intended curriculum goals, while it takes a longer time for those disadvantaged schools to shift from rote-based teaching and learning to one based on competency.

Research and Teaching

The implementation of the new curriculum and the aforementioned experimentation and innovation are supported by a Teaching Research System that provides ongoing support to classroom teaching. The system consists of teaching research institutes (mostly combined with local teachers colleges) at provincial, prefecture (municipality), and county levels. The researchers, mostly selected from the best teachers, support teachers' work by coordinating school-based research projects, visiting schools, interpreting curriculum standards, analyzing classroom teaching, developing teaching materials, administering diagnostic tests, and distilling best practices for extension (as through demonstration classes).

Practically speaking, the pedagogical study institutions play the role of operation department of the basic education system in China. Taking Beijing as an example, teachers usually devote half a day per week to district-level pedagogical research activity, and another half a day to school-level pedagogical activities. The pedagogical research institutions organize teacher training eight times a year for all teachers, and an additional eight times a year for master teachers. Also, these institutions develop and administer module-based tests and end-of-term tests. Usually one subject, such as reading, writing, and literature, is composed of twelve modules. Yet the effectiveness of these pedagogical research activities varies, being either a booster of teaching and learning when it works well, or an additional burden to teachers and students when not aligned with intended curriculum goals.

CONCLUSION

It is hard to generalize about lessons of education development, given its inherent complexity compounded by the size and diversity of such a large country as China. Indeed, curriculum reform has realized the potential of education reform in China and sparked a great deal of innovation in both learning content and method. A Chinese idiom—"Bearing global perspective (big picture) in mind, and starting from (small) concrete actions"—might best summarize the lessons in setting Chinese educational policy for the twenty-first century. Education can and will make a difference on students' learning and social well-being, when taking into consideration the tremendous changes coming in the twenty-first century and taking actions to meet these challenges and opportunities step by step.

Nonetheless, it remains challenging to realize the tridimensional goals of twenty-first-century competencies (cognitive, interpersonal, and intrapersonal) in an equitable way. In a system largely driven by the high-stakes college entrance examination—which hardly measures interpersonal and intrapersonal competencies—effective teaching and learning toward twenty-first-century competencies won't take place till the examination changes. To address these issues, the recent reform (at the end of 2014) mandated that comprehensive quality evaluation should be incorporated into the college entrance examination. The evaluation is essentially a formative assessment of comprehensive students' moral values,[25] citizenship, learning abilities, communication and collaboration abilities, sports and health, and aesthetics and behavior, in addition to assessment of traditional subject-based knowledge and skills. Such alignment between curriculum, teaching, and learning, as well as assessments, will hopefully make a difference in the implementation of the twenty-first-century competencies in China in the future.

Even so, it is foreseeable that many challenges for teaching and learning still lie ahead. First, the quality of an education system can never exceed the quality of its teachers. In China, the minimum qualification requirement for preprimary school teachers is specialized secondary education; that for primary school teachers is a short-term (two- or three-year) tertiary education degree; and that for tertiary school teachers is a bachelor's degree. Unless teacher qualifications are improved substantially, the twenty-first-century competencies called for in the curriculum cannot be realized. Second, it is challenging to design an assessment system commensurate with the new curriculum. The college entrance examination, as the guiding light of teaching and learning, basically determines what kind of curriculum is delivered in school. The twenty-first-century competencies warrant complex and authentic assessment tasks to replace the knowledge-based tests. Such tasks could presumably maximize objectivity and ensure fairness. However, it is difficult to strike the balance between fairness and efficiency of the reform.[26] Third, the challenge is to narrow the gap between developed and underdeveloped areas. Due to lack of resources, the tridimensional pedagogical strategy (knowledge and ability, process and method, and emotion, attitude, and values) has been applied much less in rural areas than in economically developed areas. The rural-urban gap makes it even harder to achieve the goal of equitable education.

The obvious conclusions are that teacher quality must be improved, including raising the qualification requirement for teachers and enhancing their professional development; that education assessments must be re-aligned with updated curricula; and that more interventions must be in place to narrow the rural-urban gap and the gap between developed and underdeveloped areas. Given the pace of the education reform in general, in the context of rapid social and economic changes, it is expected that new strategies and approaches will continue to emerge in China.

Strong Content, Weak Tools: Twenty-First-Century Competencies in the Chilean Educational Reform

Cristián Bellei and Liliana Morawietz

Center for Advanced Research in Education, University of Chile

I n this chapter we investigate how twenty-first-century competencies (21CC) have been incorporated into Chilean primary and secondary education since the mid 1990s, when these skills were introduced into the national curriculum within the context of a broader educational reform.[1] In addition, we analyze the interplay between the relevance assigned to these new competencies and the goals of the educational policies and programs designed to implement them in the actual educational system.

Our approach to twenty-first-century competencies has been framed by international literature.[2] The study uses three types of sources (see the chapter appendix for details): a detailed review of the national curriculum for secondary education, using content analysis techniques; interviews with four key policy makers and academic experts; and an analysis of official documents (such as laws, policy papers of the Ministry of Education, and ministers' speeches) as well as specialized literature on the Chilean educational reform.

The policy of introducing the 21CC approach to Chilean education has faced two main difficulties. First, curriculum reforms have to overcome several hurdles in order to transform the students' experiences at the school level; these challenges range from reaching consensus among policy makers to adopting appropriate teacher training and teaching materials for the implementation of new ideas. And second, the market-oriented Chilean educational system imposes additional difficulties, since educational authorities have weak institutional links to schools' management.[3]

Our main findings indicate that, in terms of content, the introduction of the 21CC to the Chilean national curriculum is consistent with international guidelines: it covers the system as a whole, considers 21CC both as principles and as content, remains open to the redefinition of subject matter and knowledge areas, and combines higher order thinking and interpersonal and intrapersonal skills. However, the actual adoption of 21CC by the Chilean schools has been inconsistent. For example, while the more concrete aspects, such as digital literacy and ITCs are well established, those related to the development of higher order cognitive skills or citizenship education are not. This seems to be related to a weakness in the implementation devices (teaching materials, teacher training, school improvement programs, student assessment) designed to incorporate 21CC into learning experiences at the school and classroom level. This weakness is also associated with the increasing relevance of test-based accountability policies in Chile, as a response to low student performance on both national and international standardized tests, which has resulted in a greater focus on the acquisition of basic reading, writing, and math skills.

The misalignment between purposes and implementation of the 21CC approach in primary and secondary education explains its perceived low impact and effective postponement in Chilean teaching priorities. At the same time, the growing emphasis on basic skills acquisition, driven by standards-based reforms, makes it increasingly difficult to prioritize twenty-first-century competencies at both the policy and school levels.

The chapter begins by providing the basic context of Chilean education and a brief description of the evolution of the country's educational policies. It then identifies the key sources of the Chilean curriculum reform and goes on to examine relevant elements of the twenty-first-century skills framework within the Chilean curriculum reform, discussing in detail how these ideas have been integrated into the high school curriculum.

The next section analyzes citizenship education as a key example of the Chilean reform linked to the discussion of twenty-first-century competencies within the context of returning to democracy, followed by a discussion of issues regarding implementation of the curriculum reform, including its relationship with the increasingly powerful test-based accountability policies. A final section summarizes our main conclusions and provides our interpretation of them.

CONTEXT AND EVOLUTION OF CHILEAN EDUCATIONAL POLICIES

Chilean education is made up of a primary level (eight grades) and a secondary level (four grades); secondary education is divided into general and vocational tracks, usually taught in separate high schools. There are three kinds of schools: public (municipal) schools that mainly educate students of low and middle socioeconomic status (SES), subsidized private schools that mainly educate middle-SES students, and nonsubsidized private schools that only educate high-SES students. There is an official national curriculum compulsory for all schools, though schools do have some autonomy in its implementation, as they are able to design their own study plans within the official curriculum framework.

At the beginning of the 1980s, in the context of a military dictatorship, authorities implemented a thorough market-oriented reform in education.[4] Since then, private schools, including for-profit organizations, have accessed the same public resources as public schools; all public and subsidized private schools have to compete for public funds, which are distributed using a voucher-like mechanism; private subsidized schools can also charge fees to families without losing their access to the state voucher. To encourage competition, the administration of public schools was transferred to the local governments, and the creation of new private schools was promoted, establishing minimum requirements to obtain the voucher; finally, families choose without restrictions the school their children are to attend. To stimulate a "rational choice" based on academic performance, a national standardized evaluation system was created (SIMCE), whereby students' academic achievement in language and mathematics is evaluated yearly in fourth grade (and some years in second, sixth, eighth, and tenth grades as well). School-level results are then distributed to all schools, and published on the Internet and in national and local newspapers.

Since those neoliberal reforms, private schools have quadrupled their coverage, increasing from about 15 percent to 60 percent of the national enrollment between 1981 and 2013; conversely, public education has been reduced by half in the same period, decreasing from around 85 percent to 40 percent of national enrollment. Also, the market features of the system have been associated with the high level of socioeconomic segregation of Chilean schools.[5]

Following the end of military rule in 1990, the democratic government began the implementation of a series of educational policies, later consolidated by the educational reform initiated in 1996,[6] and lasting about a decade. The basic approach of this reform was to complement the "market dynamics" of Chilean education with "state policies" of equity and school improvement.[7] It included four components: a curriculum reform for primary and secondary education; a series of compensatory and school improvement programs; a significant increase in students' time spent at school (switching from half to full school days); and massive teacher training programs to support the adoption of the new curriculum. Chilean authorities promoted the acquisition of abilities and competencies for the twenty-first century as part of this reform initiated in the mid 1990s.

Finally, since 2006, Chilean education has been shaken by a strong and sustained student movement, marked by the biggest social mobilizations in the country since the return to democratic rule.[8] The basic goal of the student movement was to end the market mechanisms that have dominated Chilean education. As a response to the 2006 student movement, the authorities designed a quality assurance system that assesses schools, classifies them according to their performance, and penalizes chronically low performing schools (with the possibility of school closure included);[9] they also increased the value of the voucher for low-SES students (the Preferential Voucher, or SEP). Nonetheless, the students considered those policies insufficient and intensified the protests in 2011.

All of these dynamics have affected the implementation of the curriculum reform. A particularly important challenge has been the extreme decentralization of the Chilean educational system: on the one hand, thousands of private suppliers are autonomous in their management; on the other, hundreds of local governments do not have an institutional link to the Ministry of Education, and all of them operate within a market framework. The government has increasingly tried new forms of state action in the field of education, emphasizing external evaluation systems, the generation of frameworks (standards) that orient the action of the decentralized agents, and the distribution of incentives and sanctions linked to measured performance. This includes a performance evaluation and a merit pay system for teachers, as well as a test-based accountability system for schools.[10]

ROOTS OF THE CHILEAN CURRICULUM REFORM

The Influence of ECLAC and UNESCO

In the early 1990s, the United Nations Economic Commission for Latin America and the Caribbean (ECLAC) and UNESCO published a highly influential report for Latin America: *Education and Knowledge: Basic Pillars of Changing Production Patterns with Social Equity*,[11] which translated the new ideas of ECLAC on economic development and social equity into proposals for the educational field. This conceptualization was based on Fajnzylber's *Industrialization in Latin America*,[12] a report elaborated for ECLAC and inspired by the experience of Southeast Asian countries with recent and accelerated growth. ECLAC-UNESCO stated the need to educate the Latin American population to "manage the cultural codes of modernity . . . to ascertain the knowledge and skills required to participate in public life, and to develop productivity in modern society."[13] It pointed out the need for a citizenry able to reflect upon itself, determine its demands, integrate internally, respond to a changing environment, and solve complex problems.

In addition to updating ECLAC's economic perspective, the report incorporated sociological ideas about the knowledge society and the growing relevance of information and communication technology, along with references to literature on new forms of business management and state restructuring.[14]

Although the 1992 ECLAC-UNESCO report was certainly a significant effort to combine economic pressures with the needs of social life and citizenship and adapt them to Latin America's educational development, the ideas, evidence, and proposals provided by the report were clearly biased toward economics, focusing on meeting the requirements of the private sector and industry.

The Commission for the Modernization of Education

The preparation of the Chilean educational reform initiated in the mid 1990s was legitimized by national agreements regarding its relevance, reach, and funding; hence, during the second democratic government, the Chilean president appointed a Commission for the Modernization of Education (1994). Led by the minister of education, the commission was composed of members from academia as well as politicians, businessmen, and representatives of the teacher union, industry, the Catholic Church, and the Freemasonry. According to José Brunner, the commission's technical coordinator, the substantial presence of representatives from the field of economics, with links to the business world, technological innovation, and vocational secondary education, was instrumental in the adoption of a future-oriented vision. Twenty-first-century skills and competencies generated a point of convergence between educators promoting educational change and personalities concerned with the intersection between education and work. The commission's final report, *The Challenges of Chilean Education in the 21st Century* (1994), would become the basis of the educational reform.

Jacqueline Gysling, who coordinated the social sciences curriculum area of the Ministry of Education during the reform, highlights the commission's emphasis on proposing "an orientation of the curriculum for life . . . a more practical approach to knowledge . . . The curriculum proposal would not be encyclopedic; it would educate students to produce knowledge, not to reproduce it exactly or mechanically."[15] In terms of curriculum change (applying Hilton and Pellegrino's 2002 skills classification), the commission proposed developing cognitive competencies (e.g., using acquired knowledge to solve problems as well as the use of appropriate procedures to obtain and organize relevant information, then make decisions based upon it), interpersonal competencies (e.g., acquiring habits, work methods, and the capacity to respond to changing situations), and intrapersonal competencies (e.g., developing collaborative abilities, basic attitudes of cooperation, tolerance, and respect).[16]

The commission's report also emphasized other competencies identified as pertaining to an education for the twenty-first century: the acquisition of basic knowledge considered educationally relevant by the Partnership for 21st Century Skills,[17] such as natural and social environment, mathematics and arithmetic, the arts, and a foreign language; and what the Pacific Policy Research Center has framed as health literacy.[18] But the competency most stressed by the commission was citizenship,[19] intended "to familiarize students with the way society functions on a daily basis, and give them the capacity and disposition to observe their duties and to demand their rights as members of a community."[20] Developing this competency was critical given the country's recent political history.

Additional Sources and Actors Driving the Curriculum Reform

The ministry's authorities and technical teams drove the curriculum reform. Moreover, the ultimate adoption of some components of the twenty-first-century agenda can be seen as the result of an internal conviction of the policy and professional elites leading the reform. Cristián Cox recognizes the relevance of the growing international literature related to educational demands posed by changes in the world of work, as articulated by authors such as Reich (1991), Murnane and Levy (1996), and most of all, due to the elaborations by the European Commission (1996) and the OECD (1994) to adopt these ideas in the field of education.[21] Additional sources for the Chilean curriculum reform were contemporary changes of the educational systems in England, New Zealand, Spain, Argentina, and some US states; the curriculum analysis of the Third International Mathematics and Science Study (TIMSS); and the national standards for the teaching of science from the US National Academy of Sciences.[22] There-fore, changes in the curriculum would connect Chilean educational con-tents with international trends.

The curriculum reform was also influenced by MECE-Media, a Chil-ean compensatory school improvement program, focused on high school, implemented between 1994 and 2000. Its key notion was to reinforce and expand the comprehensive curriculum in both general and vocational tracks, lessening both academicism and job training,[23] and making stu-dents' educational experience more challenging, engaging, and relevant to daily life.[24]

Finally, in the later stage of the design of the new curriculum, a con-sultation process was conducted within the educational system. During this phase, the curriculum reform faced some relevant restrictions in the form of conservative pressures directed toward moderating the changes in curriculum, especially those that would result in the absence of more traditional subjects or erasing their boundaries. Thus, the actual reform did not significantly alter the curricular-institutional structure, as initially proposed, and some changes related to the introduction of 21CC were moderated.

TWENTY-FIRST-CENTURY COMPETENCIES IN THE CHILEAN CURRICULUM

By the beginning of the academic year in March 2002, all Chilean stu-dents were being educated with the new curriculum, which would be only slightly adjusted in 2009 in order to strengthen its curriculum alignment. This section addresses the organization of the Chilean curriculum, focus-ing on how 21CC are incorporated and taught through it.

General Overview of the Curriculum

A main change of the reform was the way in which learning was de-fined—a conceptualization that brought it closer to 21CC as defined by Hilton and Pellegrino. The idea of education as "knowledge transfer" was replaced by one that, along with knowledge, understands learning as the development of skills and attitudes. In this scheme, "knowledge" was split into two dimensions: "information and conceptualizations" and "understanding" (i.e., "information placed in relation or contextualized, integrating greater explanatory or interpretative frameworks, and giving a base for discernment and judgment.")[25]

According to Gysling,[26] the abandonment of the centrality of content in learning processes contributed to overcoming academicism in secondary education; this change emphasized the importance of skills as learning objectives, which allowed for developing analytic capacity and critical thinking. The competencies approach would facilitate a more holistic and comprehensive approach to curriculum design and teaching. In fact, the Ministry of Education explained that the curriculum as a whole sought to develop the following capacities,[27] which are clearly linked to 21CC:

- abstraction and generation of knowledge
- systemic thinking
- experimentation and learning to learn
- communication
- collaborative work
- problem solving
- handling of uncertainty and adaptation to change

In order to deliver these competencies, the new Chilean curriculum centrally established a framework of mandatory fundamental objectives (FOs) and compulsory minimum contents (MCs) for each grade and subject matter, common to all schools at both primary and secondary levels. The curriculum considers two types of FOs: FOs for each learning sector or subject matter, and crosscutting fundamental objectives (CFOs). FOs and MCs were defined in ample reach and concise form, resembling content standards.[28] Schools were deemed free to define study plans and course programs by themselves; however, the ministry developed plans and course programs that contained pedagogical proposals for each learning area and subject matter, which were, in practice, adopted by most public and private schools in Chile.

Additionally, most of the specific changes in the curriculum also pertain to twenty-first-century competencies models. Thus, Spanish became Language and Communication, emphasizing communication skills, and History and Geography became Social Sciences in order to incorporate new content. At the same time, a learning subsector of Environment and Society was created, and a Technological Education course was incorporated into the curriculum from first to tenth grade. This subject is devoted to the development of individual and team projects. The acquisition of a foreign language (English) became mandatory from the fifth grade. In high school, among sector-specific innovations, Mathematics gained emphasis in reasoning, and History in the existence of a plurality of perspectives for each milestone or historical episode. All in all, the focus moved from preparing for higher education to knowledge and skills for real life within contemporary society.

Curriculum Analysis: The Presence of 21CC in the Chilean High School Curriculum

In this section we analyze the content of the high school curriculum, identifying the presence of 21CC as systematized by Hilton and Pellegrino.[29] We focus on high school curriculum because it better displays the view of the curriculum reform; Hilton and Pellegrino's three domains are more broadly displayed in it; it allows for better understanding of how citizenship education is approached; and it incorporates all of the CFOs. It is important to note that although the Chilean curriculum is not structured around the acquisition of competencies, it does contemplate them as outcomes of the learning process. Therefore, they are integrated in the curriculum in FOs and in MCs, which have become clearer since the 2009 adjustment. In each of the following subsections a summary table (tables 3.1, 3.2, and 3.3) shows the presence of 21CC in the different subjects and CFOs, and examples are provided to illustrate how this integration is achieved.

Our main conclusion is that the Chilean curriculum does match Hilton and Pellegrino's framework, although the three competency domains are unbalanced: cognitive skills are favored, while both intrapersonal and interpersonal competencies are postponed. Citizenship education is a special case: because of the way it is incorporated into the curriculum, this competency cannot be constrained to the interpersonal domain (as in Hilton and Pellegrino), for it mainly entails the development of intrapersonal competencies. We will later expand on the issue of citizenship education.

Cognitive skills

The development of cognitive competencies is broadly addressed by the Chilean curriculum: all of the subjects contemplate their development. Cognitive processes are addressed by most of the subjects, while the development of creativity is confined to Arts and Language and Physical Education, and only complemented by Technological Education through innovation projects.

Cognitive processes and strategies Critical thinking is one of the skills with the greatest presence throughout the curriculum documents analyzed. In Language and Communication, it is addressed by training students to read and critically analyze different types of texts (literary and nonliterary); to express—in oral and written form—their personal vision of literary works; and to critically analyze media messages. In History and Social Sciences, historical processes are stressed over memorizing events, under the premise that historical facts are complex and multi-causal. Students are expected to reach "development of their own thinking" and to be able to identify continuity and change. In Biology, as in Physics and Chemistry, critical thinking is fostered through content that shows the social, cultural, and ethical dimensions of health issues, and the social influence on scientific theories.

Technological Education approaches problem solving through the creation of a technological object in ninth grade and the design of a service process in tenth grade. In Mathematics, this competency is promoted by linking content with everyday situations and other knowledge areas, as in "Charts and Interpretation of Statistical Data from Different Contexts" or "Analyzing Statistical-Type Information in Communications Media." Also in Mathematics, mathematical reasoning is addressed in the four axes that structure the curriculum (Numbers, Algebra, Geometry, and Probabilities).

TABLE 3.1   Cognitive skills in the Chilean national curriculum

Cluster in Hilton & Pellegrino	Terms used in the Chilean curriculum	Incorporated in the Chilean curriculum in . . .
Cognitive Processes and Strategies	Critical Thinking	• Language and Communication • History • Biology, Physics, and Chemistry
	Problem Solving	• Technological Education • Mathematics • CFO Development of Thought • Biology, Physics, and Chemistry
	Analysis	• Language and Communication • History • Biology, Physics, and Chemistry • CFO Development of Thought
	Reasoning	• Mathematics
	Arguing	• Language and Communication • Philosophy
Knowledge	Information Literacy	• CFO ICTs
	ICT Literacy	• CFO ICTs
	Oral and Written Communication	• Language and Communication • CFO Development of Thought
	Active Listening	• Language and Communication
Creativity	Creativity	• Language and Communication • Technological Education
	Innovation	• Artistic Education • Physical Education

Source: authors' elaboration.

The competency of analysis is promoted in most subjects of secondary school study plans. For instance, in History, Geography, and Social Sciences, an area called "Research, Analysis, and Interpretation Skills" is included, which strengthens the ability to analyze information in different formats (graphs, maps, images), linking it to developing communication skills, using information technology and critical thinking.

Knowledge ICT Literacy is a specific CFO of the curriculum—addressed in most subjects with the incorporation of these technologies to classwork and assignments, while in Technological Education the use of ICT tools is prescribed in different project stages.

While many subjects include the development of communication skills, they are mostly found in Language and Communication, where students are expected to perform competently in different communication situations. Technological Education requires the design of a marketing strategy to facilitate the distribution of student-designed products or services; and in History students must communicate research results in the form of written essays.

Creativity Creativity and innovation are mainly stimulated in the Artistic Education subjects (Music and Visual Arts), where students develop their own projects. They are also addressed in Language and Communication by creating works of literary intent and in the production of other types of texts with diverse purposes. The core purpose of Technological Education is the generation of a service or product that responds to detected problems or needs, which is expected to develop innovation skills.

Intrapersonal skills

Intrapersonal competencies are unevenly addressed in the Chilean curriculum. While intellectual openness and positive core self-assessment are developed through specific objectives and content covered in different subject areas, work ethics is mainly restricted to CFOs (which will be discussed in the next section). To be consistent with Hilton and Pellegrino's framework, we included citizenship education in this section; nevertheless, the way in which the Chilean curriculum addresses it is closer to an interpersonal rather than an intrapersonal competency.

Intellectual openness (appreciation of diversity) is developed in History as two attitudinal dispositions: the valuing of diverse influences in building national identity, and the recognition of diverse perspectives of historical facts. Likewise, in Language and Communication, concepts such as appreciating opinions and points of view that differ from one's own are emphasized. English as a foreign language is linked to the importance of understanding and appreciating cultural diversity, and Artistic Education

TABLE 3.2   Intrapersonal skills in the Chilean national curriculum

Cluster in Hilton & Pellegrino	Terms used in the Chilean curriculum	Incorporated in the Chilean curriculum in . . .
Intellectual Openness	Appreciation of Diversity	• History • Language and Communication • CFO Ethics Formation • Artistic Education
	Intellectual Interest and Curiosity	• CFO Self-development and Assertiveness • Physical Education • Artistic Education
Work Ethics/ Conscientiousness	Productivity	• CFO Person and Environment • Physical Education
	Responsibility	• CFO Person and Environment
	Citizenship	• History • Language and Communication • Philosophy • CFO Ethics Formation • CFO Person and Environment
	Professional Orientation	• English
Self-assessment	Physical Health	• Biology
	Physical Health and Psychology	• CFO Self-development and Assertiveness • Physical Education

Source: authors' elaboration.

encourages the appreciation of different regional and historic artistic expressions. In relation to Self-assessment, health literacy is addressed in Biology when studying the immunological system, which includes a discussion on HIV/AIDS.

Interpersonal skills

Interpersonal competencies are scarcely found in the Chilean curriculum. In fact, they are almost always confined to those activities and subjects that involve teamwork. For example, teamwork and collaboration are promoted through generating team projects in Technological Education. As mentioned, citizenship education seems to be the most relevant area to develop interpersonal competencies in the Chilean curriculum.

TABLE 3.3 Interpersonal skills in the Chilean national curriculum

Cluster in Hilton & Pellegrino	Terms used in the Chilean curriculum	Incorporated in the Chilean curriculum in . . .
Teamwork and Collaboration	Teamwork	• Technological Education • CFO Person and Environment • Physical Education
Leadership	Assertive Communication	• Language and Communication • Physical Education • Artistic Education

Source: authors' elaboration.

Values and Capacities as Crosscutting Objectives

According to the official definition, crosscutting fundamental objectives (CFOs) "must permeate both the entire school's educational project and all curriculum sectors."[30] Thus CFOs are aimed at influencing the entire educational experience of students. The ethical and value-oriented education supported by crosscutting objectives may have been the reform's most emphasized element by politicians during its implementation.[31] Cox stresses the relevance of crosscutting objectives, and the continuity these have had, since they have remained virtually unmodified between 1996 and 2013.[32] CFOs intend to combine instrumental and moral dimensions of education; they provide a consensual base of society's vision of the kind of person being formed, which teachers can use as a frame of reference for their work. They also seek to guide schools on how to handle sensitive topics, such as environmental issues, sex education, and human rights, and provide schools and teachers with a way to navigate subjects that imply the expression of divergent political points of view.

CFOs cover the areas of Self-development and Assertiveness, Ethics Formation, and Person and the Social and Natural Environment for all grades; the areas of Development of Thought and Information Literacy are added in high school (ninth to twelfth grades). When compared to Hilton and Pellegrino's framework, the crosscutting objectives for primary education concern only intrapersonal (Self-development and Assertiveness) and interpersonal (Ethics and Relation to the Social and Natural Environment) skills, while cognitive competencies are added in secondary education in the form of CFOs (i.e., Development of Thought and Information Literacy).

As shown in the previous tables, the development of CFOs is amply incorporated into the Chilean high school curriculum across the three Hilton and Pellegrino 21CC domains. For instance, contents and activities in Language and Communication, Biology, Physics, and Chemistry should contribute to delivering the CFO Development of Thought, while Physical Education and the Arts enforce Self-development and Assertiveness. It also works the other way around: the CFO Ethics Formation shapes the contents of History, and the one on ICTs determines those of Technological Education.

Vocational Education

Although the previously discussed issues applied to all secondary schools, vocational high schools experienced several changes relevant to a 21CC discussion. Vocational education was reformed to provide a more flexible curriculum structure, allowing for continuous updates and increased quality in the curriculum specializations, making them more finely tuned with labor market opportunities. Students are prepared for broader sectors of the labor market rather than for specific jobs, and they acquire general skills that allow them to adapt quickly to technological changes.[33]

The reform introduced two structural changes in vocational education: it focused on the final two years of schooling (grades 11 and 12), favoring general education; and it formulated study plans and course programs for forty-six careers (instead of the several hundred that previously existed), establishing national graduation profiles for each one. The redefinition considered dynamics of employment, demands for productive development, and labor competencies. Also, student training practices were relocated from classrooms to actual companies and factories.[34]

As expected, many of the challenges vocational education faces in Chile pertain to twenty-first-century competencies in the area of working skills (as defined in Hilton and Pellegrino's "work ethic" and "teamwork and collaboration" competencies); examples of these include preparing students to learn how to learn and to interact in a wide range of situations and contexts; having teachers who encourage learning to learn and the spirit of entrepreneurship; promoting lifelong learning, and improving the quality of training opportunities.[35]

EDUCATION FOR CITIZENSHIP
IN THE CHILEAN CURRICULUM REFORM

The notion of citizenship frequently appears in the conceptual frameworks of twenty-first-century competencies, emphasizing the need to educate active and informed citizens, both globally and locally,[36] and, as mentioned, enhancing intrapersonal skills to work in an ethical and responsible way.[37] Also, the relevance of citizenship education in the twenty-first century has been stressed by UNESCO, focusing on its global dimension.[38]

From 1980 to 2002, a Civic Education subject was taught in grade 11, as part of the Chilean curriculum. Defined during the dictatorship (1973–1990), the content of the subject was centered on patriotism and institutions,[39] leaving out topics like the Human Rights Declaration, the role of political parties, or democratic elections.

During the transition to democracy, citizenship education became a priority, given the need to educate students "to value democracy, addressing the challenge of rebinding society and politics,"[40] and to become citizens committed to their society.[41] To this aim, citizenship education was defined as a cross-subject area, addressed during the entire school cycle through a competency-building approach. Thus, the Civic Education course was replaced by an area of citizenship education, which considered knowledge and skills addressed in four subjects throughout the twelve years of education: History and Social Sciences, Language and Communication, Philosophy, and Counseling.[42] The new content aimed to transmit "knowledge about the structure and functioning of the government system [and] includes abilities, values and attitudes fundamental for life in democracy."[43]

As detailed in exhibit 3.1, CFOs also make specific contributions to citizenship education.[44] Thus, in the Chilean curriculum the development of cognitive, intrapersonal, and interpersonal competencies are all expected to contribute to citizenship education.

EXHIBIT 3.1

Crosscutting fundamental objectives and citizenship

Self-development and Assertiveness

Through the development of identity, children recognize themselves as belonging to society. The abilities and competencies that will allow them to participate in the construction of an equalitarian and democratic society are: expressing and communicating opinions, ideas, feelings and convictions; solving problems; being creative, self-confident self-learners; and having a positive attitude.

Development of Thought

All subjects offer the opportunity to develop the ability to select, process, and communicate information; to develop the interest in knowing reality and finding solutions to problems for a greater good; and to express ideas and opinions clearly and efficiently. Citizens address social problems, and are committed to finding solutions.

Ethics Formation

Children acquire values expressed in the Human Rights declaration, and are conscious of the individual and collective responsibilities that come with the rights to which they are entitled.

Person and the Social and Natural Environment

School experiences promote abilities and attitudes that favor democracy, and apply democratic practices in everyday situations. Children are committed to sustainable development.

Source: authors' elaboration, based on Mineduc 2004.

During the 1990s the Ministry of Education launched as well some programs to foster democratic citizenship, in the areas of Democracy and Human Rights and Environmental Studies; additionally, the MECE program promoted youth participation in all Chilean high schools.[45] MECE supported democratic student organizations (forbidden during the military rule) and trained both teachers and student leaders to improve the quality of the student councils. Later, in 2005, the Ministry of Education mandated the incorporation of the student council presidents to the recently created school boards.

Civics knowledge among eighth-grade Chilean students was assessed by the 1999 IEA CIVED study. The results were highly disappointing. "Chilean students scored significantly below their counterparts in the rest of the world on the topics referring to human rights, the purpose of political parties, who governs in a democracy, the purpose of having periodic elections, and what characterizes a democratic government."[46] The study also showed that Chilean students did not trust their national government institutions, but they did express a higher level of trust in their schools than students in many other countries; Chilean students also demonstrated a high level of interest in public and social issues, although it was not channeled through political participation.[47]

Those results, along with the low participation of youth in elections and their expressed distrust in members of parliament, political institutions, and political parties,[48] led to the creation of a Commission of Citizenship Education in 2004, requested by the Chilean Parliament. Although the commission largely supported the key changes introduced to citizenship education, it criticized the fact that the right and responsibility of voting was not a content of the reformed curriculum.[49]

The commission also made several recommendations to reinforce citizenship education, some of which were adopted in a general update of the official curriculum in 2009. During this process, citizenship education was emphasized in high school grades, although it remained a cross-curricular learning area.[50] Citizen development was set as the main priority in History, Geography, and Social Sciences. Progress maps were created to clarify the content sequence for teaching issues like Democracy and Development and Society in Historical Perspective. Finally, objectives and content of citizenship education were relocated from ninth to twelfth grade, closer to the time students are acquiring the right to vote in national elections.

A third amendment to the citizenship education curriculum was introduced in 2013, mainly because of the formulation of a new, more comprehensive subject matter on History, Geography, and Social Sciences. Thus, currently, citizenship education is taught using the 2013 curriculum in those three subject areas from first to tenth grade, and in Counseling from first to sixth grade; while the 2009 curriculum is used to cover its content in eleventh and twelfth grades. Finally, the curriculum from 1998 is still used to approach it in the Philosophy subject matter.[51] All of these adjustments have resulted in a lessening of the crosscutting approach to citizenship education intended in 1998.

Certainly, evidence suggests that the implementation of citizenship education at the school level has been problematic. Egaña et al. asserted that, for teachers, citizenship education was the least understood area of the curriculum reform.[52] In fact, there is consistent evidence showing that, among teachers and students, a political understanding of citizenship prevails over complementary notions such as social or participatory citizenship;[53] also, students' view of citizenship emphasizes individuals over society.[54] Overall, studies have documented a significant gap between the official curriculum and its actual implementation in schools.[55]

Chilean students' civics knowledge was evaluated again by the IEA 2009-ICCS study (i.e., students schooled with the reformed curriculum). Compared to 1999-CIVED results, the average performance of Chilean students did not increase, and just as in the first evaluation, Chilean students valued local participation and social movements more than the international mean.[56] This last finding may be related to the 2006 and 2011 student movements, the largest demonstrations in Chile since the return to democracy in 1990.[57]

THE REFORM IN ACTION: IMPLEMENTATION STRATEGIES AND ACCOUNTABILITY POLICIES

The implementation of the curriculum reform was part of a more ambitious set of educational policies. In this section, based on secondary sources and interviews, we discuss some critical implementation issues that link the curriculum reform with those policies, especially the role of test-based accountability within the Chilean educational reform. We also address the issue of potential bias in the curriculum reform that may have affected its impact.

Implementation

In terms of implementing the curriculum reform, a huge effort was made to accompany it with detailed study programs, materials, guides, computers, and textbooks as support for classroom teaching. Additional policies reinforced the curriculum reform.[58] Thus, through the full-school-day policy, more instructional time was available to develop the new curriculum in school. These additional hours were seen as a condition for the implementation of the curriculum, since "higher order abilities that are the goals of the new curriculum require extended learning times."[59] Also, massive training programs for teachers on the new curriculum were implemented. Finally, curriculum change was related to a modification of the national test for college entry; the test ceased to be focused on general skills and became increasingly focused on the high school curriculum.

Although there is consistent evidence of a high degree of implementation of the reform at both primary and secondary levels,[60] the actual impact on teaching practices is more debatable, since it was difficult for teachers to translate the pedagogical message of the reform into consistent daily classroom activities.[61]

There seems to be a consensus about the idea that the means for implementing the curriculum reform were weak.[62] Gysling states that, in different ways, they all reduced, simplified, and biased the innovative message of the curriculum reform.[63] Also, although a strong effort was made to produce and distribute textbooks, Eyzaguirre affirms these textbooks were of low quality, not practical, saturated with content and summarized information in a way that made comprehensive understanding difficult; mathematics textbooks included few exercises and language textbooks had insufficient reading, which made them ineffective for teaching; finally, mathematics textbooks elaborated on conceptual levels too high for public school students and teachers, diminishing their use.[64]

Similarly, training courses for teachers were not very effective, and although the Enlaces program was fundamental to introduce ICTs,[65] Eyzaguirre does not believe significant changes were produced in the basic orientation of teaching. "Among teachers in Chile a very oral culture still persists: they do not discuss new study programs, they do not read them, they do not study them on their own. Curriculum was not considered much."[66] Gysling also thinks that the new study plans were hardly used by teachers because they were scarcely communicated to them and perceived by some teachers as being too prescriptive on how the content was supposed to be delivered; additionally, according to Gysling, instead of using the entire study plan, many teachers used shorter versions that emphasized academic content and not the competencies that were supposed to be developed.[67] Early on in the reformed curriculum implementation, Egaña et al. documented that teachers were dismissive of the reform's novelty (something they signified as a resistance to it), which they attributed, at least in part, to teachers' lack of participation in the reform's design, and to the failure by the ministry to properly communicate information about the reform once it had been approved.[68] In short, due to several implementation weaknesses, teachers had limited and superficial knowledge of the new curriculum.

A related implementation issue was that universities in charge of teacher training courses were very unfamiliar with the curriculum reform, mainly because the schools of education had not renewed their teacher preparation programs and their training was not oriented around the practical needs of the pedagogical activity in schools.[69] This implementation problem is linked to the capacity of Chilean teachers.[70] Although Chile produces twenty-first-century curriculum and implementation means, it does not have a professional teaching body with these capacities, so effective implementation of the new curriculum in the classroom is very limited and socially stratified.[71] These limitations (documented, for instance, in TIMSS 1999, 2003, 2011, and TEDS-M 2008) would particularly affect the curriculum dimensions linked to twenty-first-century competencies, which are even farther from the base of teachers' capacities. However, the problem of teacher capacities is so severe that, according to national and international assessments, a significant proportion of primary education students do not even acquire basic reading skills.

The agenda for capacity building in teachers is certainly highly complex. It faces very important limitations in the autonomy of institutions with teacher training programs and in their misalignment with the curriculum reform, the practical needs of school teaching, and the twenty-first-century agenda. The Chilean Ministry of Education has not found an effective way to modify this situation in the field of teacher training.[72] Moreover, teacher preparation programs with low selectivity that do not guarantee minimum quality have noticeably expanded in the last decade.[73] More recently, the

Ministry of Education defined standards for initial teacher training and applied the INICIA test for the assessment of beginner teachers[74] as an indirect strategy to improve teachers' capacity. The INICIA test has been criticized for emphasizing disciplinary knowledge and paper-pencil assessment for teachers, leaving aside pedagogical competencies and a more comprehensive vision launched by the reform itself.

Increasing alignment of the SIMCE test with the new curriculum was also a relevant implementation strategy.[75] Gysling and Eyzaguirre emphasize the work of the Ministry of Education to align SIMCE with the curriculum reform, and they have high regard for the efforts made at least in fourth grade to surpass a rote and mechanical assessment instrument, replacing it with questions focused on reading comprehension, problem solving, and scientific inquiry.[76]

Test-Based Accountability as a Lever for Curriculum Implementation

During the last two decades, SIMCE results played a key role in reorienting Chilean educational policy, and test-based accountability mechanisms have also increased in importance.[77] According to Eyzaguirre, "SIMCE is very powerful to establish emphasis, like accountability with SEP."[78] As explained, in 2008, SEP—the new Preferential Voucher—mandated an ambitious set of goals measured by SIMCE (language and mathematics scores), which schools have to attain over a four-year plan. Schools failing to meet the goals are subject to sanctions, including school restructuring and closure.

Certainly, this new use of SIMCE reinforced an accountability function the test already had. In Cox's view, "The questions on implementing the new curriculum in the case of Chile, cannot be separated from what is done in SIMCE in this regard and the pressure it exerts on the curriculum: you cannot drift too far because you will be in the newspapers!"[79] This view was consolidated as a reaction to the poor SIMCE results of 1999, when the idea of "bringing the reform to the classroom" was enforced with increasingly reductive means in educational aims, based on the logic of accountability.[80] According to Gysling, this is "a pragmatic vision of achieving the minimum level related to the notion of curricular focus. Anxiety for achieving equity makes everything rigid."[81] This was very clear in the new improvement programs implemented in Chile during the mid 2000s, strongly focused on increasing measured fourth-grade language and mathematics academic achievement and based on structured school and classroom level interventions.[82]

This orientation made SIMCE instrumental as a de facto control, and it became a national policy with the Preferential Voucher program requiring schools to attain very narrow learning goals, for example, by measuring the reading speed of second-grade students. For some observers, in the end, this accountability function predominated over any other potential formative use for SIMCE,[83] an issue also raised by Cox: "We have an unmatched instrument of power for capacity building and for performance assessment. [But] it is something that is unnoticed in SIMCE, in how it is publicly communicated and used, that is pure accountability and control."[84]

From this perspective, test-based accountability distorts the initial aim of the educational reform. As Gysling put it, "The problem is how accountability was done here . . . and how SIMCE turned from being an information instrument, into a control instrument for schools."[85] Additional concerns have been raised since SIMCE results did not show the same trend as PISA tests during the last decade, questioning the curriculum alignment of both instruments.[86] To be sure, in this process the new ideas that are closest to the needs of the twenty-first century are the ones that are affected the most. Nevertheless, Chilean policy makers disagree on this interpretation.

In substantive terms, Eyzaguirre did not see any contradiction or tension between acquiring traditional fundamental learning and achieving twenty-first-century competencies. She noted: "More than ever traditional school skills have become relevant in the twenty-first century because higher order thinking skills are required and they are developed by reading, by mathematics, by science that teaches abstract and hypothetical thinking. By having to learn things that are difficult, and to tolerate frustration, learning capacity is developed."[87] Therefore, since basic skills and fundamental knowledge are indispensable for higher order learning, and because in Chile a large proportion of students—especially low-income students—do not acquire them, priority should be given to developing these learning objectives. Nevertheless, Gysling disagrees with this view about learning. "The SEP expected reading speed to become a measure of reading comprehension, which is heavily questioned. It is not enough to understand reading; it is necessary to reflect upon what is read; it is not about repeating what you read."[88] Similar issues are discussed for mathematics and the natural and social sciences.

Eyzaguirre also asserts that, in order to attain high scores in SIMCE, schools need to teach higher order skills, since SIMCE was adjusted to make it consistent with the new curriculum.[89] Note that from this perspective, test-based accountability does produce curriculum narrowing, but this can be used as a tool for curriculum implementation by expanding the scope of assessment and accountability. That is what Chilean policy makers have done in recent years. For example, the number of SIMCE applications and the areas assessed by SIMCE has increased; in the last three years, the Ministry of Education applied forty SIMCE tests to the Chilean schools, compared to twenty SIMCE tests applied in the previous three years, and nine applied in the first three years of the 2000s. Another example is the inclusion of nonacademic dimensions and "soft skills"—such as motivation, self-esteem, participation, and social behavior at school—in the recently created standardized system of school external assessment and accountability, as part of a Quality Assurance System compulsory for all Chilean schools.

In turn, Brunner gives less importance to standardized measurement systems than both politicians and critics. While he thinks that relevant aspects of education for the twenty-first century cannot be measured by those tests, he also believes that SIMCE has not been an obstacle to developing these skills in the Chilean school system. "If you are going to be able to develop an educational culture around this new type of skills, it will not depend on the type of measurement. It will depend on the actual progress in teacher training, in changing practice in the classroom, and that it is not hindered by concentrating on the tests."[90]

Constraints and Bias in the Curriculum Reform

Finally, some constraints and bias may have shaped the curriculum reform, potentially affecting whether and how teachers incorporated objectives and content related to 21CC.

According to Brunner, the main constraints faced by the reform have been tradition and inflexibility in the curriculum, obstructing new views that are broader than the established disciplines. The traditional grammar of schooling seems to have been a constraint to change. In spite of the defined criteria of the curriculum reform, Brunner thinks it did not attain some key objectives, such as avoiding the encyclopedic approach and the overload of fragmentary content.[91] Gysling and Brunner[92] agree that despite the efforts, the new curriculum retained the encyclopedic and academic bias for intellectual skills while subordinating social skills, self-regulation in behavior and discipline, and new citizenship, and postponing the objectives of creativity, art, entrepreneurship, and technological education. It was these latter, nonacademic skills and objectives that had the potential of introducing a more creative approach to teaching, using such methods as team projects and practical problem solving. Thus the initial promise of the curriculum reform remained incomplete.

Another potential limitation of the curriculum reform was its appropriateness to some socioeconomic contexts.[93] Eyzaguirre argues that introducing twenty-first-century competencies (moving away from rote learning and progressing toward higher order skills) has found several limitations in schools serving low-income students, where teaching challenges are still at a basic level. From this perspective, if children are not acquiring fundamental notions of reading and mathematics, it is difficult for schools to focus on twenty-first-century skills, either because they are not pertinent or because teachers are not able to understand this more complex message. Eyzaguirre noted, "Sophistications of curriculum do not go so far there."[94]

Egaña et al. also documented a "false clarity" in the adoption of the new curriculum: since CFOs resounded with the moral purposes of education, teachers emphasized their noncognitive aspects, leaving their cognitive dimension aside.[95] Additionally, primary schools in Chile—especially in poor areas—have always been strongly directed toward basic socialization, transmitting a moral message associated with acquiring social norms and habits; thus CFOs were not considered particularly novel, according to Eyzaguirre.[96]

Finally, the new curriculum could have been involuntarily trapped in an "economic bias," which can be traced to the sources of the Chilean education reform. This potentially affected not only the balance between the varied dimensions of the curriculum, but its general relevance to the country's needs, since the developed economies in which the reform was inspired faced challenges, and required competencies, that differed in important aspects from those of the Chilean economy and society. Consequently, the curriculum was accused of being "instrumental to the requirements of contemporary companies."[97]

The curriculum reform of secondary vocational education clearly showed this asynchrony. While the reform was directed toward acquiring more general and fundamental competencies in students—changing the tradition of Chilean technical education from something more akin to job training[98]— educators warned that this new curriculum prepared students for an economy that was less represented in Chile and much more irrelevant in terms of the job market, which was still dominated by small traditional business and an informal economy.[99] As discussed, another example of unbalanced priorities was citizenship education.

CONCLUSION AND DISCUSSION

The Chilean educational reform initiated in the mid 1990s was successful in several dimensions. A greater number of children and youngsters study for more years, the school day is now longer, students attend better-equipped schools and are exposed to an updated curriculum. There is also evidence that average academic achievement of Chilean students (especially in reading) has improved over the last decade, although inequity in educational attainment is still very high. Finally, the Chilean curriculum contains relevant components of a 21CC approach to learning, although somewhat unbalanced, favoring cognitive skills and postponing both intrapersonal and interpersonal competencies. Nevertheless, it is not clear whether the aim of introducing twenty-first-century competencies to the actual students' daily educational experiences has succeeded.

Despite the limited evidence regarding this last aspect, it seems to be not particularly positive. Even though students have access to computers, it is not clear whether their use is productive in the sense of imparting useful skills or enhancing integration into the information society. Chilean students did not improve their citizenship competences during the last decade, according to the CIVED study, and the TIMSS and PISA assessments have shown consistently that only a small proportion of Chilean students achieve high performance in reading, mathematics, and science. In addition, the policy agenda seems to have lost its initial impulse in this dimension, and the effort to promote acquisition of abilities and competencies for the twenty-first century has been postponed or even abandoned.

A key example of the limitations of the Chilean curriculum is the relatively late and biased incorporation of citizenship education in Chile—a country just leaving a long dictatorship, where young people suddenly and massively stopped participating in political elections and where international comparison demonstrated huge gaps in civic education.[100] In this context, the relevance for reforming and emphasizing citizen education was too little and too late. The study program for citizenship education designed by the dictatorship in the 1980s was in force as an official program during most of the first decade of democracy. Moreover, the renewed programs did not emphasize political participation (through voting in elections) as important for democracy. Finally, the reform eliminated a subject on civic education and, although the contents and general guidelines were found in different parts of the curriculum, this would have undermined its relevance in secondary education. To address these limitations, in 2004 the government created a commission,[101] the recommendations of which were intensely used to introduce changes in the curriculum and textbooks distributed by the Ministry of Education.[102] However, the international assessment conducted in 2009 showed that Chile had made no progress in this area since 1999.[103]

What factors can explain this lack of effectiveness of the educational reform in introducing 21CC? First, the means through which the reform was communicated to teachers were not effective. Although the Ministry of Education made efforts to align the reform toward the new educational aims, the course plans, textbooks, teacher supervision, and teacher training were unable to transmit a coherent message, comprehensible and practical for teachers. This gave rise to difficulty for the teachers in incorporating the new concepts in their daily teaching activities. A more illustrative case was the teacher training programs, provided by university scholars who were not very close to the elements of the educational reform and who seemed to be unfamiliar with the ideas regarding the twenty-first-century competencies. This was critical, as the success of the educational reform depended on diminishing the gap between the capacities of teachers and the new teaching demands, but the tools used to overcome this gap were weak compared to the challenge.

Secondly, the institutional environment in which the reform was developed did not facilitate the task of aligning classroom practices, school management, and curriculum reform (along with the educational reform in general). The extreme decentralization and atomization of the Chilean school system made it difficult for the reformers to guarantee the implementation and coherence of the reform. The Ministry of Education did not have efficient instruments to accompany the improvement processes at the school level; the schools were under pressure to change and also under a market competition environment, operating as isolated management units; universities were not connected with the school system and defended zealously their autonomy from the Ministry of Education; school principals did not have a tradition of educational leadership in their communities nor of supervision of the work of their teachers; and finally, the sense of horizontal professional accountability among teachers was scarce, as the predominant tradition was of isolated work. The "message" of the reform did not find the adequate channels to be adopted by the educators, and the reform did not modify substantially those channels. In cultural issues like education, though, the message and the channel are inextricably merged.

Thirdly, the ideas associated with twenty-first-century competencies started to lose strength within the educational reform until they finally became irrelevant for educational policy. Despite the reform's comprehensive message of change and school improvement at the beginning, this message became narrower and more focused as standardized tests did not show significant improvements in reading and mathematics. The finding that a large portion of fourth-year students did not reach the minimum level in those subjects led authorities to concentrate the efforts on overcoming this situation. In order to do so, the use of achievement tests as a means for school and teacher accountability was emphasized, increasing the number and frequency of tests, linking incentives to the results, and threatening the schools that showed chronic low performance with penalization if they did not improve. All the above generated an environment of "back to basics" regarding curriculum and teaching. Also, the test-based accountability promoted dynamics that were previously present in the schools associated with market competition: selection and expulsion of students based on their potential or actual performance, and also competition for prestige in the local market ranking. Thus, the relevance of academic achievement measured by tests was exacerbated. In this environment, the twenty-first-century competencies, most of which are not evaluated by the accountability tests, were inevitably neglected.

Certainly, Chilean policy makers do not agree nowadays on how to interpret this situation and how to tackle it. Schematically, some of them do not see the tension between test-based accountability and the promotion of the 21CC, because they think basic skills (measured by the current tests) need to be developed first, or because they think twenty-first-century competencies (and other educational objectives) can be also incorporated into similar accountability mechanisms. This perspective has inspired educational policies at least since the middle of the past decade. Others perceive the accountability logic as acquiring a disproportionate relevance in educational policies, which might impose a drag on the educational process as a whole and distort school and classroom processes; therefore, it needs to be corrected. Essentially, it implies achieving equilibrium through an agenda that includes the creation of teachers' professional capacities and principals' leadership capacities that allow them to respond productively and appropriately to the increasing external pressures. Presently, the current Chilean authorities seem to endorse, at least in part, this latter view, since they have recently announced several changes to reverse the extreme market orientation of Chilean education, and have also stated their interest in revising the accountability mechanisms recently designed as part of a quality assurance system. Hence, the future of a reformist agenda that brings back the orientation toward twenty-first-century competencies to the Chilean education is currently uncertain.

Methodology

I. List of interviewees:
   A. José Joaquin Brunner. Researcher at Universidad Diego Portales and UNESCO Chair for Comparative Higher Education Policies, former coordinator of the 1994 advisory committee of the Commission for the Modernization of Education.
   B. Cristián Cox. Dean of the School of Education at Universidad Católica, director of the curriculum and evaluation unit of the Ministry of Education from 1998 to 2006.
   C. Jacqueline Gysling, academic at the Department of Pedagogical Studies at Universidad de Chile, coordinator of the social sciences area at the Ministry of Education during the high school curriculum reform (1996–2002), and coordinator of the curriculum area from 2006 to 2010.
   D. Bárbara Eyzaguirre, Coordinator of Educational Studies and Standards from 2010 to 2014.
II. Documents—all of them official documents from the Ministry of Education—reviewed for the curriculum analysis:
   A. Curriculum Fundamentals 1998 and 2009
   B. Crosscutting Fundamental Objectives
   C. All the Fundamental Objectives and Minimum Compulsory Contents (FO-MCC) from 9th to 12th grades both in 1998 and 2013 versions, of the following learning sectors and subsectors (compulsory subject matters):
      – Language and Communication
      – History, Geography, and Social Sciences
      – Technological Education (9th and 10th grade, only 1998 because it was not adjusted in 2009)

- Biology
- Physics
- Chemistry
- Mathematics
- English (as a second language)
- Philosophy and Psychology (only in 1998 because it was not adjusted in 2009)
- Physical Education
- Artistic Education

D. Learning progress maps of:
- Reading
- Writing
- Oral Communication
- Democracy and Development
- Society in Historical Perspective
- Geographic Space

III. Complementary sources: relevant national literature (see references for the entire list)

Curriculum Reform and Twenty-First-Century Skills in Mexico: Are Standards and Teacher Training Materials Aligned?

Sergio Cárdenas

Centro de Investigación y Docencia Económicas

Similar to what is observed in other Latin American countries, the performance of the Mexican education system has been a national focus of concern during the last decade. Leaders of business associations and NGOs, politicians, journalists, and parents have cited results from national and international tests as "evidence" of the ineffectiveness of the public education system, while considering the political influence of the National Union for Education Workers (SNTE) as the main factor explaining the lack of implementation of policies aimed to increase educational quality.

Public dissatisfaction with the performance of the public education system has resulted in a political climate favorable for the enactment of any reform looking to reduce the influence of the teachers union in the selection and implementation of educational policies, and it shaped a demand for a thorough change in the administration of the national education system. Thus, in 2013, the National Congress approved a constitutional amendment aimed at increasing government control over resources devoted to public education. This reform was based on the recentralization of teachers' salary and recruitment policies in favor of the federal government, the re-definition of teacher performance standards, as well as the modification of public funding allocation formulas. It also promoted greater school autonomy and established an independent national educational assessment system. All of these measures resulted in a positive perception among the public, enjoying an almost unanimous approval.[1] As the minister of education pointed out, the approval of the educational reform was possible because it "will benefit teachers, students, parents, and the whole country."[2]

The popularity of this reform in its initial stages probably compelled the federal government to expand its original goals, by including as an additional aim the definition of a "new educational model" for Mexico, to be considered as a foundation for the revision of the curriculum for basic education.

A national consultation for the definition of this new educational model started in early 2014, organized by the federal government.[3] School teachers and principals, public officials, scholars, and parents participated in a debate aimed at reaching a public consensus about the "knowledge, competencies, and values" that should be part of instructional activities for the national education system.[4] This open debate had been rarely observed in Mexico, given that curriculum reform in Mexico is usually implemented "without a deep reflection on its implications," as well as ignoring the "prevalent culture, and educational practices" in schools.[5]

Organizers of this consultation publicly explained that the revision of the national curriculum was a necessary step to guarantee that every Mexican student had an opportunity to become an "active and productive citizen."[6] Although the implementation of this deliberation did not raise great expectations, the revision opened an opportunity to explore the inclusion of new learning goals in the national curriculum, especially those related to the attainment of twenty-first-century competencies, or 21CC.

Inclusion of these competencies—broadly defined as "knowledge that can be transferred or applied in new situations [including] both content knowledge in a domain and also procedural knowledge of how, why, and when to apply this knowledge to answer questions and solve problems,"[7]— is relevant in the case of Mexico, given the tradition of emphasizing in instructional practices the "possession of specific knowledge" rather than a "conceptual understanding of complex concepts, and the ability to work with them creatively to generate new ideas, new theories, new products, and new knowledge."[8] If the new national education model proposes the inclusion of 21CC in the national curriculum, it would mean the materialization of a "society's desire that all students attain levels of mastery—across multiple areas of skill and knowledge—that were previously [considered as] unnecessary for individual success in education and the workplace."[9]

Shifting from a legal reform designed to increase control over financial and human resources, to another aimed at exploring the inclusion of different educational goals, resulted in additional challenges for decision makers. The reorientation of the reform resulted in new issues to be publicly debated, different audiences to be reached and convinced of the benefits of the reform, as well as changing expectations regarding outcomes. In addition, policy makers faced further political obstacles, given that implementing a comprehensive curriculum reform is not a popular intervention when heavy political pressure for change prevails, since change on this scale may take considerable time and may not produce immediately visible results.[10]

Considering that any curriculum "specifies what kind of knowledge, skills, and values should be taught to students [and in some cases] the desired ways of how students should be taught,"[11] any revision of the national curriculum will entail defining what a relevant competence is. An inadequate implementation of this definition process will result in schools graduating young people unable to "benefit from the emerging new forms of socialization and to contribute actively to economic development under a system where the main asset is knowledge."[12]

Unfortunately, the debate around the new national educational model has not been translated into an open deliberation about the relevance of the basic national education curriculum. Not surprisingly, just like in many other countries, public debates about educational contents and instructional practices in Mexico are scarce, usually displaced by discussions around other policy issues, like how to increase access to education,[13] or how to increase accountability.

The absence of public debate about pedagogical contents in Mexico might be partially explained by the lack of interest about the effects previous curriculum reforms have had in the operation of the national education system. In addition, there is limited evidence about how educational actors define and include in the national curriculum new competencies, including those labeled as "twenty-first century."

The lack of a public debate on the national curriculum content makes it important that policy makers understand how social actors in Mexico conceptualize and in some cases demand new competencies to be included in the national curriculum for basic education. In addition, identifying whether the current curriculum for basic education includes 21CC becomes a necessary input for the revision of the national curriculum.

This chapter aims to provide further information both on how 21CC are conceptualized in Mexico, and how these competencies are distributed across the national curriculum. It will include a description of foundations and gaps in the current national curriculum for basic education (implemented since 2011) that may inform the debate about how to include new relevant competencies.

The chapter will first describe how the Mexican public conceptualizes 21CC, based on information from a survey administered to parents, teachers, and school principals in the state of Guanajuato. It will go on to discuss the results from a content analysis of the national curriculum for basic education, to identify how instructional activities related to the promotion of 21CC have been defined in the curriculum for basic education, and whether some gaps regarding the inclusion of 21CC exist across expected learning goals. A final section will describe possible implications for policy makers.

HOW ARE RELEVANT COMPETENCIES CONCEPTUALIZED IN MEXICO?

Twenty-First-Century Competencies at the System Level

The Mexican education system, with nearly 250,000 schools, is organized into three instructional levels: basic, middle, and higher education.

These in turn are organized around three delivery models—out-of-school, in-school, and mixed—with mandatory attendance up to the high school level. It has nearly 33.6 million students enrolled in the school system (25.9 in basic education) and 1.8 million teachers (1.2 in basic education). In 2014, around 70 percent of enrolled students who started basic education in 2001–2002 graduated from lower secondary, and the national educational expenditure as proportion of the GDP is nearly 6 percent.[14]

The administration of the national education system in Mexico is formally decentralized, although the federal government has retained control for decades over strategic policies such as teacher recruitment, salaries, curriculums design, teacher professional development, educational materials design, as well as student assessment. In addition, the federal government leads planning and teacher evaluation activities, and it provides most of the public funding allocated to education in the country, around 62 percent of government expenditure.

The Mexican education system has implemented different curriculum reforms in the last few decades. However, there is a lack of solid research about how competencies necessary to survive in a globalized context are identified in the country, and how this identification may result in the inclusion of new learning goals in the national curriculum.

Among the scarce studies on the selection of competencies to be attained are the reports from the Program for International Student Assessment (PISA), published every three years by the Instituto Nacional para la Evaluación de la Educación, [INEE]. Dissemination of these reports has increased the debate about the competencies Mexican students should attain to be prepared for a globalized society.[15]

A second category of studies analyzing the identification of relevant competencies to be attained by Mexican students comprises those aimed at examining local labor markets, based mostly on the study of the perception of this topic from private employers, as well as interpreting data from national employment surveys. Among these studies are the USAID-funded study known as the *Survey of Professional Competences: What Businesses Are Looking for and Do Not Find Among Young Professionals*,[16] as well as the *Labor Market Study in Guanajuato*,[17] both examples of how relevant competencies are defined by firms and economic development agencies in Mexico.[18]

The survey of businesses depicts how employers identify the most important competencies potential employees should master. From a set of nine broad "competencies" identified by the authors of the report—general culture, communication tools, communication with others, teamwork, innovation, leadership, personal image, personal efficiency, and emotional intelligence—surveyed employers defined three competencies as the most relevant to be attained for Mexican graduates: teamwork, communication, and personal efficiency.

In the case of the labor market study researchers interviewed experts from a regional automotive industry cluster, identifying a demand for a set of competencies grouped in four categories: leadership, negotiation, personal relationships, and individual potential. The category of leadership included competencies related to individual capacities to influence and interact with others, while the second category, negotiation, included competencies related to management activities, like planning, commitment, and the search for continuous improvement. The third category comprised communication and negotiation competencies, while the fourth included competencies like self-control, innovation, and adaptation to change.

The level of influence of these studies in the public debate about the definition of educational goals and the inclusion of specific competencies in the curriculum varies widely. While reports containing opinions from employers have a minor influence, the publication of PISA reports has nurtured an interest among NGOs and business associations to promote the inclusion of educational goals different from those currently stated in the national curriculum, mostly those included in the PISA conceptual framework.[19]

Twenty-First-Century Competencies in Schools: Findings from a Local Survey

In spite of the interest in a specific set of competencies expressed by employers, there is still scarce information about how competencies are conceptualized and demanded by school communities in Mexico. Furthermore, little is known about how parents, teachers, and school principals conceptualize 21CC.

Understanding the perception of school communities regarding relevant competencies is central, given that schools and classrooms are natural places where enactment of the national curricula takes place: it is in schools where decisions are taken regarding how contents and instructional practices promoting the acquisition of relevant competencies are implemented.

To provide further information about how educational stakeholders such as parents, teachers, and school principals conceptualize 21CC in Mexico, a survey was administered to a sample of 1,257 students enrolled in 547 junior secondary schools, located in 29 municipalities across the state of Guanajuato.[20] Data was collected through four different questionnaires, administered to teachers and principals while working at schools, as well as during home visits to parents and students.

Items included in the survey were designed to identify participants' knowledge and familiarization with some of the concepts related to twenty-first-century competencies, as well as learning about competencies they considered would be necessary to obtain employment thirty years from now. Although findings are only representative for one state of the country, the data collected helps to understand whether school communities might support the inclusion of these competencies in the national curriculum.

The data showed that parents, teachers, and school principals lack familiarity with the concept of 21CC. While 94 percent of parents reported they have never heard about this concept, nearly 46% of teachers and approximately 40 percent of school principals reported the same. The main policy implication from this lack of familiarity or clarity around the meaning of this concept among parents is that it may result in a lower demand for these types of competencies from school communities, as has been pointed out in other reports and studies.[21] In other words, our findings suggest that the lack of appropriation of this concept among school actors (or the lack of knowledge about its relevance) would increase the costs of promoting the inclusion of this type of educational goals in the national curriculum.

It is important to point out that while the concept of 21CC was relatively unknown among a significant number of parents, teachers, and school principals, there was nevertheless a positive perception toward some of the competencies usually grouped under this label. For instance, the competency identified as "collaboration/teamwork" was positively evaluated in the survey by parents, principals, and teachers alike, regardless of their initial lack of familiarity with the term "twenty-first-century competencies."

Furthermore, when parents, teachers, and school principals were questioned about their personal views regarding the implementation of school activities aimed to develop in their students individual competencies grouped under the 21CC concept, a majority of respondents agreed that it would be important. Thus creativity, innovation, critical thinking, technological literacy, assertive communication, and even metacognition were all widely accepted as competencies to be developed in their schools, although this perception was observed only when specific 21CC were spelled out.

The favorable perception toward these skills depicts a positive context for the introduction of 21CC in the national curriculum. Although the positive attitude toward individual competencies may also be the result of a "social desirability" issue—just like in cases where technical concepts are erroneously associated with better educational interventions[22]—a positive perception about some of the "new" educational goals may result in a favorable environment for the inclusion of curriculum and learning goals related to 21CC in the national curriculum.[23]

An additional finding to be highlighted is the association of the concept of twenty-first-century competencies to technological literacy among school communities. When parents and teachers were questioned on the competencies their children would need to get employed in the near future, the most frequent response was "familiarity with technology." This finding points out how identification of relevant competencies among school communities may still require further debate and guidance in order to promote a more balanced and diverse perspective regarding the competencies to be attained in Mexican schools. In addition, it points out the lack of familiarity and comprehension among parents and teachers about new competencies, a situation that may result in a lack of support from school communities for the inclusion of new competencies in the national curriculum.

The information collected is just an initial step in the process of understanding how 21CC are conceptualized and defined by members of school communities in Mexico. While more explanations about the observed trends are required, it depicts some of the discussions around the process of identifying relevant competencies to be included in the revised national curriculum, and how once included, school communities may enact the curriculum. It also depicts a contrast between how learning goals are defined by curriculum designers at the national level, the demand for specific competencies by employers, and the lack of reliable information among school actors on the type of competencies their students should attain to survive in a contemporary society.

Analysis of the National Curriculum for Primary Education

Curriculum reforms implemented in Mexico can be broadly grouped into two categories, based on their pedagogical objectives and political orientation. The first group corresponds to reforms like those implemented in the postrevolution era, at a time when the national curriculum was seen as an ideological instrument intended to "support political projects"[24] to generate stability and legitimacy for the new political regime. The second category is found since the early 1990s, when curriculum reforms were considered a response to demands emerging from a "globalized and complex society," mainly through the introduction of "educational innovations" and the adoption of recommendations made by international organizations.[25]

The last curriculum reform for basic education in Mexico was enacted in 2011, and it was considered a response to the "need to update the curricula and pedagogical methods in light of recent educational research findings and so as to develop competencies for the better integration of students to contemporary society."[26]

Based on a "participatory" design, experts, academic institutions (national and international), independent scholars, state governments, international organizations (e.g., UNESCO, OEI), foreign governments (Australia and Cuba), business associations, and public interest groups participated in a consultation to guide the design of this new curriculum for basic education. The Ministry of Education in Mexico finally determined and tested the content, standards, and materials, as well as the instructional activities, creating a proposal that was validated for more than thirty thousand teachers, organized in thirty-one state groups.[27]

To identify whether competencies necessary to survive in "contemporary" or "globalized" societies were considered in this reform, a review of the new reference materials for primary education teachers (*guías del maestro*)was conducted, confirming a scattered inclusion of references to competencies considered as twenty-first-century. For instance, according to the Ministry of Education, basic education graduates who studied under the new curriculum should, at the end of their instruction, be able to do the following:

1. communicate clearly, interacting in diverse cultural settings, even in a different language such as English
2. develop arguments based on their interpretation of evidence, including evidence provided by others
3. collect, analyze, interpret, and use information from several sources
4. interpret social and natural conditions to make better decisions
5. learn about human rights and how to interact with other citizens and institutions in a democratic society
6. value social diversity
7. work in collaboration with others
8. promote health care and well-being
9. use technology to communicate, collect information, and create knowledge
10. appreciate the arts

Although there is no literal reference to 21CC in the revised material, based on the classification proposed by Pellegrino and Hilton,[28] some of the described competencies would be part of the cognitive (a, b, c, and i), intrapersonal (d, e, f, and j), as well as interpersonal (g) twenty-first-century competency domains.

In addition, other educational goals included in the new curriculum mention competencies considered necessary for life in the twenty-first century, such as the case of the standards for the attainment of "digital competencies" described in study plans for primary schools. Although the core of the definition of the digital competencies to be attained with the curriculum is formed by basic ICT activities, materials for teachers emphasize that use of technology in classrooms is an opportunity to develop six specific competencies: creativity and innovation; communication and collaboration; information management; critical thinking, problem solving, and decision making; digital citizenship; and ICT understanding.

Although no further description of mechanisms or instructional practices to achieve these goals was included, it is possible to confirm one more time a curriculum oriented (though not structured) toward developing competencies mostly described in the classification proposed by Pellegrino and Hilton.[29] Based on this classification, it is possible to conclude that competencies like creativity and innovation—as well as critical thinking, problem solving, ICT understanding, information management, and decision making—fall in the domain of cognitive competencies, while communication and collaboration might be classified in the interpersonal domain. The only competency difficult to sort based on the classification suggested by Pellegrino and Hilton is "digital citizenship," although it is still an innovative competence in the curriculum.

Finding dispersed references to 21CC in the national curriculum is still a positive sign regarding its orientation. However, a different question is whether these definitions and objectives are unambiguously linked to learning goals and instructional activities.

To examine if references to 21CC were translated to intended instructional practices, an analysis was conducted to identify how 21CC were included in the "expected learning outcomes" (ELO) defined in the curriculum for primary education.[30] By examining reference materials for primary education teachers through content analysis, it was possible to generate systematized information about the definition, orientation, and frequency of activities aimed at fostering the attainment of 21CC in the classroom, considering that teachers´ support materials in Mexico include a detailed description of learning outcomes to be achieved in each subject and grade.

The examination was conducted using content analysis, which has been widely used to assess curriculum design.[31] In fact, content analysis has been considered for decades as the "dominant solution" in social sciences, by enabling "quantitative analysis of large number of texts in terms of what words or concepts are actually used or implied in the texts," focusing on "the frequency with which words or concepts occur in texts or across texts."[32] Other authors have pointed out that this approach may also be used as an "analysis tool" to conduct the "assessment of written documents,"[33] as well as to make inferences "by systematically and objectively identifying specified characteristics within text."[34]

In order to identify educational goals and intended instructional practices in the basic education curriculum that include 21CC, a coding scheme for the analysis of teachers´ reference materials was designed, based on the "terms used for twenty-first-century competencies."[35]

Once a list of operational definitions was created (see table 4.1), this set of sampling units was used to guide the full review of textbooks and reference materials for teachers (SEP 2011a, 2011b, 2011c, 2011d, 2011e, 2011f),[36] for every subject and grade for primary education, to identify activities related to 21CC taking place in classrooms, as described in all the expected learning outcomes for primary education.[37]

To identify not just how frequently a concept related to 21CC was mentioned in any of the ELOs in primary education, but also how these concepts were distributed across grades and subjects, an analysis of units of texts was conducted considering four categories: grade, subject, domains, and clusters of 21CC within domains, as defined by Pellegrino and Hilton.[38]

Results of the content analysis can be found in table 4.2, as well as in tables 4.3, 4.4, and 4.5.[39] In table 4.2, we describe basic information about the frequency of Expected Learning Outcomes that were considered as related to twenty-first-century competencies ("ELO21") across grades, subjects, and domains in primary education. This table includes

TABLE 4.1   Phrases/codes by category

Domain	Sampling units/phrases used in the second stage of analysis
Cognitive	• Provides and supports arguments about decisions • Discriminates information based on a specific purpose • Utilizes information technology to collect information • Organizes and summarizes relevant information • Looks for solutions to solve problems under personal limitations • Improvises characters in role-playing games
Intrapersonal	• Identifies and values cultural and ethnic differences • Identifies activities to improve personal performance • Develops a positive self-concept • Evaluates consequences of decisions • Evaluates options regarding plans • Values democratic processes
Interpersonal	• Respects other people's opinions • Abides by the rules established collectively • Teamwork collaboration • Conflict resolution • Identifies differences in opinions as sources of conflict • Exchanges ideas and positions respectfully

also the percentage of ELO21 compared to the total expected learning outcomes (ELO) found in the curriculum for all the grades and subjects for primary education. This last measure provides a reference about the level of inclusion of 21CC in the general distribution of learning outcomes for primary education.

One of the key aspects to be pointed out based on this analysis is the minor proportion of ELO21 included in the national curriculum, as a proportion of the total number of ELO defined for primary education. Even though we lack evidence to suggest an adequate distribution or balance between ELO and ELO21, considering that there is an ample set of 21CC, these might well be attained in subjects currently not including a single ELO21, as in the case of arts, mathematics, natural sciences, or even geography.[40] This may suggest the implementation of a curriculum reform with a very limited definition of 21CC, or a lack of a reflection regarding how to achieve an adequate distribution of ELO across subjects and grades. This first finding highlights an absence of curricular goals aimed at promoting attainment of these competencies in the country.

TABLE 4.2 Frequency and proportion of references to 21CC in the ELOs outlined in the Basic Education Curriculum (primary level grades)

Grade	Subject	Cognitive ELO21	Cognitive PS	Intrapersonal ELO21	Intrapersonal PS	Interpersonal ELO21	Interpersonal PS	ELO21/ TELO
1	Language	4	100	0	0	0	0	8.96%
	Mathematics	0	0	0	0	0	0	0.00%
	Nature & Society	0	0	1	100	0	0	3.22%
	Civics & Ethics	0	0	4	44	5	56	45.00%
	Physical Education	0	0	1	25	3	75	26.66%
	Arts	0	0	0	0	0	0	0.00%
2	Language	3	75	1	25	0	0	8.69%
	Mathematics	0	0	0	0	0	0	0.00%
	Nature & Society	0	0	2	67	1	33	8.80%
	Civics & Ethics	0	0	3	43	4	57	35.00%
	Physical Education	0	0	1	33	2	67	20.00%
	Arts	1	33	0	0	2	67	15.00%
3	Language	2	40	1	20	2	40	9.61%
	Mathematics	0	0	0	0	0	0	0.00%
	Natural Sciences	0	0	1	100	0	0	3.5%
	Geography	0	0	0	0	0	0	0.00%
	Civics & Ethics	0	0	2	33	4	67	30.00%
	Physical Education	0	0	2	67	1	33	20%
	Arts	1	100	0	0	0	0	5.00%
4	Language	2	50	1	25	1	25	7.84%
	Mathematics	0	0	0	0	0	0	0.00%
	Natural Sciences	0	0	0	0	0	0	0.00%
	Geography	0	0	1	100	0	0	5.26%
	History	0	0	1	33	2	67	15.00%
	Physical Education	0	0	2	50	2	50	26.66%
	Arts	0	0	0	0	0	0	0.00%
5	Language	6	86	1	14	0	0	13.20%
	Mathematics	0	0	0	0	0	0	0.00%
	Natural Sciences	0	0	0	0	0	0	0.00%
	Geography	0	0	1	100	0	0	5.26%
	History	0	0	0	0	0	0	0.00%
	Civics & Ethics	0	0	1	20	4	80	25%
	Physical Education	0	0	2	40	3	60	33.33%
	Arts	0	0	0	0	0	0	0.00%
6	Language	5	100	0	0	0	0	9.43%
	Mathematics	0	0	0	0	0	0	0.00%
	Natural Sciences	0	0	0	0	0	0	0.00%
	Geography	0	0	0	0	0	0	0.00%
	History	0	0	0	0	0	0	0.00%
	Civics & Ethics	1	33	0	0	2	67	15.00%
	Physical Education	0	0	1	25	3	75	26.66%
	Arts	0	0	0	0	0	0	0.00%

ELO21: Expected learning outcomes associated to 21st-century competencies.
PS: Percentage by dominion of ELO21 included in the subject and grade.
TELO: Total expected learning outcomes corresponding to subject and grade.
21CC: 21st-century competencies.

Another aspect to be pointed out is the concentration of ELO21 in the subjects of civics and ethics, as well as in physical education. This might be explained by the fact that most of the ELO21 finally included in the national curriculum correspond to the domain of intrapersonal competencies, with an emphasis on activities promoting the "appreciation for diversity" in the case of civics and ethics, and "physical health" in the case of physical education, as well as interpersonal competencies, with the inclusion of activities promoting teamwork and teaching how to reach collective agreements.

Also worth noting is a variation in the distribution of ELO21 across subjects, observed in higher grades. After third grade, most of the ELO21 included in the curriculum are part of instructional activities conducted during physical education lessons, one of the subjects with fewer hours of instruction in the curriculum for primary education. The ELO21 for this subject in higher grades correspond mostly to intrapersonal competencies, like self-regulation. The distribution of ELO21 across grades and subjects presented in table 4.2 describe a concentration of ELO21 in a small sample of subjects. In addition, if we consider the number of subjects with at least one ELO21 included, the intrapersonal domain will be the one with the highest concentration; but if we consider the percentage of ELO21 included in each subject and grade by domain, the interpersonal domain has a higher percentage of ELO21. Furthermore, the proportion of ELO21 decreases for the last grade of this educational level.

In summary, findings reported in table 4.2 suggest that: a) there is a limited number of Expected Learning Outcomes related to 21CC in the Mexican national curriculum for primary education; b) ELO21 are scattered across grades and subjects without an apparent clear goal regarding its distribution; and c) opportunities to engage students in acquiring relevant competencies exploring different topics are missed, as in the case of natural sciences and mathematics, both subjects without any ELO21 included among the ELO described in the national curriculum.

The proportion of ELO21 and their distribution across grades and subjects suggest a lack of comprehensive planning regarding the inclusion of 21CC in the new national curriculum, and a gap between the formal definition of educational goals and the intended instructional practices to be implemented by teachers, at least when based on the guidance provided by reference materials.

Distribution of ELO21 Across Clusters of Competencies Within Domains

Another aspect to be analyzed is whether the ELO21 included in the national curriculum are focused on specific clusters of competencies within the cognitive, intrapersonal, and interpersonal domains, as defined by Pellegrino and Hilton.[41] Learning about this distribution is relevant, given the variation of competencies observed within domains: for instance, one domain (such as intrapersonal competencies) may include at the same level terms like curiosity, grip, metacognition, and integrity. Although the classification suggested by Pellegrino and Hilton is extremely useful, analysis of curriculum content requires, if possible, understanding which of the competencies prevail on the activities labeled as ELO21, thus providing a better perspective of possible gaps across competencies, decisions from curriculum designers, and of course possible differences in challenges faced by teachers given the variation in the levels of complexity resulting from the inclusion of diverse learning goals. Table 4.3 shows how learning goals and instructional activities related to the domain of cognitive competencies are focused in the knowledge cluster, partially ignoring the cognitive process and creativity clusters. This concentration is mostly explained by the emphasis on the ELO21 included regarding information/technological literacy or communication competencies. On the other hand, competencies like creativity or cognitive processes (related to critical thinking and problem solving) grouped in the same domain are relatively ignored in the ELO21 included in the national curriculum. Just like in the previous analysis of distribution across grades and subjects, there is limited evidence about how to reach an ideal distribution of competencies within domains. However, depicting this distribution helps to visualize how curriculum designers determine relevance of skills, at least when measured by its inclusion in the ELO.

In the case of competencies grouped in the intrapersonal domain, table 4.4 describes the distribution of ELO21 across grades and subjects

TABLE 4.3 Distribution among clusters within the cognitive competencies domain

Year	Subject	COGNITIVE COMPETENCIES		
		Cognitive process	Knowledge	Creativity
1	Language	■ 100%		
	Mathematics			
	Nature and Society			
	Civics & Ethics			
	Physical Education			
	Arts			
2	Language		■ 100%	
	Mathematics			
	Nature and Society			
	Civics & Ethics			
	Physical Education			
	Arts			■ 100%
3	Language		■ 100%	
	Mathematics			
	Natural Sciences			
	Geography			
	Civics & Ethics			
	Physical Education			
	Arts			■ 100%
4	Language		■ 100%	
	Mathematics			
	Natural Sciences			
	Geography			
	History			
	Physical Education			
	Arts			
5	Language		■ 100%	
	Mathematics			
	Natural Sciences			
	Geography			
	History			
	Civics & Ethics			
	Physical Education			
	Arts			
6	Language	▨ 1–25%	■ 100%	
	Mathematics			
	Natural Sciences			
	Geography			
	History			
	Civics & Ethics		■ 100%	
	Physical Education			
	Arts			

% of ELO21 for this grade identified in the correspondent cluster

☐ 0%   ▨ 1–25%   ▨ 26–50%   ▨ 51–75%   ■ 76–99%   ■ 100%

TABLE 4.4 Distribution among clusters within the intrapersonal competencies domain

		INTRAPERSONAL COMPETENCIES		
Year	Subject	Intellectual openness	Work ethic conscientiousness	Positive core self-evaluation
1	Language			
	Mathematics			
	Nature and Society	▉ (100%)		
	Civics & Ethics	▨ (1–25%)	▨ (51–75%)	▨ (1–25%)
	Physical Education	▉ (100%)		
	Arts	▉ (100%)		
2	Language	▉ (100%)		
	Mathematics			
	Nature and Society	▉ (76–99%)		
	Civics & Ethics	▨ (51–75%)	▨ (26–50%)	
	Physical Education		▉ (76–99%)	
	Arts			
3	Language	▉ (100%)		
	Mathematics			
	Natural Sciences			
	Geography			
	Civics & Ethics		▨ (26–50%)	▨ (51–75%)
	Physical Education			
	Arts			
4	Language	▉ (100%)		
	Mathematics			
	Natural Sciences			
	Geography	▉ (100%)		
	History		▉ (100%)	
	Physical Education	▨ (1–25%)		▨ (1–25%)
	Arts			
5	Language			
	Mathematics			
	Natural Sciences			
	Geography			
	History	▉ (100%)		
	Civics & Ethics		▉ (76–99%)	
	Physical Education			
	Arts			
6	Language			
	Mathematics			
	Natural Sciences			
	Geography			
	History			
	Civics & Ethics			
	Physical Education		▉ (100%)	
	Arts			

% of ELO21 for this grade identified in the correspondent cluster

☐ 0%   ▢ 1–25%   ▨ 26–50%   ▨ 51–75%   ▉ 76–99%   ▉ 100%

for the three corresponding clusters in this domain (intellectual openness, work ethic conscientiousness, and positive core self-evaluation.) There is a concentration of activities in the first two grades around the intellectual openness cluster, mostly explained by the interest in promoting the "appreciation of diversity" at an early stage. On the contrary, the positive core self-evaluation cluster has fewer mentions among ELO21, pointing out a reduced number of instructional activities aimed at promoting self-monitoring/evaluation as well as psychological health.

Finally, with regard to the domain of interpersonal competencies, table 4.5 depicts the distribution of ELO21 between the two clusters of teamwork collaboration and leadership. In this domain, most of the ELO21 belong to the teamwork and collaboration cluster as a result of the emphasis placed on conducting group activities and on fostering negotiation competencies in students in the subjects physical education and civics and ethics. Leadership, although mentioned in some of the ELO21, has noticeably fewer references among the ELO21 grouped in this domain in the curriculum for primary education.

In summary, the distribution of ELO21 across clusters within domains (tables 4.3, 4.4, and 4.5) follows a similar trend as the distribution of ELO21 across domains with respect to the national curriculum (table 4.2). There is a lack of consistent distribution across clusters, subjects, and grades, suggesting that the inclusion of ELO21 is neither comprehensive nor aligned across grades and subjects. In fact, variation not just in the allocation of activities across clusters but in the proportion of ELO21 identified in each cluster, imply an inadequate planning in the definition of learning goals associated with 21CC in the national curriculum.

Previous figures are just a straightforward representation of how designers of the national curriculum included different concepts and learning activities related to 21CC across grades and subjects in the primary education level. Although it is possible to identify where and how 21CC were included across the main subjects in the primary education curriculum with this analysis, it is still unclear how these learning goals would be aligned among grades and subjects. In addition, it is still unclear how this distribution of learning goals is actually interpreted within schools, and

TABLE 4.5 Distribution among clusters within the interpersonal competencies domain

		INTERPERSONAL COMPETENCIES	
Year	Subject	Teamwork and collaboration	Knowledge
1	Language		
	Mathematics		
	Nature and Society		
	Civics & Ethics		
	Physical Education		
	Arts		
2	Language		
	Mathematics		
	Nature and Society		
	Civics & Ethics		
	Physical Education		
	Arts		
3	Language		
	Mathematics		
	Natural Sciences		
	Geography		
	Civics & Ethics		
	Physical Education		
	Arts		
4	Language		
	Mathematics		
	Natural Sciences		
	Geography		
	History		
	Physical Education		
	Arts		
5	Language		
	Mathematics		
	Natural Sciences		
	Geography		
	History		
	Civics & Ethics		
	Physical Education		
	Arts		
6	Language		
	Mathematics		
	Natural Sciences		
	Geography		
	History		
	Civics & Ethics		
	Physical Education		
	Arts		

% of ELO21 for this grade identified in the correspondent cluster

☐ 0%   ☐ 1–25%   ▧ 26–50%   ▨ 51–75%   ■ 76–99%   ■ 100%

how effective other curriculum components are in supporting the accomplishment of goals related to the attainment of 21CC.

It is important to remember that regardless of the possible methodological restrictions content analysis may face, the results from this analysis point to a national curriculum for basic education that is unprepared for the inclusion of 21CC. Several explanations can be suggested, but further research is needed to analyze whether inclusion of 21CC in national curricula requires new approaches for curriculum planning and/or better and more specific definitions of competencies; research is also needed as to whether the translation of 21CC general objectives into specific learning goals and instructional activities faces additional challenges when compared to "traditional" competencies.

THE ROLE OF NONGOVERNMENTAL ACTORS IN THE PROMOTION OF TWENTY-FIRST-CENTURY COMPETENCIES

In order to identify some of the contextual factors explaining the inclusion of 21CC in the national curriculum, it is necessary to map out the demand for these competencies from local actors, including nongovernment organizations. The lack of clarity among school actors regarding the identification of relevant skills emphasizes the importance of involving other actors interested in influencing the national educational policy agenda by defining new contents and educational goals.

Participation of private organizations in the process of defining the content and educational goals in Mexico, including those related to 21CC, has increased in recent years, through a variety of channels. For instance, the educational foundation Unión de Empresarios para la Tecnología en la Educación (UNETE) has assumed as its main goal the development of "technological literacy" among students attending public schools. In addition, through their interventions in public schools they promote the acquisition of "cognitive competencies" like "problem solving, critical thinking, metacognition, creativity and innovation," as well as the development of "noncognitive competencies" such as communication, collaboration, and interpersonal competencies. This is perhaps the most explicit and comprehensive intervention about 21CC from NGOs in Mexico. The NGO Confederación Patronal de la República Mexicana (COPAR-MEX), in contrast, has developed its own educational model. Although their model lacks specific competencies to be included in the curriculum, this organization describes and demands the recognition of four specific goals for the national education system: the development of intelligence, the transmission of values and knowledge, social interaction, and training for jobs. Other organizations like Mexicanos Primero are key actors in the promotion of public debates in Mexico about education, including the dissemination and thorough analysis of PISA results, endorsing the inclusion of relevant competencies suggested by this assessment.[42]

Other interventions from NGOs and private foundations working collaboratively with school communities have defined and highlighted competencies that students in public schools should attain to survive in a contemporary society. Among these is the Young Citizens Program implemented by the NGO Via Education. By implementing a research-based youth participation model,[43] this organization promotes "genuine participation" by students. Through its participatory model, primary school students attending public schools debate community problems, identify solutions, and reach agreements before implementing interventions aimed to solve them. These activities altogether aim to develop competencies such as democratic participation, problem solving, and teamwork.

Chipi-chape is another organization implementing independent interventions aimed at developing specific competencies beyond those considered in the national curriculum, through the design and promotion of educational materials intended to foster innovation and creativity. Designed as a nontraditional, out-of-school activity, its materials are distributed to children, along with the implementation of professional development activities for teachers. Another example of an organization promoting the development of 21CC in Mexico is INOMA. Based on the development and distribution of instructional games, available through the Internet, INOMA promotes not only technological literacy, but also aims to develop specific competencies like creativity, along with the reinforcement of "traditional" or curriculum-based learning.

Considering the limited inclusion of 21CC in the national curriculum, the lack of a public debate about relevant competencies, as well as the limited understanding of relevant skills among school actors, understanding how other actors may influence curriculum content is relevant.

Given the current context of the Mexican education system, nongovernmental organizations may be a "bottom-up" source of innovations to identify relevant competencies to be included in the revised national curriculum. The restriction in the national legislation against complete local adaptation of the national curriculum or the use of educational materials different than those approved by the national government, may explain why the curricular innovations aimed at promoting the attainment of new competencies have been implemented so slowly and usually on such a small scale. However, the experiences of NGOs working in the arena of building 21CC may still be considered as a source of possible interventions, and a laboratory to understand how relevant competencies might be included in the national curriculum for primary schools.

CONCLUSION

Understanding how 21CC are included in national curricula is a necessary step toward a more effective implementation of curriculum reform processes aimed at increasing the number of goals and instructional activities promoting the attainment of new skills. Although research on the implementation of these processes still has many other questions to be explored, analysis of the results of curriculum reforms (measured by the number and type of learning goals, as well as the distribution across grades and subjects) may shed some light on key aspects about how societies identify, conceptualize, and define relevant competencies, as well as how this definition is finally translated by educational administrators in the inclusion of new instructional activities in curricula.

This chapter described in its first section how 21CC are conceptualized by members of school communities in one Mexican state, pointing out the lack of a clear definition among school actors for these types of competencies. It also described how school communities consider technological literacy as the most important competence for the near future, ignoring other competencies that the available literature suggests are necessary for a successful integration into a globalized context. Even though both aspects may be seen as possible barriers to the implementation of 21CC curriculum reforms, there is also a welcoming environment among school communities and NGOs toward the possibility of including 21CC in instructional activities.

The positive environment highlights a need for starting an informed public dialogue about how to adapt the current educational system in response to the shift in the demand for competencies resulting from the increasing number of networks emerging across countries. Informing this discussion is a priority in order to improve the implementation of curriculum revisions.

A second aspect pointed out in this chapter is the inadequate implementation of the most recent curriculum reform in Mexico, at least if measured by its inclusion of 21CC considered as relevant in the literature review conducted by Pellegrino and Hilton.[44] The content analysis reflected a lack of alignment across grades, subjects, and domains, suggesting that inclusion of ELO21 in the national curriculum is neither comprehensive nor adequately aligned. Furthermore, the analysis suggests that the inadequate distribution of learning goals may result in an ineffective curriculum implementation.

This condition suggests that in order to successfully implement 21CC curriculum reforms, it is necessary to conduct further relevant research about curriculum planning, and probably to identify models of curriculum design that have been developed to promote the acquisition of new competencies in public schools.

Just as available research identifies ideal routes to attain specific knowledge regarding cognitive or "traditional" skills, it is necessary to widen the empirical knowledge base about how school communities should help students to attain 21CC in a scalable and effective manner. On this matter, comparative studies will be a must to validate and learn about different strategies implemented in other contexts.

Absence of an adequate understanding and a common conceptualization of 21CC suggest that beyond the traditional challenges faced by the educational systems regarding identification of competencies to be demanded in the near future, it is still necessary to promote a common understanding about which competencies should be included in the national curriculum. On the other hand, while it could be argued that the inadequate distribution of learning goals across subjects is a result of a trade-off in the inclusion of new and traditional competencies, the current distribution still does not correspond to the need employers express about the relevance 21CC in the workplace, based on the information provided by the scarce number of available studies analyzing the demand for specific competencies in the country.

This situation will result in a mismatch between supply and demand of specific competencies for the labor market,[45] and the possible exclusion of graduates who may not be able to attain these skills in a timely manner. In addition, if the lack of alignment is ignored in the ongoing curriculum revision, it is likely that most of the learning goals related to 21CC will remain just as an "intended curriculum," but not "enacted" or "learned," like in other educational reforms.[46]

Translating standards and learning goals related to 21CC into effective instructional practices in schools, seems an additional challenge for educators. Answering questions about how potential employers define demands for new competencies, how parents and teachers identify relevant competencies to be attained in the school, how curriculum designers should balance and allocate instructional time and activities among cognitive and noncognitive competencies, and how to identify effective instructional practices for 21CC included in the national curriculum, are pressing challenges both for educational researchers and policy makers. Furthermore, these questions must be addressed at the same time as different activities aimed at increasing a public demand for these skills should be implemented.

There are, however, a few relevant aspects to be considered in the process of including new competencies in the Mexican national curriculum.

In the first place, key actors (parents, teachers, and school principals) must be convinced that all students, in all schools, should attain these new competencies. In an educational system that is already unequal and unfair, great care must be taken when including new competencies not to increase the gaps among different population groups.

The process of including new competencies in the national curriculum should also take into account the results of previous curriculum reform strategies. Three aspects in particular should be pondered:

- An adequate evaluation of the implementation of curriculum reforms requires long periods of time.
- Curriculum reforms should not ignore the "prevalent culture, and educational practices."[47]
- Implementation of a real participatory planning process will increase the odds of including new competencies valued by actors ignored in previous reforms, such as businessmen and NGOs.

Although these aspects seem obvious, the ongoing revision of the national curriculum suggests that it remains a centralized and closed design and implementation process, similar to previous reforms.

Finally, there is an evident gap in available research about the different processes explaining how new competencies become part of the curriculum, and once included, how students should attain these competencies in an efficient and equal manner. More reliable comparative evidence is needed about the demands these new competencies pose for teachers, particularly about how to identify effective instructional practices, and how to accommodate a curriculum including 21CC for the multiple populations served by the public system.

It is clear that there are more aspects to be considered about the design and implementation of a new curriculum in Mexico. New interrogations about how to include 21CC in the curriculum will be added to other relevant questions about how to increase school effectiveness for the attainment of other relevant skills. Uncertainty about which competencies will be demanded from basic education graduates in fifty or a hundred years, and how educational systems will respond to that question, is permanent. However, in spite of this ambiguity, ignoring the shift in the demand for new competencies observed in the last decades across the world, is a policy option no educational system can afford.

Twenty-First-Century Competencies, the Indian National Curriculum Framework, and the History of Education in India

Aditya Natraj, Monal Jayaram, Jahnavi Contractor, and Payal Agrawal
Piramal Foundation, India

This chapter presents India's vision for twenty-first-century learning as articulated in the National Curriculum Framework 2005 (NCF2005).[1] The framework presents the larger and aspirational aims of education in India and includes possible pedagogies to be used for implementing them; these aims are then further broken down into learning goals in Indian textbooks for different grades.

We argue that while India has a robust curricular framework for twenty-first-century learning as seen through the NCF2005, it faces huge challenges for student learning implementation. The curricular goals view education from a "holistic" perspective and balance the twin aims of social transformation with economic growth for the country. However, leaders at various implementation levels appear to be struggling with implementing a smooth shift toward twenty-first-century learning principles as articulated in the NCF2005.

Our analysis indicates that there are some significant and nuanced differences observed between the goals outlined in the NCF2005 and the competencies outlined in the Hilton and Pellegrino framework for education for life and work in the twenty-first century.[2] We conclude that there are significant differences as a result of the difference in contexts and needs of a historically complex country like India and other developed countries. The NCF articulation significantly emphasized a learning that is global and at the same time grounded in the local communities and the personality of the child. Unlike the Hilton and Pellegrino framework, the NCF envisions education as a tool to cause social transformation and thus provides specific space to the role of rationality, deductive reasoning, and dignity of labor. And where the Hilton and Pellegrino framework focuses on developing competencies in teamwork and collaboration in the workplace, NCF envisions creating an autonomous learner who is capable of making decisions for himself or herself in the work and social spheres and of living a more socially responsive life.

The NCF2005 recognizes teacher and head teacher capacities, new syllabi and textbooks, and the translation and interpretation of new textbooks as well as NCF2005 materials into each state language and context as the key mechanism for the implementation of the framework. It also takes into account local contextual realities when designing education for the global world of tomorrow. The country showcases exemplary initiatives of successful implementation by local, nongovernmental organizations, where students have developed the desired learning outcomes in accordance with the Indian goals for education. However, implementation on a large scale via public systems is rather fragile. Our hypothesis is that leadership at various implementation levels struggles with skills and attitudes necessary to recognize the regressive impact of hierarchical thinking and the related consequences in making the shift toward an inclusive education system.

Based on Michael Fullan's theory of change in education[3] and the analysis of interviews with government officials, policy makers, educationists, and education change leaders in the country, we understand that leaders at various implementation levels needs to be equipped with the knowledge and skills of managing social transformation and change. We present this as a possible solution to move the Indian education system from its current position of low student learning, nonaligned teaching content and learning processes, and apathetic teaching attitudes, in order to make NCF2005 a reality.

RESEARCH METHODOLOGY

In writing this chapter we have followed a qualitative research methodology that included analysis of secondary resources as well as interviews conducted by the authors.

Data from the secondary sources, such as Indian educational policies, were analyzed, which involved content analysis, review, and coding of the following: the National Curriculum Framework 2005 and its associated position papers; the Indian National Five-year Development Plans (NDP); language and math textbooks of primary grades and social science textbooks from grade 6 onward; the Indian National Policy on Education 1968 (NPE1986);[4] documents on Continuous Comprehensive Evaluation (CCE); the Right to Education Act (RTE) 2009;[5] and the Hilton-Pellegrino Framework for twenty-first-century competencies. Secondary sources such as websites of civil society organizations like Digantar, Design For Change, Barefoot, and Lend a Hand India, were reviewed to analyze their role in initiating twenty-first-century learning in the country.

Twenty-five interviews were conducted, followed by analysis and synthesis of the content. Those interviewed included twelve practitioners from a combination of low-resource schools and English teaching medium-resource schools, both run by civil society organizations;[6] two policy makers who have spearheaded different committees;[7] two business leaders;[8] four government leaders;[9] one spiritual leader and four change makers in education leadership development.[10] The names of the interviewees and their organizations are listed in the chapter appendix.

THE INDIAN CONTEXT FOR TWENTY-FIRST-CENTURY EDUCATION

The Indian context for twenty-first-century education comes from its need to address contemporary socioeconomic inequities.

India's vision for twenty-first-century education is elucidated in its current National Curriculum Framework, which was revised in 2005 to address the inherited problems of the past, the current realities, and the future requirements for a developing India in a globalized twenty-first-century world.[11] India's recent National Education Policies are focused on the right to education for all, specifically the disadvantaged members of society, including the girl child.[12] The country has a decentralized federal structure[13] with national educational policies that guide and support state educational organizations. The various educational organizations include the National Council for Education, Research and Training (called SCERT at the state level) that develop textbooks and related trainings; and the National Council for Teacher Education (NCTE) that sets the benchmarks for teacher education and recruitment norms. They support local District Institutes of Education Training (DIETs) to ensure district level training and monitoring for policy implementation.

To provide a contextual understanding of India's vision for education, we have divided the history of India into four time periods: the ancient era (pre-1757), the colonial period (1757–1947), the post-independence period (1948–1990), and the post-liberalization period (1990 onwards).

Ancient India (Before 1757)

Ancient Indian society was marked by caste-based segregation,[14] varied religious identities, multiple regional kingdoms, and linguistic diversities. While the regional kingdoms were wealthy and had self-sufficient systems, inequities existed, where people in the lower levels of the caste system had lesser opportunities for social and economic mobility.

In this context, education was a tool that maintained the caste system.[15] Most ancient wisdom and knowledge of sciences, arts, yoga, and spiritual understanding was available for higher castes only. Lower castes were assigned menial work, and their education was based on a father passing on the knowledge associated with that menial profession to his son.

Additionally, the practice of untouchability and gender subjugation were built into the social system. Eventually these social, religious, and gender-based prejudices became deeply rooted in the ethos of the people.

Colonial Period (1757–1947)

The colonial period was a complex period in which the British system provided formal education to a select few while the general population was increasingly drawn to the freedom struggle and social awareness movements. The British allowed the traditional caste system to continue unchanged from ancient times. Formal education was offered only to the upper castes, who were then reeducated in the British value system and ways of thinking. The purpose of the British education system was thus primarily to build a group of administrators who perceived themselves as British and who served them and their empire.

However, this created a stir among the reeducated upper castes who were influenced by the industrial revolution and the influx of Western ideas, and who experienced a confluence of cultures. They started questioning the ancient beliefs and social prejudices. Thus, while the purpose of the British education system was not really for equity or social reengineering, the broader perspective exposed Indians to a new set of ideas like freedom, democracy, equality, equity, and critical thinking.

In this context, education was seen as a tool for social reform and political awareness. Social reformers and freedom struggle leaders like Raja Ram Mohan Roy, Rabindranath Tagore, Jyotiba Phule, B. R. Ambedkar, Lala Lajpat Rai, and Mahatma Gandhi recognized education as a means of raising the collective consciousness and mobilizing people toward a nonviolent struggle against the colonial rule.

Post-independence (1947–1990)

The idea of creating a resurgent India marked the post-independence period. India's freedom struggle inspired people to envision a society moved by a democratic ethos. Education continued to be seen as a tool for social and economic reform by many. The focus was on developing technical knowledge and a scientific mind-set that challenged traditional beliefs such as caste and gender subjugation. The aim of education had a civic frame, including the goal of uniting disparate regional identities and creating a socially cohesive democratic nation.

The policy also aimed at celebrating India's traditional knowledge, cultural diversity, and plurality. To meet manpower needs for industrial growth and development, policy makers focused on delivering modern education in science and technology. The practice of untouchability was declared illegal under the new constitutional laws. Policies to support the lower castes through positive discrimination aimed to break down caste prejudices and divisions in the society. There was an emphasis on educating the girl child, increasing access to schools, and increasing the number of female teachers. The government focused on social and economic reconstruction to combat poverty, unemployment, social segregation, and a large influx of refugees.

The mixed economic model of planned development led to a slow but sustained growth of local industries and the modernization of agriculture. However, despite this growth, economic and regional disparities increased. Urbanization led to unemployment, urban poverty, and reduced development in rural areas. The urban-rural divide widened, and many in rural India aspired to life in a city. This in turn led to a declining interest in indigenous means of livelihood, especially in rural areas. As the demand for modern education increased and outpaced the creation of jobs that matched the new skill sets of the population, more and more educated Indians entered the ranks of the unemployed and underemployed.[16]

Various education commissions recommended increasing investment in education and ensuring common school systems for equitable education for all. However, the investment as a percentage of GDP declined from 1947 to 1986. The National Policy of Education[17] in 1986 reversed this trend and stressed the need for Universalising Elementary Education (UEE) and the retention of children in schools up to age fourteen.[18] The Seventh Five-year Plan recommended that the Indian education system focus on the following: the achievement of universal elementary education;

the eradication of illiteracy in the fifteen- to thirty-five-year age group; development of vocational and skill-training programs; updating and increasing the rigor of education standards to provide effective links with the world of work, with special emphasis on science, environment, and value orientation; the provision of facilities for high-quality education in every district of the country; and the modernization of technical education.[19]

Post-liberalized Era (1990 to Present)

Unemployment and socioeconomic inequities marked the post-liberalization period.[20] As Indian industrial, manufacturing, and agricultural sectors reeled under the effects of globalization, Indian education policy makers focused on teaching information technology, and by 1990 pushed for policies to develop twenty-first-century competencies for innovation and entrepreneurship. To reduce rural-urban disparities, the National Policy on Education Programme of Action 1992 (POA1992) recommended measures to promote diversification and dispersal of employment opportunities.[21]

Education was seen as a human right for all children, especially those from disadvantaged and weaker communities. Though untouchability and gender discrimination were declared illegal, effects of historic stratifications continued to cause unequal access to education. For example, at the dawn of the new century, 28.5 percent of India's population of 1.27 billion was under fourteen years of age, and policy makers realized that while India had the world's largest youth population, it also had a skewed sex ratio and therefore must ensure quality education to all for social and economic equity and justice. The NPE1986 and POA1992 emphasized that "equality of education to all" meant not only equal access to education for all, but also equitable conditions of success. The policy makers believed that the inherent equality of all would be achieved through the creation of a common core curriculum. The purpose was "to remove prejudices and complexes transmitted through the social environment and the accident of birth."[22]

India became a key player in the new liberalized global market. Indian industries were exposed to competition from international organizations.

The ongoing technological changes and the depletion of natural resources led to unemployment that brought about rapid changes in living and working conditions. Agriculture and manufacturing processes became increasingly homogenized to suit global market needs, ignoring local diversities and contexts. Thus, the changing realities of India in the globalizing economy of the twenty-first century required that education must enable innovative learning to promote, for example, entrepreneurial ventures that are suited to local needs and contexts yet successful, competitive, and sustainable in the rapidly changing global market.

Formation of the National Curriculum Framework 2005

The NCF2005 was created against the backdrop of the new liberalized world where each nation strives to leverage the ongoing globalization process to its advantage. The creation of the framework took into account data showing that Indian society at the beginning of the new century faced the dual challenges of "economic growth without employment"[23] and the historic social inequities that had persisted through the years. The NCF2005 recommended a series of education reforms in curriculum, teaching methods, and assessments to address these contemporary issues. The Right of Children to Free and Compulsory Education (RTE) Act of 2009 further made it mandatory for the government to ensure quality education to all.

According to District Information System for Education, in 2013–2014 there were 1.52 million schools spread over 662 districts across 35 different Indian states and Union Territories.[24] Due to varied geography, linguistic pluralities, and cultural, social, and economic disparities across a vast country, the NCF2005 was designed to be a flexible guiding document that is open to interpretation according to the varied local contexts. Numerous rounds of focus group discussions incorporated the views of scholars, education experts, teachers, parents, and practitioners from NGOs, as well as academicians in various fields like science, math, social sciences, and art.[25]

The NCF2005 is thus a product of multiple discussions and deliberations involving more than three hundred people and resulting in twenty-one position papers. It is the inclusive product of a large number of people as opposed to a limited group of policy elites making decisions on their own. It consolidated the lessons from the past NCFs in 1975, 1988, and 2000, and took into account the recommendations made by various education commissions based on their studies of previous education policies of 1968 and 1986 as well as from schemes such as UEE. The curriculum thus is based not merely on an abstraction but on a wide range of perspectives coming together. The next section elaborates in detail various twenty-first-century competencies and educational goals that the NCF2005 articulates.

NCF2005: AN ALTERNATIVE APPROACH FOR TWENTY-FIRST-CENTURY LEARNING

The NCF2005 proposes twenty-first-century learning for Indian students as a means of developing human capabilities for social and economic empowerment.

The NCF2005 provides an alternative view of education by locating it in India's contextual needs in the global world, rather than merely responding to an outside context of global demands. It aims to enhance human capabilities to empower learners and achieve social and economic equity. The goal is to develop learners' individual competencies so they are empowered to make choices to favorably transform their own lives and society. The NCF2005 is a flexible curriculum suited to its varied regional contexts and has emerged from numerous discussions, deliberations, and sociological perspectives. This section elaborates a few guiding principles along which the NCF2005 is designed.

Work-Centered Education

NCF2005 recommends Work-centered Education—practical applications to transition from the academic world to the world of work and develop social entrepreneurship.[26]

Work-centered education enables generic subject competencies, learning strategies for transferring theory into practice, and finding meaning through experiential learning. Historically, Indian education has emphasized theoretical knowledge that is cut off from practice and has inadequately prepared the learner for the challenges of a workplace, leading to educated unemployment and underemployment.[27]

NCF2005 thus stimulates entrepreneurship, problem solving, observation, decision making, brainstorming, and evaluating solutions as competencies to be acquired by a learner with an aim to adapt to changing work situations. These competencies enable lifelong learning that is essential in industrial, agricultural, or corporate workplaces. The proposed pedagogy in all subjects is centered on collaborative projects, such as fieldwork, field research, surveys, and managing local farms leading to learning activities that encourage applied knowledge to a practical issue.

For example, a school in one of the states included field research in their social studies classroom. Students conducted field research on the issue of famine that was most relevant for the state that year. Students interviewed elders in the village and recorded a local history of famines in the village. They thus learned about local scientific knowledge related to crops, water sources, flora and fauna, and the environment.[28]

Head, Heart, and Hands

NCF2005 recommends Head, Heart, and Hands—a hands-on and minds-on education that promotes dignity of labor.

Head, heart, and hands enables respect for the dignity of labor and the local nonformalized expertise of people such as artisans and farmers. Historically, Indian caste stratification was based on the perceived superiority of "intellectual" work leading to disregard for "manual" work, looking down upon local indigenous wisdom. In such a context, NCF2005 seeks to change this mind-set by legitimizing a local, experience-based approach to education.

NCF2005 also empowers the learner as well as the community by bringing artisans, carpenters, and farmers into the formal school as resource teachers, thus stimulating cognitive, affective, and psychomotor domains in a holistic way. The proposed pedagogy involves observing and learning from local practitioners, who demonstrate the practical application of theoretical knowledge in math, science, and other subject areas. For example, a rural municipal school[29] invited a carpenter who demonstrated to students how he creates circles, squares, and rectangles. Students tried the same, and at the end of his session, 90 percent of the children could explain the difference between a square and a rectangle and identify and draw various geometrical figures. The learners here learned by doing, analyzing, and being receptive to the local wisdom.[30] Thus, NCF2005's focus on head, heart, and hands addresses India's need to inculcate the value of dignity of labor and reduce intellectual class and caste divisions.

Higher Order Thinking

NCF2005 recommends Higher Order Thinking—developing a scientific way of thinking along with mathematical and linguistic abilities across all subject areas.

Higher order thinking competencies enable learners to lead their own learning processes, actively participate in constructing their own knowledge and understanding, and go beyond textbook content. Historically, the Indian education system is based on rote learning. It rewards the skill to reproduce textual knowledge, follow the teacher's words unquestioningly, and accept events in nature without getting into the rationale. In contrast, NCF2005 seeks to develop critical thinking and scientific temperament, as both are key competencies needed in the evolving world of innovation and the rapid technology transitions in the twenty-first century. It empowers the learners to become independent thinkers and solution finders rather than waiting for an authority to provide answers.

The proposed pedagogy involves teachers asking questions, encouraging students to ask questions, and enabling learners to come up with out-of-the-box solutions. For example, in the mathematics classroom, the NCF2005 recommends that teachers inspire students to look for different ways of arriving at a solution, as by asking how many different ways you can use two numbers to arrive at the sum of 24. This motivates students to explore different possibilities, such as 20 + 4, 10 + 14, 7 + 17, and so forth, promoting critical reasoning competencies.[31] The grade 4 and 5 environment studies textbooks published by the National Council for Education Research and Training (NCERT)[32] each include a chapter on sources of water, and poses critical thinking questions to sensitize students on caste, class, and gender. Teachers are expected to facilitate discussions on such questions as how water is unequally supplied and how some people do not get equal access to water; the textbooks also recommend asking questions such as who fetches water from the well—is it always the women of the house? Thus, NCF2005 posits critical thinking and reasoning as key abilities for preparing the learner for the workplace while also recognizing the role of rationality and deductive reasoning in social transformation.

Aesthetic Appreciation

NCF2005 recommends Aesthetic Appreciation—
an education that exposes learners to India's multicultural
art forms and varied traditions.

India has inherited a rich legacy of varied arts that was long neglected due to the colonial influence, contributing to Westernized notions of aesthetic appreciation and a low esteem for Indian artefacts. Education in the arts enables learners to develop aesthetic sensibilities and discover their own talents and potential. It promotes artistic sensibilities and empowers learners to express the self, widen their experiences, and gain exposure to varied art forms.

The proposed pedagogy involves exposing learners to varied art forms such as literary arts, performing arts, and crafts of varied regions. For example, teachers can integrate art education in all subjects by organizing field trips to museums or historic sites in the community to showcase folk art and architecture. Schools can organize a Bal-Sabha[33] where children get a platform to showcase their artistic talents. While developing artistic appreciation is favored, NCF2005 additionally aims to promote Indian art heritage and develop aesthetic sensibilities that will help resist the homogenizing influences of the market forces in the new globalized world.

Democratic Citizenship

NCF2005 recommends Democratic Citizenship—an education
to make active, responsible citizens who respect diversity in
beliefs and opinions and develop a democratic ethos.

Education for democracy enables learners to develop social awareness and to learn to be democratic and responsible citizens with respect and appreciation for social, cultural, religious, economic, and gender diversities. After independence, the Indian government's goal was to unite regional states and develop a socially cohesive democratic country. Democracy was required to be established as a way of life rather than a system of governance. In such a light, an education for democracy empowers learners to take initiative and responsibility and to develop leadership capabilities.

The proposed pedagogy of NCF2005 involves exposing learners to democratic culture where they get the space to voice their opinion, take the lead, and assume responsibility. For example, many schools have Bal-Sansad,[34] or children's parliament, where every academic year school elections are held, students vote for their representatives, and a student council is formed.

The NCF2005 goals locate citizenship as a skill under work ethics and conscientiousness as part of developing intrapersonal competencies, with a focus on developing citizens for a society where democracy is a way of life and not just a system of governance.

Flexibility and Creativity

NCF2005 recommends Flexibility and Creativity—
building creativity, flexibility, and autonomy through
developing the learning process.

Education that is flexible and creative enables leaners to co-construct understanding, develop creativity, and take into consideration the varied local contexts of India so that elements of diversity that are embedded in the country, such as linguistic diversity, are looked at inclusively rather than as detriments to be overcome.[35]

Historically, education in India was rigid, homogenized, and dictated by curricular content; it did not allow space for students' voices, varying contexts, or independent reflections on the existing diversities and indigenous ways. The change incorporated into NCF2005 empowers learners to develop confidence and lead their own learning process. The proposed pedagogy allows learners to bring their own independent thinking, knowledge of the local context, and collective understanding to the classroom. For example, a school[36] allowed students to go beyond their science textbook content on environmental science and do a project to identify various trees in their village by talking to elders and creating a database of all the trees, their special characteristics, their flowering season, and so forth. NCF2005 thus highlights the need for intellectual openness and autonomous self-led learning processes as integral to teaching and learning for the twenty-first century.

Education for Peace

NCF2005 recommends Education for Peace—appreciating differences, becoming makers of peace, and resisting intolerant and violent means of resolving conflicts.

Education for peace enables learners to build a culture of peace, develop nonviolent conflict resolution skills, and solve contemporary problems peacefully. Historically and culturally, the Indian society has a legacy of peaceful coexistence amidst varied religious and cultural identities. India's freedom struggle was a nonviolent movement. The current global context, however, is marked by increased intolerance and terrorism, making education for peace both relevant and important given the spate of communal tensions and the political strife between India and Pakistan. The NCERT Education for Peace position paper calls for a curriculum that empowers students to learn to make value-based decisions, reflect on their actions, and choose peaceful means over violence, thus enabling learners to become "makers of peace rather than only consumers of peace."[37]

The proposed pedagogy of NCF2005 involves creating classroom processes where learning activities give opportunity for peaceful coexistence and nonviolent conflict resolution.[38] For example, teachers can help children resolve interpersonal conflicts through peaceful dialogue, and invite influential writers and experts to speak on contemporary issues and expose students to India's varied cultural and religious diversity. The framework thus finds conflict resolution as a critical goal for education, and nonviolence and peace as key attributes for learners to imbibe as part of their education.

The Challenges of Implementing NCF2005

The NCF is a robust framework, but it is not implemented uniformly across the varied schooling systems of India.[39]

India's decentralized system gives varied school systems and textbook development organizations flexibility to interpret the NCF2005 recommendations in line with their local contexts. In fact, the NCF2005 is articulated in a series of position papers across twenty-one subject areas, enumerating the aims of education, the recommended curricular content to achieve each aim, the pedagogical process to be used for it, and how it should be assessed. However, it does not articulate a list of specific learning outcomes or competencies that the country's education system must develop in all its citizens.[40] This often leads to misinterpretation or misunderstandings regarding which specific learning outcomes or student competencies need to receive focus. Unlike in many other countries, where student competency rubrics are typically specified at the national level, educators and textbook writers in India may choose to interpret the guidelines according to their own understanding, thus making it difficult to ensure effective and uniform implementation of the NCF2005 guidelines across the country.[41]

However, as we discuss in the next section, in those organizations where the NCF2005 is accurately interpreted and followed, and where leadership systems are aligned, the result has been a comprehensive approach to education that is exemplary. In these organizations student learning outcomes have reflected the NCF2005 vision. Thus, re-articulation of the competencies in terms of learning outcomes would help to align the varied systemic processes such as textbook content, assessment practices, and teacher development toward meeting the recommended goals of NCF2005. The next section describes a few case studies to exemplify this observation.

SUCCESSFUL IMPLEMENTERS OF TWENTY-FIRST-CENTURY LEARNING AS ARTICULATED IN NCF2005

Models exist in the country that demonstrate
twenty-first-century learning resonating strongly with
educational aims as articulated by NCF2005.

This section documents the efforts of four organizations that have been working in alignment with the NCF principles and have demonstrated ways in which they have been effectively interpreted to benefit students.

Digantar: A Model for Developing Competencies to Counter Social Stratification

Digantar has contributed significantly to the discourse
on critical thinking skills while working on the social
transformation aim of NCF2005.

Digantar is an independent nonprofit focusing on alternative education. Along with running two schools, Digantar develops curriculum and organizes training workshops for education workers. They also conduct education research and publish an education journal as well as workbooks for children and other supporting curriculum materials for educators. Digantar has recognized the persistent hierarchies of caste, economic status, and gender relations as key components that have contributed to India's uneven social and economic development.[42] Their educational approach therefore deeply influences access to education and participation in school by the girl students and students from affected castes and religions. They have enabled girls in their program to pursue university education. These girls find themselves empowered enough to question traditional gender constraints and claim their rights.[43]

Digantar has established classrooms as safe and democratic spaces where children learn to make their own decisions and enquire into social traditions and systems that are generally assumed to be beyond question. Their pioneering work has led to the development of an alternative teacher training model to equip teachers to address challenges in teaching as well as to become reflective practitioners who can create their own solutions appropriate to the situation.[44]

Teaching the child to become a self-motivated and independent learner with the ability to think critically is the central theme of the solution designed by Digantar. Empowering the children with critical thinking skills, Digantar aims to create an alternative approach to engage with children in a fearless democratic way and develop them as sensitive, respectful, and caring members of the society.[45]

Lend a Hand India: A Model for Balancing the Competencies of Head, Heart, and Hands

Lend a Hand India has established an approach to teaching entrepreneurship skills while integrating the work-based education aims of NCF2005.

As of 2012, twelve thousand students from over one hundred villages in Maharashtra, Karnataka, and Goa are associated with Lend a Hand India programs. Lend a Hand India has recognized the impact of ignoring the integration of diverse work traditions of India in its curriculum.[46] Their educational approach strives to minimize the alienation of children due to this inferior treatment by including the rich experiential base of their communities and positioning it on a par with intellectual work. Integrating basic technology training in education according to children's local socioeconomic contexts so that they can practice in their own surroundings and achieve self-sufficiency is the inspiring idea behind this initiative. Empowering the students with entrepreneurship skills, Lend a Hand India is making school education practical and relevant by providing job and life skills training, aptitude testing, career counseling, and bridge loans for microenterprises.[47]

In sum, the program has established a bridge between school education and the opportunities, skills, and exposure necessary for students to achieve their full potential and earn a livelihood, contributing immensely to children's confidence and self-esteem. Their work has set up an alternative solution that addresses the problems related to the unemployment of rural youth and their migration in substantial numbers to cities in search of employment. The program has influenced the motivation of children positively toward school and learning, leading to increased enrollment, enhancement of academic performance, reduction in the dropout rate, and a higher number of secondary school graduates opting to receive a technical education.[48]

Barefoot College: A Model for Developing the Competencies for Democratic Citizenship

Barefoot College has transformed the thinking on citizenship skills while working on the democratic participation aims of NCF2005.

Every year three thousand children elect their members of parliament, their government, and their prime minister as a part of Barefoot College.[49] Barefoot College's educational approach focuses on institutionalizing child parliaments in their night schools to enable all learners to claim their rights as well as to contribute to society and the polity equally. This intervention has allowed students to experience real power in their hands to make decisions and take responsibility for the management of their school. Barefoot College has acknowledged the critical role of teaching students to exercise their rights and make wise choices.[50]

Barefoot College has foregrounded the respect for basic rights of children in the education process by allowing children's voices to be heard in the decision-making process and by creating the space for them to be equal and responsible members of the society. Their work also has set up a successful locally relevant model of education for children who must work during the day in order to survive and who remain deprived of opportunities to learn skills that guarantee a sustainable living in rural communities through setting up night schools.[51]

Giving children the opportunity to learn about their rights and make decisions that enable them to influence matters that are important to their lives is the core focus of their approach. Empowering young people with citizenship skills, Barefoot College's child parliaments are increasing the stake of children in school management as well as in community issues like child marriage and the exploitation of children by organizing children as a parliament to take collective decisions.[52]

Design for Change: A Model for Developing Competencies of Flexibility and Creativity

Design for Change (DFC) has pioneered the work on design thinking skills while working on the creative expression aims of NCF2005.

More than one hundred seventy thousand students participated in the DFC challenge between 2009 and 2013, impacting twenty-two million people through 3,279 stories of change led by brilliant ideas all over the world. All these children found themselves empowered to challenge age-old superstitions in rural communities and to earn their own money to finance school computers to solve the problem of heavy school bags. Design for Change recognized the loss of learning opportunity in the narrow focus on using textbooks as the main source of curriculum. Their educational approach moves beyond the traditional subject-based approach of organizing the curriculum with examinations and instead emphasizes areas that are "rich in potential for the development of skill, aesthetics, creativity, resourcefulness, and teamwork."[53]

Design for Change has created space in the education process for children to engage with thoughtful action in life through opportunities that equip them to make sense of the world, study its contradictions, and learn the competencies to negotiate its challenges so that they are prepared for the rapidly changing global world. DFC designed its solution on the premise that exposing children to the belief that they have choices and that they can change the world can prepare them to face the real world. DFC teaches students about skills like empathy, collaboration, and digital literacy by inviting them to come up with creative solutions through a structured problem-solving approach. Their innovative model has demonstrated that transformative student participation is possible and that they can create alternatives to counter the sense of helplessness within communities where they do not feel empowered to solve their own problems.[54]

These efforts highlight the relevance and scope of possibility of the NCF2005 in India's context, when its principles are implemented faithfully. There is, however, a need to closely examine the factors that impede its implementation on a large scale and build a momentum to integrate these smaller initiatives into the public school system.

THE IMPLEMENTATION DEFICIT OF TWENTY-FIRST-CENTURY LEARNING AS ARTICULATED IN NCF2005

Systems at different implementation levels are not always designed to counter the sociocultural biases that obstruct the development of twenty-first-century learning as articulated in NCF2005.

This section highlights the major systemic gaps at various implementation levels to ensure the development of twenty-first-century competencies in children as articulated in NCF2005 at a national scale. Despite a carefully designed decentralized education system, there are systemic concerns regarding content development and teacher preparation that, when addressed, could better ensure that policy recommendations are carried out.

State Level Gaps

One of the missing pieces in ensuring that policy directives are implemented faithfully is the lack of robustness in systems to ensure that content design and staff selection processes rise above the existing social inequities in India. For example, textbook reviews conducted by government and nongovernment organizations have disclosed that stereotypes about social inequities continue to exist in the choice and presentation of the content. Decision processes guiding what kind of indigenous content is worth bringing into textbooks have lacked empiricism and research-based data. The reviews have highlighted a lack of systemic focus on the need to strictly adhere to national goals and to develop the process, expertise, and systems needed to address any neglect of those goals. For example, a Gujarat state social science textbook was found to be perpetuating religious or caste-based biases by mixing history with mythology and presenting factual inaccuracies.[55] Also, a gender review exercise by the National Council for Education Research and Training[56] revealed that the textbooks of Uttar Pradesh and Madhya Pradesh states continued "gender stereotypes."[57]

These inconsistencies are amplified by the fact that in different states the preparation of syllabi and textbooks is taken up by different agencies such as SCERT, examination boards, state textbook boards, and private publishers. All states have independent mechanisms for preparation and approval of textual material, making consistency challenging. In addition, a subcommittee set up by the Ministry of Human Resources to review the procedures for textbook production observed that the "textbooks are created mechanically without really addressing the core curricular concerns defined in the education policy."[58] Because of the varied systems across states for textbook production, the goal of coherence in the content according to the national goals also gets compromised. While policy has proposed the use of multiple content and a range of teaching-learning methods, the review committee discovered that teachers were employing didactic teaching methods to teach content in the textbooks. The state leadership is responsible for ensuring that curricular content is aligned to national guidelines, and they could do better to ensure higher standards and consistency.

The state leadership is also responsible for ensuring that all schools have teachers in accordance with the guidelines prescribed by the National Council for Teacher Education,[59] including the mandate by the Right to Education Act 2009 to design and execute teacher eligibility tests (TETs) to ensure the minimum level of professional quality of teachers.[60] Reports on the status of teacher assessments, however, reveal one of the most important critiques of TETs. In some states, teams without adequate expertise or training on content and psychometrics have been entrusted with conducting these assessments. For example, on tests administered in certain states, many questions were focused on rote and recall. In some cases the tested items were not based on sound psychometric principles and were ambiguous; some had multiple answers in the choices given; some had no applicable answers in the choices given; and in some, the questions were irrelevant to teaching and learning.[61]

Additionally, the lack of an adequate number of teachers, and the fact that not all states have been complying with the needs of the TET, has proven to be a stumbling block for the recruitment of professionally qualified teachers in the country.

In its curriculum framework on teacher education, the National Council for Teacher Education acknowledges the challenges and states that students in teacher education programs "need to be exposed more and more to the realities of school and community. Internship, practice of teaching, practical activities, and supplementary educational activities need to be better planned and organized more systematically. The curriculum, pedagogy and evaluation of teacher education programs need to be made more objective as well as comprehensive." It further goes on to say that "if teachers are to make positive contribution to the realization of the constitutional goals, pre-service and in-service education of teachers needs to give up its neutral stance and commit itself to attaining these goals." The Indian cultural ethos and philosophy of education must be integrated.[62]

District Level Gaps

Systems to prepare teachers to come out of their hierarchical mind-sets lack rigor.

The District Institutes of Education Training were envisioned as academic lead institutions to provide guidance to all academic functionaries in the district.[63] All states attempt to carry forward implementation of the educational goals through the decentralized systems of DIETs. They are expected to conduct research to improve and innovate teaching and develop contextually relevant material for schools.

However, the quality of training runs a risk of being substandard, since the trainers in this system are a mix of people experienced in training but inexperienced in teaching and classroom processes. Additionally, DIETs in several states are said to be headed by bureaucrats who lack pedagogical experience.[64] Training events and decisions on training needs are not driven by empirical research based data, and lead to training that promotes socio-cultural gaps rather than questioning them. DIETs also lack infrastructural support like libraries and laboratories for different subjects.[65] States which have invested in infrastructure reveal low utilization of such facilities due to a lack of understanding and vision about the ways of using such infra-structures for training.

Research on culture and classroom reform reveals that transform-ing teacher's attitudes toward social inequities calls for rigorous mind-set shifts. It requires trainers to rework their own world views and then to ini-tiate the questioning and unlearning of belief systems while at the same time providing a safe, thoughtful environment for the teacher-learner to construct a new belief system. The same research suggests that the hierar-chical social systems that the teacher traditionally carries along "restrict[s] them to come down to child's level." In spite of their enhanced ability to use aids and ask questions to children, newly trained teachers are still fail-ing to let children generate knowledge through experience-based activi-ties and by sharing with each other.[66] This leads to a vacuum of reflective teacher training practice where the teacher continues to be the authority figure with the students instead of a facilitator of learning.

School Level Gaps

Systems to prepare school leaders to shift from an authority
figure to an instructional leader are inadequate.

The school leadership is responsible for contributing to the contextualiza-tion of the school curriculum and preparing teachers to teach it. Some In-dian states have initiated head teacher aptitude tests, but there have not been any standardization attempts like the teacher eligibility test to select school leaders. The school leaders continue to be promoted into a head teacher's role on the basis of seniority rather than aptitude.

Instructional leadership in schools runs a risk of being substandard since systems to equip school leaders to interpret policies appropriately to their contexts are not in place. NCF2005 documents the fact that the autonomy and expertise of school leaders to choose culturally and geographically relevant content have not been given adequate attention.[67] School leaders therefore do not find themselves equipped to take curricular decisions for their schools and continue to believe that policy changes are really not required. There is a wide gap between how the role of school leader is envisaged and what they actually end up doing. At present they are seen largely as the administrative authorities in schools.

Since head teachers come from the same cadre as teachers who struggle with caste, gender, and class biases, the head teachers too continue the legacy of these prejudices and hierarchies. The authoritative behavior of school leaders toward children often extends to teachers. There is a continuous expectation for teachers to perform without giving them much support or even identifying their training needs. This limits the school leader's capacity to identify explicit and subtle discriminatory attitudes toward students, parents, or teachers from certain background because their own belief system aligns to these prejudices.

These systemic gaps, along with a weak political will in the country for positive change, preclude the realization of progressive measures that policies sought to bring about to change the educational experience of children. Some recommendations, such as improving teacher selection processes, do not get implemented because the implementation systems are not equipped to usher in the change, while other recommendations, such as increased teaching hours and planning time, remain only on paper due to a lack of political will.

POSSIBLE SOLUTIONS TO THE IMPLEMENTATION OF TWENTY-FIRST-CENTURY LEARNING AS ARTICULATED IN NCF2005

Role-specific skill building of leadership at each implementation level would be required to shift the perspectives of hierarchy that is deeply rooted in the Indian mind-set.

This section aims to propose an investment in education leaders in terms of appropriate skills and attitudes as a solution to the implementation deficit that India faces. The hypothesis is that well-equipped leaders at various implementation levels can ensure that the institutions they lead function in consonance with the responsibilities endowed on them.

As this chapter has indicated, India has in place a robust curriculum framework that explicitly recognizes the changes required in processes ranging from teacher selection and development to assessment systems to content and pedagogy, keeping in mind both the contextual reality of India as well as the learning needs of children. However, putting policy recommendations into practice and improving the quality of learning in schools have taken a back seat owing to historically inherited hierarchies and bureaucratic administrative culture. Varghese points to the "need for developing organizational arrangements to facilitate educational planning in a decentralized framework" and the "absence of planning competencies at various implementation levels which is a major constraint in operationalization of decentralized planning."[68] In effect, the clarity in curricular vision has not necessarily resulted in implementation.

Setting up a unit of educational planning with the DIETs in the 1980s was one of the steps that have been taken in hopes of bridging this gap. Another was the establishment of the State Institute of Education Management and Training (SIEMAT) to build professional competencies of planning at local levels within the state in the 1990s, following the recommendations of NPE1986.[69] However, the SIEMATs were unable to meet the expected goals of building the skills and knowledge of education functionaries and instead ended up being defunct organizations.

The hypothesis here, then, is that developing the leadership abilities of officials and leaders in the system could play a key role in institutionalizing systems and processes through which the policy vision promoting twenty-first-century learning could be translated into practice. Leadership could build a larger environment in which reflection on the deeply seated sociocultural beliefs and mind-sets of people is not only possible but considered a necessary process for transformation.

Based on the work of Michael Fullan, this chapter proposes to incorporate action points that he suggests are crucial for systemic change. Since the implementation is on a large scale, Fullan's work seems appropriate in the process of designing solutions.

State-Level Leadership for Twenty-First-Century Learning

State leadership, if prepared for building a shared vision and adaptive policies, could align stakeholders to move toward a common direction espoused in the NCF2005.

A shared vision and understanding of the expected change is an important determinant of success in leading change. "Shared vision and ownership is more an outcome of a quality process than it is a precondition. This is important to know because it causes one to act differently in order to create ownership."[70]

State leadership, which is the first level of decentralization for policy implementation where decisions regarding the contextualization of policy and the broader implementation plan are made, could play an instrumental role in creating this shared vision. A shared vision could set the expectations from each level and the role that each stakeholder is required to play in the process. This could also establish processes for change such as evidence-based enquiry and reflective practice as essential to integrate in the current way of functioning.[71]

In one of the interviews conducted for this chapter an education leadership change manager referred to the disintegrated understanding of the NCF2005 which leads to a lack of focus on social transformation in the implementers' minds. In this regard, state leadership that is equipped to bring everyone together around the core values of a policy change could ensure that there is minimal dilution in understanding the real essence of a policy, and that processes like content development and teacher recruitment integrate principles articulated in the NCF2005.

Statewide change also requires coherence and alignment across multiple stakeholders. State leadership equipped to understand the need to foster these elements needs to be adaptive in nature to face challenges that large-scale system change encounters.[72]

District-Level Leadership for Twenty-First-Century Learning

*District leadership, if prepared for designing capacity-building
programs with a focus on results and reflective practice, could prepare
practitioners to bring in deep changes in teaching-learning practices.*

A capacity-building program with a focus on results is crucial for change to transpire. This is a perfect combination of the pressure and support principles that Fullan identifies for effective large-scale reform. According to Fullan, emphasis on accountability for results alone can become a kind of negative pressure; he calls for positive pressure by which he means emphasis on results along with motivational support accompanied by resources for capacity building.[73]

The district level has a significant role in the capacity building of teachers in order to implement change. Once a direction and expectations are set from the state leadership, district leadership could continue moving in the same direction by preparing teachers to understand the need of fundamental changes in their practice.

District-level leadership could also begin to integrate a bias for reflective action in their engagement with teachers and other practitioners (principals and administrators) so as to emphasize the value of learning by thinking about what one is doing.[74] Deep changes in teaching practice for twenty-first-century learning are possible when a comprehensive teacher development is in place that includes both technical and reflective aspects of learning.

School-Level Leadership for Twenty-First-Century Learning

*School leadership, if prepared for fostering contextual learning
and instructional leadership, could create conditions for teaching
and learning that lead to improved student learning.*

Learning in context is identified by Fullan as an important strategy for reform. Quoting Elmore (2004), Fullan says that "improvement is more a function of learning to do the right things in the settings where you work."[75] One of the critiques of standards-based reform is that it does not encourage educators to change the settings in which they work.[76]

Schools leaders—who are the most decentralized unit in the chain of implementation, where content and teaching practices can be contextualized according to the needs of the school—could be equipped to organize teacher development in the context of their own schools. They could create opportunities for teachers to observe each other in their own classrooms and create a sustained learning about their practice.

Instructional leadership, characterized by expectation setting, teacher development, resource allocation, safe environment, and quality teaching, could equip school leaders with comprehensive leadership practices.[77] In the Indian context, where school leaders are still perceived as administrative heads of the school with limited autonomy or expertise, a shift toward developing them as instructional leaders may support decentralization of policy efforts.

CONCLUSION

A close reading of NCF2005 highlights the human-capability approach to education that is embedded in the framework along with an articulation of twenty-first-century learning competencies. It also emphasizes the importance of analyzing the challenges and capacities required to implement such a framework in a vast and diverse country like India.

NCF2005 is a balanced model for twenty-first-century learning
The framework balances values like peace and dignity of labor with economic growth—values that are crucial for countries like India that are transitioning toward globalization and are struggling to balance their national traditions with a global reality. It presents a strong case for balancing larger humane values with attitudes and skills that are required in order to maintain one's cultural heritage along with achieving economic growth.

NCF2005 views education as a tool for social change
The framework considers contribution to social change as a crucial aim of education as opposed to preparing children primarily to be employed. It

believes that a global outlook devoid of deeper understanding of immediate realities and engagement with them could lead to alienation from their own roots and culture.

NCF2005 is a broad framework that requires contextual interpretation

The framework was designed to meet the diverse challenges of India in such a way that teaching-learning practices reflect the realities and traditions across geographies and cultures. This creates space for creativity and autonomy for textbook developers, supervisors, and teachers to choose the content. At the same time this very characteristic demands that educators use these tools to their highest capacity and apply the new content well.

The framework implicitly assumes a proactive leadership role for all those who are active in education: teachers, head teachers, school supervisors, and curriculum and textbook designers. It assumes that they would be able to correctly interpret and internalize the curricular goals enlisted in the NCF position papers. It also implicitly hopes that the state governments would be able to ensure curricular materials and that support is made available in varied languages for its effective implementation. In the last ten years efforts have been made by government agencies to develop textbooks at the national level that are aligned to the NCF2005, and different states in the nation are at different stages in translating and contextualizing the textbooks to their requirements.

Twenty-first-century learning as articulated in NCF2005 depends on leadership development and mind-set shifts

The National Curriculum Framework for Teacher Education was also developed in 2009 in alignment with the NCF2005. This document provides a framework on "preparing professional and humane teachers."[78] The SCERTs and other training agencies in each state are making attempts to improve their training.

However, successful implementation of NCF2005 faces a challenge in the absence of clearly articulated objectives and actions that need to be taken at various leadership levels. The flexibility of interpretation and comprehensive curricular expectations place rigorous demands on all the people involved in the education system—teachers, school leaders, and the entire education bureaucracy. Fostering coherence and shared understanding of the NCF2005 is necessary for it to percolate to schools in the form of teaching-learning practices.

A leadership equipped to facilitate these changes would ensure that India is able to move beyond the various sociocultural and economic inequities that challenge the development of twenty-first-century learning competencies in children.

Interviewees and Their Organizations

No.	Interviewee	Designation / Organization	Category
1	Goverdhan Mehta	Researcher and chemical scientist; National Research Professor, School of Chemistry, University of Hyderabad; former director, Indian Institute of Science	Policy maker
2	Rohit Dhankar	Dean of education, Azim Premji University National Curriculum Framework, member, National Steering Committee	Policy Maker NCF 2005
3	Atul D. Patel	Gujarat state senior BJP leader; chairman Nagar Prathmic Shikshan Samiti NPPS Surat, Gujarat	Government leader
4	Hitesh J. Makheja	Administrative officer, Nagar Prathmic Shikshan Samiti NPPS Surat, Gujarat	Government leader
5	Shyam S. Agrawal	Additional chief secretary, School Education, Sanskrit Education, Higher Education and Technical Education, Rajasthan, Jaipur	Government leader
6	Hanuman Singh Bhati	State project director, Sarva Shiksah Abhiyan, Rajasthan	Government leader
7	Swami Swatmanand	Director (West Zone) All India Chinmaya Yuva Kendra, Chinmaya Mission	Spiritual leader
8	Reena Das	Digantar	Educationist
9	Rohit Kumar	Akanksha Foundation, Mumbai, manager, Service Learning Program	Educationist
10	Kiran Parab	Muktangan, Mumbai, teacher trainer, Socioemotional Development Department	Educationist
11	Jayanthi Nayak	Muktangan, Mumbai, teacher trainer, Science Department	Educationist
12	Purvi Vora	Founder, Reniscience Education, Mumbai	Educationist
13	Tamara Philip	Teacher and coordinator, Avsara Leadership Fellows, Mumbai	Educationist
14	Stephan Philip	Maths teacher, Avsara Leadership Fellows	Educationist

No.	Interviewee	Designation / Organization	Category
15	Elizabeth Mehta	Muktangan founder	Educationist
16	Poorvi Shah	Akanksha Foundation, Director, Student Enrichment	Educationist
17	Ramlal Gurjar	Teacher, Digantar	Educationist
18	Sunita	Teacher, Digantar	Educationist
19	Usha Pandit	Mindsprings founder	Educationist
20	Rajesh Jain	Founder and managing director, Netcore Solutions Pvt Ltd	Business leader
21	Nirav Modi	Founder, Nirav Modi Foundation	Business leader
22	Vivek Sharma	Programme director, Piramal Foundation	Change maker in Education leadership development
23	Niraj Lele	Programme director, Piramal Foundation	Change maker in Education leadership development
24	Manmohan Singh	Programme director, Piramal Foundation	Change maker in Education leadership development
25	Nandita Raval	Programme director, Piramal Foundation	Change maker in Education leadership development

Mapping the Landscape of Teaching and Learning for the Twenty-First Century in Massachusetts in the Context of US Educational Reform

Fernando M. Reimers and Connie K. Chung

Global Education Innovation Initiative,
Harvard Graduate School of Education

This chapter discusses how education policy in the United States frames the purposes of public schools in terms of preparing students to thrive in the twenty-first century. In it, we argue that in the United States, the current dominant approach to increasing educational quality consists of clearly defining a narrow set of outcomes that are mostly cognitive, measuring student performance, and creating various incentives to support school improvement aligned with the achievement of those outcomes. This approach has produced many successes as measured by state, national, and international assessments, but this success in turn has limited also the possibility of transitioning schools and school systems to an adaptive culture where educators and students embrace more and more complex tasks and goals. The very instruments that were successful in focusing attention on a narrow set of outcomes to ensure academic excellence have contributed to crowding out from the curriculum the opportunities to develop the skills which policy makers, teachers, members of the business community, and the public at large increasingly recognize as central to thriving in the twenty-first century.

We focus on Massachusetts in our study about the United States and twenty-first-century competencies because of the state's high performance in many education accountability measures and because of the historically state- and locally-driven nature of education policy creation and implementation in the United States that make the state, rather than the country, the sensible unit of analysis; we will, however, refer to the national policy context when relevant.

INTRODUCTION

The Commonwealth of Massachusetts was the birthplace of public education in the United States, leading the expansion of educational opportunities in many ways throughout its history. 1635 saw the establishment of the Boston Latin School, the first public school in the American colonies; in 1647, the Massachusetts Bay Colony was first to mandate by law that every town of fifty or more families support a school;[1] in 1789, Massachusetts laws required that public schools serve females as well as males; and in 1852, Massachusetts passed the first compulsory school laws in the United States. Almost 150 years later, Massachusetts was one of the first states to adopt standards-based education reform in 1993; the reform consisted of defining standards, assessing the performance of students in those standards using tests, and using various policy instruments to support improvement in student achievement against those standards.

In part as a result of this early adoption of standards-based accountability measures, Massachusetts has been noted for its student performance levels that exceed those of average student performance in the United States, with the state also regularly ranking among the top OECD participants. These consistently high results in standardized assessments also helped give the state's education system a reputation, within the United States at least, of functioning well; of having achieved and benefited from significant consensus among the policy elites and therefore of having had a continuity in policy over a relatively extended period of twenty years in the context of short-cycle educational reform initiatives; and of having overall good levels of capacity in education administration and in the teaching force.

Against this background, which in many ways demonstrates real success, this chapter examines the following question: what do policy makers and educators in Massachusetts believe students need to know and be able to do to prepare themselves for life in the twenty-first century, including thriving at work, at home, and in society? We will answer this question by first briefly reviewing relevant research literature about historical and political contexts for policy discussions about purposes and goals of education in the United States; we then give a short summary of the most recent reforms in Massachusetts in the context of changes taking place in the rest of the country using policy documents, research literature, and interviews with educational policy leaders; we next draw on these interviews to discuss how educational leaders describe the knowledge and skills that K–12 public schools should help students gain in the twenty-first century; and we go on to provide a content analysis of the current curriculum frameworks for high school students in Massachusetts, including the recently adopted national Common Core standards for literacy and math, comparing these against the framework presented in a recent National Research Council report reviewing social and behavioral research on key competencies needed for the twenty-first century.[2] Drawing on interviews with key policy actors and a review of relevant policy documents, we discuss the principal instruments which were used to attempt to advance twenty-first-century education in Massachusetts. We conclude with a discussion of the key lessons drawn from the Massachusetts experience to align the purposes of schools with the expected demands that society poses on graduates in the twenty-first century.

A BRIEF SUMMARY OF HISTORICAL AND POLITICAL CONTEXTS FOR THE PURPOSES OF PUBLIC EDUCATION IN THE UNITED STATES

In the United States, public schools emerged as local institutions, with strong ties to the towns that funded them. As a result, there has been a strong tradition of favoring local and state control over the purposes and functioning of schools; for example, the Common School Movement, extending from 1830 to 1860, had the goal of advancing state control over schools as well as making teaching a profession.[3] The design of the public school curriculum has traditionally been a prerogative of teachers, often within frameworks defined by school departments and school districts.

The influence of the federal government in education in the United States is relatively recent, with the creation of the Department of Education in 1979 as a presidential cabinet- level agency; it replaced a federal Office of Education within the Department of the Interior which had existed since 1867, mostly to gather and distribute information, but which had been disbanded in 1972 following the repeal of the law that had established it. In fact, because the Tenth Amendment of the US Constitution reserves to the states those powers not delegated to the federal government nor prohibited to the states by the Constitution, most education policy is decided at the state and local levels.[4] Further, the 1979 law that established the Department of Education strictly limits its scope:

> No provision of a program administered by the Secretary or by any other officer of the Department shall be construed to authorize the Secretary or any such officer to exercise any direction, supervision, or control over the curriculum, program of instruction, administration, or personnel of any educational institution, school, or school system, over any accrediting agency or association, *or over the selection or content of library resources, textbooks, or other instructional materials* by any educational institution or school system, except to the extent authorized by law.[5]

Without a strong central governing body, educational policies and programs in Massachusetts, as in the rest of the United States, are the result of a number of forces that converge on the schools: education policies set by district, state, and federal institutions; organized programs of diverse members of civil society and educational product companies; and individual projects of teachers and parents, among others. Public schools in the

United States are, by design and by tradition, institutions where the practice of democracy is exercised by members of the community, and the independent spirit of the citizens of the Commonwealth of Massachusetts is exercised in few places with the same vigor as it is with regards to influencing the learning opportunities of the next generation, whether in or out of school.[6] Aware of such impetus for civic engagement in education, the Massachusetts Department of Education works with existing and ad-hoc mechanisms for consultation and participation, including district officials, school boards, and various education advocacy coalitions.[7]

Indeed, the purposes and goals of education have been in contention in the United States for as long as the country has been independent from Great Britain. As early as the period after the Revolutionary War, Thomas Jefferson argued that the new nation needed a tax-funded education system, and that it should go beyond basic skills to build knowledge of the classics, sciences, and education for citizenship.[8] But his plans for a nationally directed education system were ignored, and schools were locally established. By the 1780s Noah Webster's grammar, reader, and speller had been introduced, and in the 1830s McGuffey's graded readers appeared and dominated curriculum for the next hundred years.[9] The 3 R's (Reading, wRiting, and aRithmetic) were core, but the common theme of American curriculum and educational goals being works in progress and moving targets was evident even then, as reformers added spelling, geography, history, the US Constitution, nature study, physical education, art, and music in the schools.[10]

While curriculum writers covered academic content, and largely dictated the purpose of schooling, discussions about the purposes and goals of schooling have often included other voices, with those of business leaders being among the most prominent. In 1906, a *Report of the Massachusetts Commission on Industrial and Technical Education* recommended the introduction of industrial and vocational education in public schools, claiming that "old-fashioned" schooling caused large numbers of children to leave school early, unprepared for their professions.[11] Instead of a "literary" education, the report argued, children should be trained with vocational and commercial studies for jobs in industry. This was to be one of the first of a long series of reports and statements made by captains of industry, echoing similar themes of students being poorly prepared for the future.

The concerns expressed by the business community alternated or were in tandem with those concerns articulated about the general national welfare of the United States; for example, the Soviet launch of Sputnik in 1957 led to handwringing over the state of education, and stimulated a round of federal educational legislation that envisioned education as part of the national security agenda, as national leaders saw Sputnik as a "major humiliation for the country, [and] proclaimed it a dangerous threat to the nation's security."[12] The National Defense Education Act of 1958 (NDEA), as a consequence, supported technical education, geography, area studies, English as a second language, school libraries, and educational media centers, focusing resources and incentives to improve the quality of education.[13] A recent 2012 Council of Foreign Relations task force produced a report titled *U.S. Education Reform and National Security*, cochaired by Joel I. Klein, the former chancellor of the New York City Department of Education, and Condoleezza Rice, the former US Secretary of State; it echoed this commingling of concerns about the quality of public education and national security, concluding that "America's failure to educate is affecting its national security."[14]

This common theme of fear about the individual and collective future driving the educational agenda is perhaps best exemplified by the electrifying title of the seminal report, *A Nation at Risk*, released in 1983 by the National Commission on Excellence in Education. It observed that "the educational foundations of our society are being eroded by a rising tide of mediocrity that threatens our very future as a Nation and a people."[15] It was in this document that the possibility of a shared national common core curriculum as a solution to the low quality of public education was first articulated, and a report issued by the Carnegie Foundation for the Advancement of Teaching in 1985 provided data to support the negative findings of the report, noting that "nearly 75 percent of the major U.S. corporations it surveyed were forced to offer their employees courses in reading, writing, and computation" and that each year, American companies were noted to be spending more than $40 billion to educate their workers while on the job.[16] The same year, the Committee for Economic Development, an independent organization of more than two hundred business executives and educators, issued another report linking concerns over academic underperformance to concerns about the economic future of the United States: "Education has a direct impact on employment, productivity, and growth, and on the nation's ability to compete in the world economy,"[17] it observed. Business leaders became involved in state education affairs, from companies such as Westinghouse Electric awarding grants to innovative teachers and principals to businesses in South Carolina urging their legislators to levy a one-cent sales tax increase to help increase teachers' salaries.[18] With these and other supports from the business community, by 1990 things had changed, with the National Center for Education Statistics finding that nearly 40 percent of high school graduates met the core curriculum requires recommended in *A Nation at Risk*, compared to less than 20 percent who met those requirements when the report had been issued seven years earlier.[19]

As these concerns about national security were being expressed in discussions about the quality of public education, the country's complicated racial history was also playing out in its public schools, and particularly in regard to access and equity in education. The 1954 Supreme Court ruling in *Brown v. Board of Education* stated for the first time that black and white students were receiving different levels of education and ruled that separate schools for black and white students were unconstitutional; it required schools to integrate. At the time, just sixty years ago, seventeen of forty-eight states required segregated schools; sixteen forbid it, while four allowed it, and only eleven did not have laws pertaining to segregation. In South Boston, parents demonstrated belligerently against school desegregation, and it was only in the late 1970s that the last holdout school systems desegregated.

The broader civil rights movement of the 1960s, with its federal programs of War on Poverty and Great Society, saw education as a mechanism to address social issues. The 1965 Elementary and Secondary Education Act (ESEA), for example, based aid to education on the economic condition of the students and not on the needs of the schools. It focused on equity and increased funding, with emphasis on the education of low-income families, libraries, instructional materials, teacher training, help for children with disabilities, bilingual education, equal access, and promotion of parental involvement. While the act forbid the establishment of a national curriculum, it ushered in an era of standardized testing as a way to monitor the academic progress of different racial and socioeconomic groups of students. The 1966 publication of the report commissioned by the US Commissioner of Education, Harold Howe, and authored by Professor James Coleman, *Equality of Educational Opportunity*—more commonly known as the Coleman Report—began a series of research studies into the causes of gaps in student achievement between low-income minority students and middle-income white students, now commonly known as the "achievement gap."[20] The question of which strategies were more likely to equalize educational opportunities for poor minority students—compensatory education or racial integration—has been a central question driving much of educational reform in the United States since the 1960s.

RECENT EDUCATIONAL REFORM IN MASSACHUSETTS AND THE PURPOSES OF EDUCATION

These concerns—economic and national security, as well as the issue of equity and access to high quality education among different racial and socioeconomic groups—influenced much of the most recent educational reforms in Massachusetts. A decade after *A Nation at Risk* decried the "rising tide of mediocrity" in American public education, Massachusetts passed the Massachusetts Education Reform Act of 1993 (MERA). As in the rest of the country, the business community played an important role in placing education on the state's education reform agenda. A former secretary of education for Massachusetts noted that in addition to concerns about raising academic expectations, "most of the people, both in the State House and in the business community who worked hardest on ed reform . . . tipped their hat to . . . civics and citizenship. They felt this ought to be part of a regular education system."

MERA, however, is currently most known for impacting academic curricular content, by making dramatic changes in Massachusetts public education over a seven-year period. Among the major provisions of the act were distributing greater and more equitable funding to schools, including accountability for student learning, and changing statewide academic requirements for students, educators, schools, and districts. Prior to 1993 the only statewide educational requirements had been in history and physical education. MERA, however, called for statewide curriculum frameworks and learning standards for all students in all core academic subjects. These guidelines were designed for teachers to use in preparing their daily lesson plans and for districts to use in planning their curriculum.

In an unprecedented effort to document systemwide academic performance in public education and increase transparency and accountability, a new statewide test, the Massachusetts Comprehensive Assessment System (MCAS), was created with the intention of measuring the effectiveness of schools in supporting students to achieve the academic standards stated in the curriculum frameworks. MERA required that the MCAS be given to students in grades 4, 8, and 10, mandating that all students pass the state's tenth-grade test, in addition to meeting local requirements, in order to receive a diploma, beginning with the class of 2003. The purpose of the assessment system was to identify individuals and schools that needed attention in particular areas, placing emphasis and attention on student achievement as measured by test performance; it was the first time that data was publically made available on a large scale to show how individual students, classrooms, and schools were performing.

These reform efforts were successful in focusing the attention of school leaders and society on whether students were learning a common statewide set of academic standards. Approximately twenty years after the standard-and-test-based reform was implemented, Massachusetts students lead their peers in the United States on a range of test scores. According to the 2012 PISA results, Massachusetts[21] students tied for fourth among the sixty-five participating countries and education systems in reading literacy, trailing only students from Shanghai-China, Hong Kong-China, and

Singapore. In mathematics and science literacy, Massachusetts students tied for tenth and seventh places, respectively.[22] Of the nine US states that participated independently at grade 8 in TIMSS, four states—Massachusetts, Minnesota, North Carolina, and Indiana—had public school average scores that were higher than both the TIMSS scale average and the US national average in mathematics, while Massachusetts, Minnesota, and Colorado had public school average scores that were higher than both the TIMSS scale average and the US national average in science.[23]

Superintendent Paul Dakin of Revere, Massachusetts, where 75.8 percent of the students are classified as being from low-income households, said that prior to the reforms, "there were no AP courses, [and] very few of the kids were completing an algebra sequence. There was only a two-year math requirement. In the last twenty years of education reform, however, [the high school] bolstered the rigor of the curriculum to [offering] multiple AP courses."[24] When we interviewed him in April 2014, he had just learned that five students in his district had been accepted to Ivy League schools. Noting that one of the four primary guiding principles of his district is "rigor," he observed that "the eas[ier] thing to do is build a rigorous curriculum."[25]

In spite of these positive quantitative and qualitative indicators of success, however, MERA and test-based educational reforms have not been without their critics. In February 2013, some 170 professors and researchers from twenty schools in Massachusetts signed and submitted a public statement to the state Board of Education, urging it to stop overusing high-stakes standardized tests to assess students, teachers, and schools. The endorsers of the statement specifically noted the following:

> Given that standardized tests provide only one indicator of student achievement, and that their high-stakes uses produce ever-increasing incentives to teach to the test, narrow the curriculum, or even to cheat, we call on the BESE [Board of Elementary and Secondary Education] to stop using standardized tests in high-stakes decisions affecting students, teachers, and schools.[26]

They were part of a larger groundswell of protests across the country forming against high-stakes testing. Six hundred seventy Texas school boards and nearly one-third of all New York State principals expressed similar sentiments, among others.[27] A National Research Council report in 2011, *Incentives and Test-Based Accountability in Education*, reviewed and synthesized relevant research from economics, psychology, education, and related fields about how incentives work in educational accountability systems and found that, broadly speaking, incentive programs for schools, teachers, and students aimed at raising standardized test scores are largely unproductive in generating increased student achievement. They noted that standardized tests commonly used in schools to measure student performance "fall short of providing a complete measure of desired educational outcomes in many ways."[28]

Massachusetts' reform efforts are an example of how the current broad education agenda in the United States, as reflected in policy and priorities, has remained mostly focused on priorities expressed in *A Nation at Risk*, which underscored the need for academic and economic competitiveness in the nation's high school graduates:

> We live among determined, well-educated, and strongly motivated competitors. We compete with them for international standing and markets, not only with products but also with the ideas of our laboratories and neighborhood workshops. America's position in the world may once have been reasonably secure with only a few exceptionally well-trained men and women. It is no longer . . .
>
> In a world of ever-accelerating competition and change in the conditions of the workplace, of ever-greater danger, and of ever-larger opportunities for those prepared to meet them, educational reform should focus on the goal of creating a Learning Society. At the heart of such a society is the commitment to a set of values and to a system of education that affords all members the opportunity to stretch their minds to full capacity, from early childhood through adulthood, learning more as the world itself changes.[29]

This emphasis on the need to prepare for global economic competition and the focus on the need to give everyone—not just the elite few—the opportunity to "stretch their *minds*" (emphasis added), in fact, presaged the current official mission of the federal Department of Education, some thirty years later, "to promote student achievement and preparation for global competitiveness by fostering educational excellence and ensuring equal access."[30]

Indeed, much of the conversation about public education quality in the United States among policy elites has been dominated by workplace preparation and performance on state, national, and international tests, exclusive of broader discussions about the purposes of education. Recent national reform movements in the United States have focused on increasing the quality of education within public education with the tools of standardization, accountability, and assessments. The recent federal initiatives of the No Child Left Behind Act of 2001 and of federal programs such as Race to the Top (RTTT)—a $4.35 billion Department of Education–sponsored competition begun in 2009 to spur states to innovate and implement educational reforms, particularly around the Common Core standards—support this policy thrust.

The Common Core itself was an initiative that began in 2009 with the National Governors Association, the Council of Chief State School Officers, and Achieve, an educational nonprofit created in 1996 by a bipartisan group of governors and business leaders. The development of the Common Core standards that were released in 2010 was conducted by a small organization called Student Achievement Partners, with twenty-seven writers. Perhaps because of the lack of teeth given to the federal Department of Education by law, the entire process was mostly funded by the Bill and Melinda Gates Foundation, to develop, evaluate, promote, and implement the standards in forty-two states and the District of Columbia. As would be expected, in a country with such a long-standing tradition of local control, the Common Core initiative has met much contention and resistance from various ideological camps. However, these newly instituted assessments and standardization have largely driven the content and curriculum of public schools in the United States, most recently with the aim of increasing the quality of education and narrowing gaps in academic performance as measured by test scores between racial groups in the United States.[31]

HOW DO EDUCATION LEADERS IN MASSACHUSETTS TALK ABOUT TWENTY-FIRST-CENTURY SKILLS?

The desire to increase educational quality in the face of perceived threats to individual and national economic security is just one of the many factors that affect education agendas. Large-scale changes in technology, infrastructure, and the world that impact the ways in which we work and live also drive educational change. To begin to address this issue of rapidly changing demands on the education system, a 2012 consensus report conducted by the United States National Research Council (NRC), *Education for Life and Work: Developing Transferable Knowledge and Skills in the 21st Century*, synthesized the best available scientific evidence on a comprehensive range of skills necessary for life, citizenship, and work in the new century. Grouping those skills into three broad categories—cognitive, intrapersonal, and interpersonal—the report summarized a vast body of psychological and educational literature on what is known about the short- and long-term effects of those competencies and how they matter in preparing people for work, as economies are transformed as a result of globalization; for citizenship; and for longer, healthier lives as life expectancy increases. The NRC researchers note that these skills have been "valuable for many centuries, rather than skills that are suddenly new, unique, and valuable today."[32] The difference, they emphasize, however, is in society's desire that all students attain levels of mastery rather than just a select few, echoing the observation made in the *Nation at Risk* report some thirty years earlier.

Given such historical and political contexts and such concerns driving recent educational reforms, we wanted to find out how educational leaders in Massachusetts spoke about twenty-first-century competencies. In interviews, education leaders—including current and past commissioners of education, the former state secretary of education, and a district leader—all spoke about the importance of twenty-first-century skills. They mentioned skills such as critical and creative thinking, communication skills, the ability to collaborate and work on projects, global languages and global awareness, as well as skills for civic participation as part of twenty-first-century competencies. Some spoke about the importance of skills for lifelong learning.

Massachusetts leaders we interviewed referred to these competencies as skills that are helpful to the world of work—for example, collaboration and working in teams, communication, creativity, critical thinking, awareness of the rest of the world—as well as to civic participation. They observed these competencies to be important, but noted that they are not being deliberately taught in most K–12 schools at this point.

These themes that policy makers identified with twenty-first-century skills reflected the broad themes identified in the 2008 report of the Task Force on 21st Century Skills, which cited the Partnership for 21st Century Learning (P21)[33] documents: information and communications, thinking and problem solving, interpersonal and self-direction, global knowledge and understanding. Reflected in that report, but rarely mentioned by those we interviewed, were also financial, economic, and business literacy and entrepreneurial skills. Even more influential than the 2008 report of the skills task force in shaping the discourse of policy elites in the state was the 2012 report of a task force on college and career readiness, as this report was cited and referenced more frequently by those interviewed.

In contrast to the twenty-first-century skills presented in the National Research Council Report, those mentioned by policy elites in Massachusetts were less specific and at a higher level of abstraction; they emphasized cognitive domains, and to some extent interpersonal competencies, with very little mention of intrapersonal skills. Most of the competencies mentioned were cognitive, with a particular emphasis on cognitive processes and strategies. Cognitive processes that were not explicitly mentioned included analysis, reasoning/argumentation, interpretation, decision making, executive function, and adaptive learning. The interpersonal competencies mentioned were teamwork and collaboration, with no mention of leadership. These references lacked the specificity and granularity of the NRC report when referring to the same competencies. There was virtually no mention of the intrapersonal competencies included in the NRC report—such as intellectual openness, work ethic/conscientiousness, or positive self-evaluation—nor of such interpersonal competencies as empathy, trust, service orientation, conflict resolution, responsibility for others, assertive communication, self-presentation, or social influence.

A number of those interviewed referred to these twenty-first-century skills as competencies that were especially important to disadvantaged students, but recognized two challenges to supporting them: the fact that they were not the focus of the assessment instruments used to establish accountability, and the fact that the short duration of the school day limited the possibility of enacting the pedagogies that would support the development of such competencies given the urgency to support student learning in the core subjects of English and mathematics.

HOW DO CURRENT MASSACHUSETTS STANDARDS REFLECT CONTEMPORARY SCIENCE-BASED RESEARCH ABOUT TWENTY-FIRST-CENTURY SKILLS?

In addition to canvasing educational leaders about their thoughts on twenty-first-century competencies, we were also curious as to how the current Massachusetts curriculum frameworks[34] compared to research-based competencies named as being critical for the current century. To assess how the state curriculum frameworks in Massachusetts compared to the taxonomy of competencies for the twenty-first century as proposed by Hilton and Pellegrino, we constructed a coding system using the NRC report. We used the three broad categories of Cognitive Competencies, Interpersonal Competencies, and Intrapersonal Competencies, as well as their subsets of clusters (e.g., Processes and Strategies, Knowledge, and Creativity, under the category Cognitive Competencies) and synonymous terms (e.g., both Creativity and Innovation under the subcategory Creativity) as our etic code system (see chapter appendix).

As we coded the English, math, science, and social science high school standards as outlined in the state curriculum frameworks, emic codes emerged, including those such as Mathematical Knowledge, which were used to code standards outlining subject area knowledge that did not fit into other preexisting NRC categories, such as "Calculate the distance between numbers in the complex plane as the modulus of difference, and the midpoint of a segment as the average of the numbers at its endpoints."[35] Each standard was assigned at least one code; some standards, with emphasis on multiple skills, were coded more than once. All told, 1,015 segments were coded in the four primary subject areas. We did not code frameworks in arts, foreign languages, health, and vocational technical education frameworks. The chapter appendix shows the results, noting examples from each category.

The majority of the standards asked students to summarize, explain, identify, describe, or communicate information particular to content areas, such as math, politics, history, science, economics, and culture. For example, the following standard was labeled as "non-US cultural, historical, or political knowledge":

> Summarize the major reasons for the continuity of Chinese civilization through the 19th century, [including] the role of kinship and Confucianism in maintaining order and hierarchy; the political order established by the various dynasties that ruled China; and the role of civil servants/scholars in maintaining a stable political and economic order.[36]

In Bloom's Taxonomy,[37] for example, most of these standards would fall under the lower category of Comprehension or Knowledge rather than the higher order activities of Application, Analysis, Synthesis, or Evaluation. While these standards could be taught using engaging and challenging pedagogy,[38] without an explicit articulation in the curriculum frameworks, there is no guarantee that teachers and students would be engaged in these higher order activities.

More complex tasks that asked students to relate what they were learning to contemporary real-world situations were rare and mostly emerged in the math standards, and particularly in the modeling standards within the math curriculum framework:

> Modeling links classroom mathematics and statistics to everyday life, work, and decision-making. Modeling is the process of choosing and using appropriate mathematics and statistics to analyze empirical situations, to understand them better, and to improve decisions. Quantities and their relationships in physical, economic, public policy, social, and everyday situations can be modeled using mathematical and statistical methods. When making mathematical models, technology is valuable for varying assumptions, exploring consequences, and comparing predictions with data . . .
>
> Real-world situations are not organized and labeled for analysis; formulating tractable models, representing such models, and analyzing them is appropriately a creative process. Like every such process, this depends on acquired expertise as well as creativity.
>
> Some examples of such situations might include:
>
> • Estimating how much water and food is needed for emergency relief in a devastated city of 3 million people, and how it might be distributed . . .
> • Designing the layout of the stalls in a school fair so as to raise as much money as possible . . .
> • Modeling savings account balance, bacterial colony growth, or investment growth . . .
> • Analyzing risk in situations such as extreme sports, pandemics, and terrorism.[39]

The tasks suggested in the modeling standards offer a contrast to the previous standard about Confucianism in China; both are interesting topics and full of possibilities, but the modeling standard is more explicit in incorporating creativity, analysis, exploration, expertise, and relevance to students in its outline.

The section in the science curriculum frameworks that describe the steps of the engineering design process was also another place where students were asked to conduct a multistep process of identifying a need or problem, research the issue, explore options, develop possible solutions by using their math and science knowledge, select the best solution, construct prototypes, test and evaluate the solution, communicate the solution, including a discussion of the societal impact and trade-offs, and then redesign it to improve the product. Standards that asked students to work with other students to develop intrapersonal and other competencies were rarer, and included one instance in the history and social sciences standards: "Together with other students, identify a significant public policy issue in the community, gather information about that issue, fairly evaluate the various points of view and competing interests, examine ways of participating in the decision-making process about the issue, and draft a position paper on how the issue should be resolved."[40]

Not surprisingly, among the three broad categories outlined by the NRC study, the cognitive competencies overwhelmingly outnumbered the other two categories in their representation in the state curriculum frameworks, with 952 segments out of 1,015 being coded as cognitive; within it, the knowledge cluster had 711 segments while the processes and strategies cluster had 235 standards coded as such. The creativity cluster, among the cognitive competencies, came in last, with just 6 segments out of 1,015 being coded as encouraging experimentation or creativity.

The interpersonal competencies appeared just 17 times, with intellectual interest and curiosity appearing 4 times, perseverance or grit appearing 3 times, and professionalism/career orientation appearing 2 times. The intrapersonal competencies appeared 13 times in the high school Massachusetts standards in English, math, science and social studies. Standards were coded as teamwork and collaboration 6 times, communication twice, and empathy/perspective taking twice.

Indeed, William Mathis[41] notes that the "dominant" national educational policy since *A Nation at Risk* was published in 1983 has been "test-based and cognitive;" the Equity and Excellence Commission report issued in 2013 to the secretary of education agrees, noting that "the directions of school reformers over the past thirty years has been guided by the polestar of world-class standards and test-based accountability."[42] The requirements for state standards in Goals 2000 and the No Child Left Behind Act of 2001 further supported this emphasis. The 2013 report by the US Education Secretary's Commission on Equity and Excellence concluded that the approach has not worked very well, and a 2011 National Research Council report noted that gains, with these reforms, are "concentrated in elementary grade mathematics" and are "small compared to the improvements the nation hopes to achieve."[43] Noted effects include curriculum narrowing and an increase in drop-outs when tests are tied to graduation requirements.

These findings are echoed in a recent survey of Massachusetts business leaders and employers commissioned by the Massachusetts Business Alliance for Education, with 69 percent of those surveyed reporting having had challenges finding people with the skills necessary for the positions they needed to fill, and believing the K–12 system was ineffective in preparing young people for employment.[44] Only 20 percent of the respondents believed that the K–12 public schools prepare students for the workforce. CEOs reported an inability to fill entry-level positions "due to lack of soft skills, professionalism, and reliability of candidates."[45] When asked to rate how well the K–12 system helped students gain a number of work-related skills, business leaders provided grades of A or B for their employees' ability to follow directions (49%), ability to work together in groups (48%), ability to write clearly (24%), oral communication and presentation skills (23%), independent and critical thinking (22%), awareness of work-appropriate behavior (19%), and setting meaningful goals (15%).[46] Most business leaders interviewed (63%) noted that too much time is spent preparing students for standardized tests, at the expense of applied skills and STEM fields. Respondents attributed to the excessive focus on testing an inability to prepare lifelong learners, and to develop skills necessary outside of schools.

How did this curriculum narrowing occur? In the next section we describe how key stakeholders explain what happened in Massachusetts as they considered implementing broader competencies deemed to be necessary for the twenty-first century into the state education system.

IMPLEMENTING TWENTY-FIRST-CENTURY COMPETENCIES IN MASSACHUSETTS

Building on the successes of the 1993 reforms and following a political transition in state leadership, the new state secretary of education convened the Task Force on 21st Century Skills in 2008. The twenty-two-member committee included members of the Massachusetts Board of Elementary and Secondary Education, along with educators, business leaders, and other civic leaders, such as heads of foundations. The charge to the task force was to develop "a set of recommendations for ways to integrate 21st century skills into the state's educational program through improvements to existing standards, assessment tools, measures of accountability and professional development efforts."[47] The commission received strong support from a number of key players, including the Broad Foundation, the Boston Foundation, Cisco Systems, and the Massachusetts Association of School Superintendents, who all issued statements of support for the findings of the task force.[48]

In a statement presenting the report of the task force, then-Secretary of Education Paul Reville highlighted the growing skills and knowledge demands for civic and economic participation, and for participation in families and communities. He underscored the need to have the skills for lifelong learning, and presented the task force as a direct response to the plea of employers:

> [Business leaders] are telling us, more urgently with each passing year, that we are not preparing enough of our students to do the jobs of the present and future. They tell us too few can make coherent oral presentations, solve complex problems using either creativity or technology, too few understand the complexities of the US in its relationship to the other countries of the world, too few can work effectively as part of a group or team, and too few have the motivation and work ethic needed for success.[49]

With the support of Governor Deval Patrick, Massachusetts had been accepted as a leadership state in the newly formed national Partnership for

21st Century Learning in 2007, and Secretary Reville asked the task force to draw on the work of the partnership, adopting their framework and definitions. The final white paper from the Massachusetts Task Force on 21st Century Skills focused on five levers for change, which were comprehensive and far-reaching in scope:

1. Overhaul the state's teacher training and professional development programs to recruit and retain high achieving educators who have a background in and up-to-date knowledge of 21st century skills.
2. Raise the state's bar on rigor by embedding 21st century skills and content through the Commonwealth's curriculum frameworks in every subject.
3. Become a national leader in assessment by integrating the measurement of 21st century skills throughout the Massachusetts Comprehensive Assessment System (MCAS).
4. Hold teachers, administrators and the state accountable for incorporating 21st century skills into the curriculum in a complementary way and hold students accountable for learning them.
5. Establish demonstration vehicles, including: a) establishing up to five 21st Century Districts and up to ten 21st Century Schools, b) expanding the number of Expanded Learning Time Schools to 100 or more, c) establishing the Creative Teaching Partners Initiative, and d) striving to place up to 1,000 artists, scientists and/or engineers-in-residence in schools part-time over the next five years.[50]

The report also outlined a process to manage the implementation of this plan, which included specific recommendations for the department of education, creating an advisory council charged with building support, including the various professional education associations of teachers, superintendents, and school committees in this process, and collaborating with other states in New England.[51]

There was some opposition to the work of the partnership in Massachusetts from the Pioneer Institute, an "independent, non-partisan, privately funded research organization that seeks to improve the quality of life in Massachusetts through civic discourse and intellectually rigorous, data-driven public policy solutions based on free market principles, individual liberty and responsibility, and the ideal of effective, limited and accountable government."[52] They issued a rebuttal to the report, a twelve-page paper titled *A Step Backwards: An Analysis of the 21st Century Skills Task Force Report*,[53] in which they identified both the positive contributions of the report and the points over which they disagreed. While they agreed with the task force that "students need an array of social, technical, and communication skills to compete successfully in a global economy, including 'critical thinking,' 'problem-solving,' and 'financial, economic, and business literacy,'" they saw these skills as "already explicitly embedded in the state's current academic curriculum frameworks," and agreed that these competencies will "continue to need further emphasis."[54] They also "strongly" supported the task force recommendation to redesign teacher preparation systems to recruit and retain "high-achieving candidates."[55] The Pioneer Institute characterized the task force as distracting Massachusetts from the position of a clear leader in core subjects and from the clear emphasis on rigor established by the 1993 reform, and particularly expressed concern about both the lack of research on how twenty-first-century skills can best be taught or measured; they also argued that these skills were a particularly poor priority on which to focus, considering the low academic performance of students in urban school districts within Massachusetts where more students from lower socioeconomic status were concentrated.

There was also a matter of timing and competing priorities for the department of education. The task force had issued its report in November 2008, and in July 2009 the US Department of Education announced its Race to the Top grants initiative with potentially $10 billion being available to states and districts to implement standards-based reforms.[56] Given its limited amount of time and attention, the priority of the state department of education shifted to applying for a RTTT grant, which the state won, in phase two of the initiative, in August 2010.[57] When asked about the possibility of there being a twenty-first-century competencies emphasis on a national scale, the former Secretary of Education Paul Reville reflected:

> There's always an opportunity for an administration to use the bully pulpit—the president and the cabinet and the secretary of education to incentivize . . . [They] could have put in Race to the Top: 21st Century Skills. That would have changed the game altogether, [and] that's all it would have taken. Because you'd have now . . . thirty or forty states who would have taken that bait, made policies, made changes and moved in that direction, if only to get the money. Because that's how we do things here is incentivizing competition. You can do it, but you're going to have to have some top leadership who says this is important, [and] then is willing to help, not just get people to change policies, but also to build the capacity to really be able to do it.[58]

In spite of the fact that the recommendations of this task force did not receive political or financial support for effective follow-up and implementation, there were a number of outcomes of this work, including a) the redefinition of college and career readiness, a definition that was approved by the State Board of Elementary and Secondary Education (SBESE) as well as by the State Board of Higher Education in 2010, and b) greater impetus to a series of programs to promote career readiness in high schools, including a report produced in 2012 by another SBESE task force focusing on college and career readiness. This group, called the Task Force for the Integration of College and Career Readiness, included many of the same members as the 2008 Task Force on 21st Century Skills, and even had the same chairperson. Based on what they had learned from the failures of the 2008 report to garner traction for implementation of the recommendations, the 2012 task force had a much sharper focus and made recommendations that fell directly within the authority of a single unit in the department of education.

The 2012 report, *From Cradle to Career: Educating Our Student for Lifelong Success*, emphasized the importance of more intentionally preparing students for work: "Students who are able to gain experience and exposure to the world of work while in high school are better prepared to persist in and complete a postsecondary education and succeed in pursuing livable wage careers."[59] The 2012 report proposed a new definition of career readiness, encompassing knowledge, skills, and experiences that draw on academic knowledge, workplace readiness, and personal and social development: "Career readiness means an individual has the requisite knowledge, skills ,and experiences in the academic, workplace readiness, and personal/social domains to successfully navigate to completion an economically viable career pathway in a 21st century economy."[60] It included the diagram in figure 6.1 to communicate their essential purpose.

FIGURE 6.1   Diagram in *From Cradle to Career: Educating Our Student for Lifelong Success*

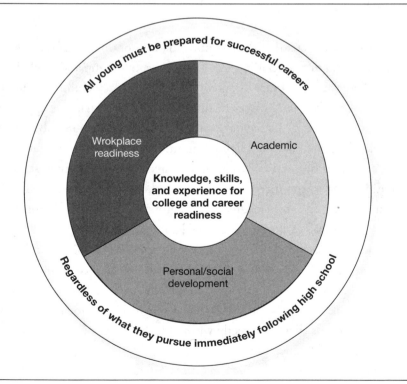

The report proposed incorporating career readiness into a Massachusetts recommended course of study; strengthening school, employer, higher education, and community partnerships; improving the role of school counselors in career readiness education; incentivizing schools to create career readiness strategies; promoting college and career readiness; and identifying personnel to execute the recommendations of the task force.

The department of education, with renewed priority as a result of this report, developed Connecting Activities, a series of programs to support career readiness that included promoting work-based internships, workplace exposure, and mentoring and training for high school students, and it developed a rubric to assess the competencies that students should gain in those internships.[61] The 2012 report also led to the development of a new definition of college and career readiness which was approved jointly by the Board of Elementary and Secondary Education as well as of higher education. This definition represents an expanded understanding of the skills and competencies that students need for careers. The Massachusetts Definition of College and Career Readiness underscores the need of "knowledge, skills and abilities that are necessary to successfully complete entry-level, credit-bearing college courses, participate in certificate or workplace training programs, and enter economically viable career pathways."[62] The definition explicitly goes beyond career-ready levels of competency in English language and mathematics, to include a foundation in the disciplines in the MassCore course of study and competencies for workplace readiness as identified in the 2012 report. The definition specifies in some detail the language and mathematical competencies necessary, as well as workplace readiness, which include: work ethic and professionalism and effective communication and interpersonal skills.

The following competencies are specified in the definition:

Essential Competencies
1) Academic preparation to read and understand complex texts independently; write effectively; build and present knowledge through integration, comparison and synthesis of ideas

2) Academic preparation in mathematics to solve problems involving major content with connection to mathematical practices; solve problems involving additional and supporting content; express mathematic reasoning constructing mathematical arguments; solve real world problems, engaging in modeling

Workplace Readiness Competencies

3) Work ethic and professionalism: attendance and punctuality; appropriate appearance; accepting direction and feedback positively; motivation and initiative and ability to complete projects; understanding workplace culture, including respecting confidentiality and workplace ethics

4) Effective communication and interpersonal skills: oral and written communication; attentive listening; interaction with co-workers individually and in teams

The definition on college and career readiness emphasizes the following abilities:

Higher order thinking skills (analysis, synthesis, and evaluation)

Critical, coherent, and creative thinking

Ability to direct and evaluate own learning

Motivation, intellectual curiosity, flexibility, self-advocacy, responsibility, and reasoned beliefs

While this change is too recent to have translated into specific programs, it is possible that, over time, it will lead to tangible outcomes.

DISCUSSION: OPPORTUNITIES AND CHALLENGES TO TWENTY-FIRST-CENTURY EDUCATION IN MASSACHUSETTS

Massachusetts schools have demonstrated remarkable continuity in their sustained efforts to improve education, which received significant impetus from the 1993 Education Reform Act. These efforts have produced significant and very important results: a greater focus on instructional quality and improvement, a more consistent set of academic expectations across schools, greater transparency and accountability in the governance and operations of public schools and districts, sustained improvement in those outcomes currently measured in the assessment system, an increase in high school graduation rates, and greater awareness and focus on the persistent gaps in educational achievement and attainment between students in different ethnic and socioeconomic groups. These are all very important achievements.

In spite of these gains, however, education leaders and business leaders increasingly point out that schools are not adequately preparing students for the jobs of the present or future Massachusetts economy or with the skills they will need for life and engaged citizenship. This is to some extent paradoxical, that a system with the demonstrated capacity to achieve what it set out to achieve, and where leaders recognize the importance of a more expansive set of goals for schools, has yet to deliver on the opportunity for students to develop those competencies. In particular, this failure is puzzling given that the secretary of education appointed a task force that produced a remarkably clear and compelling road map articulating the urgency of twenty-first-century skills along with a series of concrete steps to begin that journey. Why were so few of those steps implemented? What could explain this paradox?

Massachusetts was one of the early starters of the education reform movement, needing (and attaining) political consensus across the two main political parties in order to do so. The early success in achieving this consensus and in setting the main directions of reform—defining standards and measuring student achievement—created a momentum that made the education system relatively immune to subsequent efforts to engage the state in the broader national coalition for twenty-first-century skills. The language used to describe the focus of those efforts on "soft skills" was viewed by important stakeholders in Massachusetts as antithetical to the "rigor" that had been the focus of the 1993 reform. This opposition was perceived as threatening the political consensus undergirding the reforms, and as a result there was little political support for a more expansive focus on twenty-first-century skills. Also significant was the fact that the task force on twenty-first-century education was appointed at a time when the country was coping with a serious economic downturn, which constrained the capacity of the education department to take on additional initiatives.

While Massachusetts did sign on as a partner state to Partnership for 21st Century Learning, and produced a very cogent white paper endorsed by the Board of Elementary and Secondary Education, the impetus of the ongoing 1993 reforms, plus the new initiatives advanced by the federal government with the Common Core and the Partnership for Assessment of Readiness for College and Careers (PARCC), all modulated, and to some extent diminished, the influence of the twenty-first-century task force report. No political capital was invested in supporting the recommendations of the report. There has been follow-up to some of those recommendations, but the road map developed by the commission was never implemented by the department. In the words of the founding executive director of P21: "I believe that the 21st century skills as a statewide matter have taken a back seat to PARCC and Common Core implementation. It's not a surprise, but I just don't think we have the ardor at the state level for these competencies."[63] In different words, a former secretary of education concurred:

> The [21st-century-skills] report was very well done I thought, but the Department, in the midst of Race to the Top, etc. was just taxed beyond its capacity and this was not a priority much as I wished it would be . . . It got a lot of attention. Some super[intendents]s used it to make the case for changes at the local level, but overall, I believe the ball was dropped. Sad to say.[64]

As a result, the actions that had been outlined in the report were not implemented. While it provided language and symbolic support to those districts that were already doing work in this area, the 2008 effort did not lead to programmatic initiatives that would cause districts that were not attending to teaching twenty-first-century skills to do so. Indeed, even though the task force that was appointed for this purpose described these skills using concepts and language very much in line with those of the Partnership for 21st Century Learning, no investment was made to communicate and educate relevant stakeholders around these ideas, and to explain how those ideas were illustrated in practice, with the result that when education leaders speak about such skills in Massachusetts the concepts that are used are at a very high level of abstraction, with little operational definition, and there is no coherence in the use of those concepts across leaders at different levels of governance and management.

The most significant effort at scale to specifically support twenty-first-century education is the program to support career readiness through the creation of internships and other workforce opportunities in high schools, a program currently reaching three thousand of the three hundred thousand students in the state. There are also a number of initiatives and programs to advance twenty-first-century education in individual institutions, but none of them have achieved a scale beyond that of a single institution. For example, the Worcester Technical High School was mentioned as a site that was providing exemplary technical education with an emphasis in preparation for the world of work.

Contributing also to the lack of penetration of twenty-first-century learning in schools and classrooms, is the fact that the conversation about twenty-first-century skills in the state has been one with active participation of representatives of the business community and of senior education leaders. Noticeably absent from this conversation have been schools of education, political and civic leaders, or grassroots participants at the community level, where much education policy is still shaped in the state.

Absent from these policy initiatives of the education department also are more intentional initiatives to influence how teacher capacity is built. While the Department of Higher Education has statutory authority to approve and regulate programs of teacher education, efforts to align those programs with the goals of the education reform initiatives have been lacking. In the report on twenty-first-century skills prepared by the 2008 task force, teacher preparation was recognized as critical; however, no specific initiatives focused on inducing changes in teacher education have yet been implemented.

CONCLUSION

An analysis of the frameworks and of the discourse of policy makers does not tell the whole story of how an educational system functions or what it emphasizes. Because the educational priorities are so many, a school district leader like Dr. Paul Dakin of Revere has the ability and the need to direct the effort and attention of the district toward a more explicitly articulate vision. It is at the level of school districts that much educational opportunity is shaped, and for those districts with stable leadership it is possible to support twenty-first-century education initiatives. With his background in computer science and engineering, Dakin had this to say:

> If there's any advantage I can bring to my urban kids, it is to close that technological divide. Because if I don't close the technological divide, that is going to contribute to the educational divide growing. Technology has to be one of the things we stay abreast with because I honestly believe learning is accelerated with the proper use of technology. If kids in the suburbs are getting that, and my kids aren't, then it's going to accelerate their learning even more, and we're going to have more of an educational gap than we have. I've got to have a technology network that can feed these kids, and technology expertise that can. If I do it even better than others, I have a chance, in my belief, to close the divide.[65]

The urban context of his school district is not far from his mind as he determines how he will ask his teachers to address the rigor, relevance, relationships, and resilience emphasized in his district vision. Dakin explained how the school staff's interpersonal competency of building relationships with students and making learning relevant to them, as well as the school leaders' ability to cultivate the intrapersonal competency of resilience in both students and staff, sustain the district's focus on rigor:

> It has to become a belief system. The adults have to believe that kids, despite the fact that they come to our schoolhouse with a gap,

an inherited gap . . . with some of them not knowing their colors or numbers because of the[ir] life situation, [can do rigorous work]. There has to be a belief system, and it involved the four R's. We can't stop on rigor. You [have to]... mak[e] the learning more relevant with urban kids. If you build relationships with them, we know that they are going to work with you more. In our work, we [also] have to fuel our own resiliency . . . How do we bolster our own resiliency as educators . . . so that we can keep pressing the other three R's? . . . We [speak] to students so that they can become more resilient and understand that despite the fact that their parents may have not gone to school or even high school, or come from other countries that don't even speak the language . . . they can be a success in the American education system and reach any dream they want to reach. It takes years to build that psychology with a staff . . .We work to it all the time.[66]

Indeed, to this experienced educator, the recipient of the Massachusetts Superintendent of the Year Prize in 2013, curricular rigor is the easiest "R" to implement, while intrapersonal skills such as resilience are tougher and even more important to cultivate in both students and teachers in his district.

At the core of these controversies are the questions of whether public schools should focus on a minimalist set of aspirations versus a more expansive set of goals, as well as the question of whether these goals should be established nationally or locally. There is an inherent complexity to educating for the twenty-first century, resulting from the multidimensional nature of the competencies involved, which makes it challenging to influence by the blunt instruments of policy. Thus, even when education leaders have placed twenty-first-century education on the agenda, the topic has not received traction. The success of the Massachusetts Education Reform Act is illustrative of this conundrum, of how to help an education system make adaptive changes in line with broader education purposes, when it has been very successful making incremental improvements in a narrower set of goals.

Analysis of the Massachusetts State Standards Vis-à-vis Hilton and Pellegrino framework

	COGNITIVE COMPETENCIES		
Cluster	**Subcategory/ Terms used for 21st Cent Skills**	**# of Segments**	**Example**
Creativity (6)	Creativity	3	"Write narratives to develop real or imagined experiences or events using effective technique, well-chosen details, and well-structured event sequences." (ELA Standards)
	*Experimentation**	3	"Experiment with transformations in the plane." (Math Modeling Standards)
	Innovation	0	
Knowledge (642)	*Scientific Knowledge*	147	"Identify Earth's principal sources of internal and external energy, such as radioactive decay, gravity, and solar energy." (Science Standards)
	Political Knowledge	94	"Define and use correctly the following words and terms: Magna Carta, parliament, habeas corpus, monarchy, and absolutism." (History and Social Science Standards)
	Mathematical Literacy	93	"Use the relation and the commutative, associative, and distributive properties to add, subtract, and multiply complex numbers." (Math Standards)
	Economics and Capitalism	84	"Define the use correctly mercantilism, feudalism, economic growth, and entrepreneur." (History and Social Science Standards)

COGNITIVE COMPETENCIES			
Cluster	**Subcategory/ Terms used for 21st Cent Skills**	**# of Segments**	**Example**
Knowledge (642)	*Historical Knowledge*	71	"Interpret and construct time- lines that show how events and eras in various parts of the world are related to one another." (HSS Standards)
	Non-US Cultural, Historical, Politi- cal Knowledge	65	"Explain how Korea has been both a battleground and a cultural bridge between China and Japan." (HSS Standards)
	Oral and Written Communication	40	"Demonstrate command of the con- ventions of standard English gram- mar and usage when writing or speaking." (ELA Standards)
	Information and Communication Tech Literacy, i ncluding research using evidence and recognizing bias in sources	43	"Use technology, including the In- ternet, to produce, publish, and update individual or shared writing products in response to ongoing feedback, including new arguments or information." (ELA Standards)
	World Religions Knowledge	14	"On a map of the Middle East, Europe, and Asia, identify where Islam began and trace the course of its expansion to 1500 AD." (HSS Standards)
	Real World Situations	10	"Recognize and explain the con- cepts of conditional probability and independence in everyday lan- guage and everyday situations. For example, compare the chance of having lung cancer if you are a smoker with the chance of being a smoker if you have lung cancer." (Math Standards)
	Active Listening	1	"Evaluate a speaker's point of view, reasoning, and use of ev- idence and rhetoric, assess- ing the stance, premises, links among ideas, word choice, points of emphasis, and tone used." (ELA Standards)

	COGNITIVE COMPETENCIES		
Cluster	**Subcategory/ Terms used for 21st Cent Skills**	**# of Segments**	**Example**
Processes and Strategies (284)	Analysis	56	"Cite strong and thorough textual evidence to support analysis of what the text says explicitly as well as inferences drawn from the text, including determining where the text leaves matters uncertain." (ELA Standards)
	Problem Solving	46	"Reason quantitatively and use units to solve problems." (Math Standards)
	Reasoning/ Argumentation	45	"Write arguments to support claims in an analysis of substantive topics or texts, using valid reasoning and relevant and sufficient evidence." (ELA Standards)
	Abstract/ Conceptual Thinking	34	"Model with mathematics." (Math Standards)
	Interpretation	34	"Interpret plans, diagrams, and working drawings in the construction of prototypes or models." (Science Standards)
	Critical Thinking, including evaluating information	32	"Delineate and evaluate the argument and specific claims in a text, assessing whether the reasoning is valid and the evidence is relevant and sufficient; identify false statements and fallacious reasoning." (ELA Standards)
	Executive Function, including Strategy and Pattern Recognition	14	"Use appropriate tools strategically." (Math Standards)
	Adaptive *and Applied* learning	14	"Interpret and apply Newton's three laws of motion." (Science Standards)
	Decision Making, including making inferences	9	"Make inferences and justify conclusions from sample surveys, experiments, and observational studies." (Math Standards)

INTERPERSONAL COMPETENCIES

Cluster	Subcategory/ Terms used for 21st Cent Skills	# of Segments	Example
Intellectual Openness (14)	Personal and Social Responsibility, including Cultural Competence	[7]	"Explain the meaning and responsibilities of citizenship in the United States and Massachusetts." (HSS Standards)
	Intellectual Interest and Curiosity	[4]	"Conduct short as well as more sustained research projects to answer a question (including a self-generated question) or solve a problem, narrow or broaden the inquiry when appropriate; synthesize multiple sources on the subject, demonstrating understanding of the subject under investigation." (ELA Standards)
	Artistic and Cultural Appreciation	[3]	"Describe the origins and development of the Renaissance, including the influence and accomplishments of Machiavelli, Michelangelo, Leonardo da Vinci, Raphael, Shakespeare, and Johannes Gutenberg." (HSS Standards)
	Appreciation for Diversity	[0]	
	Continuous Learning	[0]	
	Flexibility and Adaptability	[0]	
Work Ethic and Conscientiousness (6)	Perseverance or Grit	[3]	"Make sense of problems and persevere in solving them." (Math Standards)
	Professionalism and Career Orientation	[2]	"Attend to precision." (Math Standards)
	Citizenship	[1]	"Identify specific ways for individuals to serve their communities and participate responsibly in civil society and the political process at local, state, and national levels of government." (HSS Standards)

Cluster	Subcategory/ Terms used for 21st Cent Skills	# of Segments	Example
INTERPERSONAL COMPETENCIES			
Work Ethic and Conscientiousness (6)	Self-Direction or Initiative	[0]	
	Responsibility for Self	[0]	
	Productivity	[0]	
	Precision	[0]	
	Type 1 Self-Regulation, including Forethought, Self-Reflection	[0]	
	Integrity and Ethics	[0]	
Positive Core Self-Evaluation	Physical and Psychological Health	[0]	[May be contained in the Health Standards]
	Type 2 Self-Regulation	[0]	
INTRAPERSONAL COMPETENCIES			
Teamwork and Collaboration (10)	Collaboration, Cooperation, and Coordination	[6]	"Initiate and participate effectively in a range of collaborative discussions (one-on-one, in groups, and teacher-led) with diverse partners on grades 11–12 topics, texts, and issues, building on others' ideas and expressing their own clearly and persuasively." (ELA Standards)
	Communication	[2]	"Work with peers to set rules for collegial discussions and decision making (e.g., informal consensus, taking votes on key issues, presentation of alternate views), clear goals and deadlines, and individual roles as needed." (ELA Standards)
	Empathy Perspective Taking	[2]	"Compare the point of view of two or more authors for how they treat the same or similar topics, including which details they include and emphasize in their respective accounts." (ELA Standards)

	INTRAPERSONAL COMPETENCIES		
Cluster	**Subcategory/ Terms used for 21st Cent Skills**	**# of Segments**	**Example**
Teamwork and Collaboration (10)	Interpersonal Skills	[0]	
	Service Orientation	[0]	
	Trust	[0]	
	Conflict Resolution and Negotiation	[0]	
Leadership (2)	Self-Presentation	[1]	"Come to discussions prepared, having read and researched material under study; explicitly draw on that preparation by referring to evidence from texts and other research on the topic or issue to stimulate a thoughtful, well-reasoned exchange of ideas." (ELA Standards)
	Assertive Communication	[1]	"Practice civic skills and dispositions by participating in activities such as simulated public hearings, mock trials, and debates." (HSS Standards)
	Social Influence with Others	[0]	
	Responsibility for Others	[0]	

*Categories not in the Hilton and Pellegrino frameworks are in italics.

Theorizing Twenty-First-Century Education

Fernando M. Reimers and Connie K. Chung

BROADENING THE GOALS OF EDUCATION IN THE TWENTY-FIRST CENTURY

In this comparative cross-national study of the purposes of education in six countries—Chile, China, India, Mexico, Singapore, and the United States—we found that in all countries those purposes, as outlined in national curricular frameworks, have been expanded over the last couple of decades to include the development of a broader range of competencies, cognitive as well as social and intrapersonal. To varying degrees, the six countries have broadened the goals of education as the understanding has expanded about the kinds of competencies needed to empower people so they can live well in the world. The expansion of those aspirations has increased the demands on the work of teachers and school administrators, and with it, the perception that schools are failing to meet these new demands. This results in a paradox: in a time of great expectations for education, support for traditional ways of schooling is dwindling, because there is increasing awareness that students are not learning what they need to learn. This perception persists in spite of the fact that schools may be improving in their capacity to support the basic cognitive development of students. This concluding chapter unravels this conundrum, summarizing the key findings of our study, highlighting important differences across countries, and discussing how the goals outlined in curricular frameworks changed—what strategies were followed to support the execution of those changes, what the sources of innovation were, and what explains the persistent gaps between curricular policy intentions and practice. First, however, we offer a brief summary of each country's recent changes in curriculum frameworks and how they came about.

In Singapore, curricular reform in 2011 introduced the notion of a "values-driven, student-centric" education, emphasizing that the holistic education of individuals was essential to functioning in the twenty-first-century workplace and society. This values-driven phase built on a prior phase of education reform, started in 1997, that emphasized learning outcomes (the ability-driven phase), as distinct from even earlier phases of reform that focused on access and efficiency. In announcing the 2011 reform, Singaporean authorities emphasized the importance of placing values and character education at the core of the educational process, in response to the changing demands of a global work environment. In particular, the government leaders felt that the multiracial, multicultural nature of Singaporean society demanded inculcating in its citizens a shared set of values, particularly in terms of appreciating diversity, in order to support social cohesion and harmony. One of the basic tenets of this curriculum reform was a much greater emphasis on personalization of education, adapting it to meet various learners, and of creating multiple pathways to support the development of every child, regardless of ability or achievement level, with the significant revamping of technical education as an example of this policy objective.

A distinctive feature of the new Singaporean framework of twenty-first-century competencies is that it spells out each competency in detail, describing what learners should be able to know and do to demonstrate that they have mastered the competency. The key core values in Singapore's framework are respect, responsibility, integrity, care, resiliency, and harmony. The socioemotional competencies include self-awareness, self-management, social awareness, relationship management, and responsible decision making. The emerging twenty-first-century competencies are civic literacy; global awareness and cross-cultural skills; critical and inventive thinking; and communication, collaboration, and information skills. This operational expression of core values and competencies reduces ambiguity and facilitates clear communication among key educational stakeholders such as ministry officials, schools, principals, and teachers.

In China, the intended curriculum reflects a broad range of cognitive, interpersonal, and intrapersonal skills. These were introduced via the 2001 Outline of Basic Education Curriculum Reform, which resulted from a series of ordered steps: 1) surveys of teachers, parents, researchers, and local authorities and communities, 2) a draft of the document prepared by researchers, practitioners, and administrators, 3) consultation with schools, teachers, and local government officials to solicit their opinions on the relevance and feasibility of the drafted policy, 4) a pilot of the policy in four provinces, and finally 5) amendment of the policy document for nationwide implementation.

In Chile, the national curriculum reflects the broad range of cognitive, interpersonal, and intrapersonal skills, with more emphasis on cognitive competencies and comparatively less emphasis on the other two. These were introduced in the context of a curricular reform implemented between 1996 and 1998, and subsequent adjustments in 2009 and 2013. This in turn was part of a broader educational reform led by the government, which was heavily influenced by a policy document formulated by UNESCO and the United Nations Economic Commission for Latin America and the Caribbean, with a focus on economic development and social equity. As the authors write in their chapter, increasingly, the poor results achieved by Chilean students in national and international assessments of student learning in the basic literacies have narrowed the focus of the reform to those basic skills as measured by standardized tests, rather than on the broader aims attempted in the curriculum.

In Mexico, recent curriculum reforms included adding several of the competencies in the cognitive, social, and intrapersonal domains as outlined in the Hilton and Pellegrino framework. However, cognitive learning outcomes are dominant, followed by interpersonal competencies and, to a much lesser extent, by intrapersonal competencies. Important milestones in the introduction of these twenty-first-century competencies include a new approach to civic education in the late 1990s, and the growing interest and attention to the results obtained by students in Mexico in the PISA assessments.

In India, the government sponsored twenty-one focus group discussions and deliberations among three hundred people representing various constituencies such as educators, researchers from government think tanks, principals, teachers, and professors to begin their curriculum reform process. These discussions resulted in a series of position papers that informed the development of the National Curriculum Framework of 2005, and included such broad-ranging topics as education for children with special needs, education for peace, and physical education, reflecting the wide range of stakeholders invited into the discussion. The curriculum framework proposed the development of "holistic" learning, a view very much aligned with and even beyond the concept of twenty-first-century competencies as proposed by Hilton and Pellegrino and discussed in this book. In addition, India also developed national-level textbooks that presented a grade-by-grade and step-by-step approach to achieving these competencies.

In the United States, a concern about preparing students for a new knowledge-based economy that required higher levels of education, as well as concern over the pervasive stratification of educational opportunity by students' race and socioeconomic background, drove much of the recent reforms. In particular, the No Child Left Behind Act of 2001—the most recent iteration of the Elementary and Secondary Education Act of 1965 and the largest source of federal spending on elementary and secondary education—authorized funding to institute annual standardized student assessment of all students, and highlighted gaps in academic achievement among different groups. In part, as a response, the Common Core standards were developed by a small group of writers in a nongovernmental advocacy group, supported by a bipartisan group of governors and business leaders, and funded by the Gates Foundation, as a way to institute a common set of academic goals for all states, beginning with the subjects of English language arts and mathematics. Given the emphasis on academics, it is not much of a surprise that the analysis of the standards vis-à-vis the Hilton and Pellegrino framework showed a strong emphasis on developing cognitive competencies and less so on the interpersonal and intrapersonal competencies.

In these six countries in general, the purposes of education were expanded both as a response to the perception that the demands for labor participation were changing, to a great extent because of transformations generated by the development of information technology, and also as a response to the perception that civic participation would require greater sophistication and responsibility. In all cases, broadening of curricular aims was predicated on the premise that education could contribute to positive national development and, in the cases of Chile, India, Mexico, and the United States, to the empowerment of individuals.

The forces that provided impetus to these reforms of curricular aims were local as well as global. National governments were the key actor initiating these curricular framework reforms in all cases, although various groups in civil society participated in consultations about reforms in most countries, and also in designing and piloting education programs that embedded the expanded curricular aspirations. As governments developed new narratives about curricular goals, they drew on a range of sources, including narratives developed by supranational institutions, such as UNESCO's Delors Commission report on education for the twenty-first century (*The Treasure Within*); the UN Commission for Education in Latin America and the Caribbean report on *Education and Knowledge: Basic Pillars of Changing Production Patterns with Social Equity*; or the various publications of the OECD, especially those comparing results of cross-national tests.

While the curriculum broadened its aims in all countries, there are also important distinctions in curricular emphasis among countries. In most countries cognitive goals dominate; they reflect the most established and accepted purposes of schools, deeply ingrained in the traditional grammar of schooling. Singapore stands out, among the countries examined, with its strong emphasis on values-based education. Chile and Mexico stand out by their focus on democratic citizenship education. India's curriculum framework is arguably the most holistic and broadest in terms of its goals. The United States and China emphasize higher order cognitive skills.

Underneath these various emphases, however, there are more commonalities than seem apparent on the surface. The DNA of curricular purposes differs from the particular language used to describe the emphases and programs to advance those purposes, and similar competencies may undergird different programmatic emphases. For instance, citizenship education in Chile and in Mexico invokes many of the same interpersonal and intrapersonal competencies that are reflected in Singapore's twenty-first-century education or in India's emphasis on global citizenship and education for peace. Most importantly, all countries recognized that educational goals for all students needed broadening.

STRATEGIES TO IMPLEMENT TWENTY-FIRST-CENTURY EDUCATION

While the goals of educational reform in the six countries treated in this book were similar in many ways, the paths taken to implement those goals differed significantly from one country to the next, depending on their social, political, and historical contexts. Below we summarize the main strategies, policy instruments, and mechanisms these countries used to implement twenty-first-century education, and we discuss the underlying themes that emerged from our analysis.

In Singapore, a particularly effective partnership between the Ministry of Education (MOE), the National Institute of Education, and the 360 schools in the nation, has produced a unique combination of goal alignment, systemic coherence of expectations, and synergistic mechanisms that together support the implementation of policy directives set by the ministry. In particular, the MOE sets the overall direction and ensures that there is congruence across different stakeholders in the system. Thus the Ministry of Education developed a twenty-first-century competency conceptual framework and a framework spelling out the "desired outcomes of education," which were broadly communicated to all actors in the system at all levels.

However, similar to China, rather than imposing a completely top-down system, the MOE used a balanced "autonomy versus standardization" framework in guiding key educational stakeholders in the implementation process. Discussions and interactions were carried out with key stakeholders before changes were introduced systemwide, starting at the primary school level, and then extending to the secondary and postsecondary levels. As the authors of the chapter report, the MOE stressed a collaborative framework of shared values and goals that were aligned to a unified outcome.

A particularly salient aspect of Singapore's efforts of continuous education improvement efforts is the alignment between teacher and school principal preparation—both initial preparation and ongoing support for further development throughout their careers—and the changing education goals. Following the introduction of the framework for twenty-first-century competencies and student outcomes in 2010, for example, Singapore launched an experimental program with five secondary schools from 2011 to 2013 to co-develop whole-school approaches to twenty-first-century development. Additionally, it scanned global good practices and engaged local and international experts.

In China implementation of the curriculum framework has depended on a governance structure balancing centralization and decentralization, reflected in a three-level curriculum structure including national, local, and school-based curricula. The national curriculum accounts for 80 percent of the curriculum, with local and school-based curricula accounting for 20 percent of what students learn as a way to express the principle of "common basics, diversified options." The Ministry of Education develops the national curriculum framework, while local (including provincial, prefecture/municipality, and county/district) authorities devise local curricula for schools in their respective administration. The textbooks for the national curriculum are accredited by the National Textbook Review Board and endorsed by the Ministry of Education. The textbooks for local curricula are accredited by provincial authorities. It is up to the district/county governments to select textbooks. Schools develop implementation plans for the curriculum responding to local social and economic conditions, traditions, strengths, and student interests and needs. Schools also decide school-based curricula, including what elective courses to offer.

As in Singapore, this curriculum is closely aligned with teacher preparation and ongoing learning. China's educators are supported by a Teaching Research System that supports teachers' classroom teaching; this includes teaching research institutes and local teachers colleges at provincial, municipal, and local levels. Researchers are selected from the best teachers; they support teachers' work by coordinating school-based research projects, visiting schools, interpreting curriculum standards, analyzing classroom teaching, developing teaching materials, and identifying best practices for extension. Pedagogical research institutions organize teacher training eight times a year for all teachers, and an additional eight times for master teachers. Teachers spend half a day each week in district-level pedagogical research activity and another half day in school-level pedagogical activities.

In Chile, the curriculum reform was part of a more ambitious set of education policies that included detailed study programs, materials, guides, computers, and textbooks to support classroom teaching; the adoption of a full school day; and several school improvement programs promoting collaboration among teachers. As part of these policies, massive teacher professional development was offered, but not necessarily aligned with the new curriculum. Also included in the reforms was aligning the periodic student test with the new curriculum and modifying the national test for college entry; in turn, tests results were increasingly used in a variety of forms to align both school management and classroom practices.

In Mexico, the main policy instruments to support the implementation of the new curriculum included the publication of the national curriculum; the redesign of educational materials, including textbooks; and the implementation of technology programs in schools. A constitutional reform with a new focus on accountability has also fostered discussion of the need of new educational models. While there has been investment in teacher professional development, these programs have not been aligned with the new curriculum.

In India, the following approaches were used to implement the National Curriculum Framework of 2005: teacher and principal preparation, new syllabi and textbooks, and the translation and interpretation of textbooks into regional languages. A national curriculum framework for teacher education was developed translating the NCF2005 expectations to expectations for teacher knowledge and skills. In the past ten years, efforts have been made to develop textbooks at the national level that are aligned to the NCF2005, and different states in the nation are at different stages in translating and contextualizing the textbooks to their requirements. But as the authors of the chapter note, the implementation has fallen short, particularly as teachers still lack the capacity to implement the curriculum.

In the United States, the key approaches to support twenty-first-century learning included aligning assessment with higher order competencies in the fundamental literacies of language arts, mathematics, and science; gradual alignment of teacher standards with the new curriculum; and policies to stimulate partnerships with business and nonprofit organizations to enrich the curriculum. Dating back at least two decades, policy has stimulated partnerships with nongovernmental organizations for the development of innovative programming aligned with twenty-first-century curriculum. Public and private funding has supported different approaches to reform and other modalities of teacher preparation to support innovative pedagogies aligned with deeper learning. More recently, public policy has encouraged the development of charter schools—public schools run often by nonprofits that are released from some of the constraints of regular schools with the explicit goals of facilitating improvement in academic performance. Public policy and funding have also supported selective expansion of the duration of the school day, for the purpose of allowing academic curricular enrichment.

These policies across countries were implemented in diverse institutional contexts, with various degrees of centralization and decentralization, resulting in various perceived degrees of alignment between policy and implementation programming. Singapore, a relatively small education system including only 360 schools, exhibits much greater capacity for policy implementation alignment, to a great extent because a single institution, the National Institute of Education, is responsible for the development and implementation of programs to build teacher capacity aligned with curricular aspirations. In addition, a very strong partnership between the Ministry of Education, the National Institute of Education, and the schools, translates into frequent communication of curricular aspirations, and into regular and rapid feedback loops that support policy implementation and adjustment. Similarly, China, with its strong, centralized education ministry, had a rather straightforward, sequential roll-out of its curricular reforms, in spite of its much larger size relative to Singapore. In contrast, in Chile, another small education system among those included in this study, the efforts of the Ministry of Education to develop a twenty-first-century curriculum were hampered by relatively limited authority over schools, resulting from previous and current reforms to decentralize and privatize education in a market-oriented framework which significantly diminished the ministry's regulatory authority. Chile's system, with 12,000 schools, is decidedly larger than Singapore with 360 schools, even as it is much smaller than the education systems in China, India, Mexico, or the United States. In spite of these differences, however, in many ways the Chilean government shared similar challenges with the larger countries in terms of having to navigate a decentralized system that limited the authority of the central government to influence implementation of curriculum reform and other educational policies.

India, Mexico, and the United States, large nations with large and complex education systems, had many more levels of intermediation from curriculum policy to execution at the school and classroom level, due to more levels of government bureaucracy as well as a larger number of institutions involved in key complementary functions of teacher preparation and the development of instructional and student assessment materials. As a result, coherence and alignment between those functions and the new curriculum was a greater challenge in these nations than it was in Singapore or China.

In addition to the varying institutional settings, countries differed in the strategy and policy mix used to support the implementation of their twenty-first-century curriculum. Undergirding these various strategies are diverse program theories. These theories are not built on a specific conceptualization of the supports necessary to advance twenty-first-century education, but rather are extensions of more general managerial theories to support instructional improvement. They range from those that emphasize measurement of student learning outcomes and the use of incentives to hold teachers and administrators accountable for student performance (i.e., that improve the accountability and efficiency of the education system), to those that emphasize the development of skills and capacity among teachers and adults (i.e., that promote professionalism). Significantly less salient were approaches that promoted education redesign and innovation. This typology (accountability, professionalism, and innovation) does not mean that national education systems either increased accountability through standards and assessments or else enhanced the professionalism of teachers; all did a mix of both, but countries varied in the fundamental underlying approach to improvement. This distinction is most visible in the contrast between the United States (emphasizing accountability) and Singapore (emphasizing the development of professionalism).

A question emerging from the country case studies is whether the same program theory that can sustain technical improvements in education—that is, improvements in the technical efficiency of school performance (for example, getting schools to improve their capacity to deliver on long-established goals)—is also adequate to sustain improvements in getting schools to embrace new purposes, such as improvements in relevancy of the kind attempted by the curricular reforms examined in this study. The cases of Chile and the United States, and to some extent China, suggest that the use of a theory for technical improvement of education (standards-based reform and accountability) may undermine efforts to increase the relevance of education. At the conclusion of this chapter we sketch the elements of a theory of improvement for twenty-first-century education.

Because many of these countries instituted curricular reforms on what appeared to be an ad hoc basis, there was often a lack of alignment between the strategies pursued to advance a twenty-first-century education and those pursued to advance other goals. For example, Chile's reforms prioritized improving educational equity in a system where privatization and radical decentralization had segregated students of various social strata into schools of different quality. To achieve that objective, the education strategy emphasized accountability and targeting support to the most disadvantaged schools. This strategy led to concentrating the large investments in teacher professional development on teaching the basics, as that was the focus of the accountability reforms. However, to some extent this decision was at odds with the broad reform of curricular goals, and particularly with the emphasis on developing competencies for the exercise of democratic citizenship which required greater innovation in supporting the development of pedagogical capacity to achieve the new curricular goals, not measured in the assessments that were part of the accountability system. These potential tradeoffs were not openly confronted, and the strategy did not explicitly articulate the priority to be given to each of these policy objectives. In contrast, in Singapore, the most recent emphasis on twenty-first-century education built on and reinforced the preceding priority assigned to the development of critical thinking and higher order skills in schools. In fact, the Singapore case study is an exemplary story of continuous improvement over a very long period where each phase of reform builds on the previous phase, and new emphases capitalize on synergies with those of preceding reforms.

In addition, different countries placed their bets on different parts of the education system. China and Singapore, for example, made teacher preparation a key component of the implementation strategy, and while student knowledge was assessed routinely, this was not the central driver of implementation of the curriculum reform. Chile and the United States, in contrast, enacted the implementation of the twenty-first-century curriculum in a context largely driven by standards-based reform, an approach to instructional improvement that relied heavily on assessing student performance on a narrow range of student knowledge and skills and on using that information to enhance accountability.

Countries varied also in the approaches used to stimulate pedagogical innovation. India and the United States fostered the participation of organizations of civil society in the development of innovative approaches to advance twenty-first-century education, often to support the development of new ideas in learning and pedagogy and the provision of teacher preparation. While teacher preparation was an important element in the policy mix in all countries studied, the alignment between teacher preparation efforts and the novel aspirations of the curriculum varied greatly. It was more tightly coupled in Singapore, and significantly less so, at least for government-supported programs, in Chile, Mexico, or the United States. In China and India, local pilot programs, advanced by both local education authorities and nongovernmental organizations in the case of China, and by nongovernmental organizations alone in the case of India, produced teacher professional development programs that clearly aligned with the new curricular approaches.

THE CHALLENGES OF IMPLEMENTING TWENTY-FIRST-CENTURY EDUCATION

The chapters in this study demonstrate that the implementation of twenty-first-century education is weak in most cases, at least at scale and in ways that benefit all students.

Singapore identified that one of the primary challenges of moving to a broader set of learning competencies was to ensure that their teachers were ready for teaching twenty-first-century competencies, as well as to be equipped with the knowledge and ability to inquire and be role models for students in their learning. Previously, pedagogy had traditionally been based on teacher-centered, subject-based curriculum, and largely shaped by national high-stakes assessments. Changing the culture of schools to create an environment conducive to learning in the new century is a challenge. Another challenge for Singapore has been how to engage parents, business leaders, and community members in ways that support a broader array of educational goals that go beyond doing well in national examinations. In particular, parents are strong supporters of assessment milestones and national examinations, which are perceived to reflect the country's value of education as a pathway in a meritocratic system—where performing well and hard work pays off as stature, privilege, and respect from society; thus, doing well in assessment milestones and national examinations remains critical in the minds of parents and students alike, and enhancing cognitive skills remains the ultimate focus for most. This embrace of a narrow focus by key stakeholders may challenge schools' freedom to innovate.

Similarly, in China pedagogy is still driven by examinations and textbooks, and textbooks remain the principal means to implement curricular aspirations. Thus, intended competencies mandated in the curriculum standards are often diluted in the classroom after being translated into textbooks and examination specifications. Most examinations are paper-and-pen-based, and focus on a limited range of subjects. Those exams focus principally on low order cognitive skills and do not cover interpersonal and intrapersonal competencies. While the government has recognized and emphasized that college entrance examinations should test a more comprehensive set of skills, and while more ability-related items have been incorporated into the college entrance examinations, in general, exam papers involve limited measurement of noncognitive competencies.

In Chile, in spite of a high degree of implementation of the intended activities of the education reform at the primary and secondary levels, impact on teaching practices and classroom processes remains elusive. Means for implementing the curriculum reform would not have been very effective as they consisted largely of traditional training courses for teachers. Universities in charge of teacher training courses were unfamiliar with the intended goals of the curriculum reform and were too far from the realities of practice and of the pedagogical activity in the schools to be able to adequately prepare teachers in the development of robust pedagogies that could support twenty-first-century education.

In India, while the curricular goals are robust, the implementation of these goals is weak systemwide, and not focused on supporting elements like leadership development. Systems at each implementation level are not designed to counter sociocultural biases that obstruct the development of twenty-first-century competencies as articulated in the National Curriculum Framework of 2005. For example, teachers and school principals reflect a hierarchical and authoritarian mind-set that is antithetical to twenty-first-century learning, and robust systems are required both for ensuring that content design and staff selection in each state rise above social inequities, and for preparing teachers and school leaders to shift their mind-sets.

In Mexico, there are two key challenges: inadequate curriculum design and lack of demand for twenty-first-century skills from parents and teachers. There is no shared vision across school communities of which competencies are relevant for students, and there is no evidence that pedagogy has changed in any ways that reflect the broader curriculum aspirations.

In the United States, the recent educational reforms have focused on accountability measures that in effect narrowed the curriculum to what was "test-based and cognitive,"[1] a judgment with which the 2013 Equity and Excellence Commission report agrees, noting that school reformers over the past thirty years have been guided by "the polestar of world-class standards and test-based accountability,"[2] as exemplified by the recent Common Core movement. While education leaders in Massachusetts in 2007 put time and resources into a task force that identified ways to implement educational policy that paid explicit attention to support districts, schools, teachers, and students for twenty-first-century education, the matter of timing and competing priorities that privileged standards-based reforms supported by the federal government led them to put the task force recommendations on hold. Only recently, through one section of the Department of Elementary and Secondary Education, did the Massachusetts education leaders begin to make the connection to career and college readiness a priority, and more recently to realign standards for teacher preparation with the Common Core. While examples of inspiring, creative, and expansive notions of education for the twenty-first-century exist in schools and networks of schools within the United States, such as the Deeper Learning Network of schools supported by the Hewlett Foundation, the challenge of taking these schools and efforts to scale with systemwide support and linkages to teacher education remains.

With these findings, we suggest that the difficulty in achieving the goals of a twenty-first-century education, as expressed in the many documents produced in recent decades calling for such reform, is due to the lack of an explicit and effective systems theory that supports an adequate implementation strategy. Indeed, in spite of a rich knowledge base outlining what students should learn and be able to do in the new century, there is a critical void in the research literature about how to produce system-wide change to enable teachers and students to teach and learn in today's world. Consequently, as schools have aspired to an expanded list of competencies that students need to acquire, the gap between these aspirations and the enacted grammar of schooling has grown. This has created a paradox: as societies become more aware of the crucial role of education to prepare the young to invent the future, and as consensus emerges about the multidimensional nature of the competencies necessary to be empowered to do so, dissatisfaction with the performance of schools to deliver these rising expectations also grows. The challenge is that this paradoxical state of affairs may lead to less support for schools, and to disengagement from public education, at a time when such support is needed more than ever, if schools are indeed going to be able to deliver on a curriculum designed to empower individuals and to support economically and civically viable nation-states that are responsive to the global challenges of the twenty-first century.

Another challenge with the practice of twenty-first-century education arises from the perceived tension between investing in supporting effective practices aligned with the traditional literacies versus supporting practices aligned with twenty-first-century competencies in schools that perform very poorly in the traditional literacies. The argument goes that since schools cannot even get children to learn the basics, it is better to go back to those basics, and to hold teachers accountable to them, than it is to set higher aspirations. A variation of this challenge focuses on the possible tradeoffs between investing in back-to-basics for the poor versus investing in twenty-first-century education for more privileged students.

A third challenge affecting implementation concerns the lack of sound developmental theory to support a pedagogy and effective systems theory for twenty-first-century education, including an approach to appropriate teacher education and school and system leadership development. There is not yet an integrated developmental theory that articulates how the competencies listed in the various twenty-first-century frameworks develop, or that does so in ways that reinforce and complement one another. As curriculum has focused on cognitive development for a longer period of time, presumably the scope and sequence used to teach the traditional subjects—of language or mathematics, for example—reflect that theoretically informed understanding. But the absence of sound theory is particularly salient for intrapersonal and interpersonal skills. These curricular frameworks identify, for example, that a trait such as perseverance is important, but do not explain how perseverance develops. Most of the individual traits and components of intrapersonal and interpersonal skills draw on psychological research and, as a result, there is a theoretical foundation to explain the development of those traits, on which extensive applied work has been based to help cultivate them. Examples include self-efficacy, a key intrapersonal competency—the confidence in one's ability to succeed—as theorized by Albert Bandura;[3] the theory of multiple intelligences—an alternative to the concept of intelligence as a single construct—as developed by Howard Gardner;[4] the construct of growth mind-set—the belief that abilities can be developed through hard work—as developed by Carol Dweck;[5] and the concept of grit—the passion and motivation to achieve particular goals—as studied by Angela Duckworth.[6] But while the individual study of isolated traits helps advance theoretical understanding, as well as the design of interventions to develop those traits, the challenge of twenty-first-century education is to support the development of a range of traits simultaneously and to ensure a coherent set of opportunities for students across subjects and grades. The lack of an integrated theory that brings all these traits together into a single theory of human development, in a way that is comprehensive but also parsimonious, is a limitation to the development of practical approaches to the design of learning experiences intended to achieve a balanced set of twenty-first-century competencies.

We need theory to inform the development of a sequence of experiences that help students gain those competencies, integrating across the cognitive, interpersonal, and intrapersonal domains. Scholars and practitioners may use the theory of human development to inform the development of a sequence of experiences that can support learning across all those domains, and not just in some of them. In the absence of such theory, education systems are attempting to develop twenty-first-century competencies largely by drawing on approaches that were designed to support cognitive development. We have no reason to think that the same mechanisms and approaches should work in helping students develop interpersonal and intrapersonal competencies, and some reason to question that they work to develop some cognitive competencies, such as innovation and creativity.[7] Mexico, for example, has attempted to develop citizenship competencies in the subject of civics, largely relying on didactic pedagogies; in contrast, Chile tried to accomplish the same goal differently, infusing learning objectives across various disciplines, but teachers were not prepared to teach "transversal" objectives that did not follow the traditional subject-centered grammar of schooling. Compounding these challenges resulting from the lack of an integrated theory of the development of twenty-first-century competencies are, first, the absence of a theory of how adults (teachers and school administrators) learn the competencies that support a twenty-first-century pedagogy, and second, how collaborative practices translate into a coherent and integrated set of educational experiences for students across subjects and grades.

We also could benefit from a more robust and explicit discussion about the goals and purposes of education, in the context of our current and anticipated social, political, and economic contexts, and an explicit discussion of the anticipated needs, challenges, and opportunities of the twenty-first century and beyond. In countries such as India and Singapore, where such discussions were facilitated, the outlined competencies are more comprehensive and robust.

SOURCES OF INNOVATIVE PRACTICE

In spite of the fact that there is limited evidence of large scale implementation of twenty-first-century education, in all the countries examined in this book there are models that demonstrate twenty-first-century learning, albeit at a small scale. While this was not an explicit focus of our study, emerging evidence suggests that the analysis of the sources of innovative practices to support such learning is one that deserves further investigation.

The following discussion should be treated as suggestive of the necessity of such research, rather than as offering definitive conclusions regarding the sources of innovative practices in each of the countries studied.

In Singapore, schools have modified curriculum and assessment to teach twenty-first-century competencies in academic content subjects. Content across all subjects was reduced by 30 percent to allow time in the school curriculum to promote critical thinking and self-directed learning. Thinking skills were integrated in tests and examinations assessing students' skills in evaluating, synthesizing, decision making, and problem solving. Project-based learning was implemented in every school as a way to develop curiosity, creativity, resourcefulness, and teamwork. All primary schools implemented the Programme for Active Learning, which uses entertaining activities in sports and games and in the performing and visual arts to facilitate students' holistic development. Schools are also developing multiple forms of co-curricular activities to develop twenty-first-century competencies and values. One of the key initiatives was the introduction of comprehensive integration of Information and Communication Technology into curriculum and pedagogy; six model schools, known as FutureSchools@Singapore, are experimenting with ways to seamlessly integrate ICT into curriculum.

The other countries in our study have not implemented their reforms as thoroughly across the education system as in Singapore. In China, local education authorities and schools decide the extent to which interpersonal and intrapersonal competencies are taught via local and school-based curriculum. Effectiveness of teaching and learning depends on their capacity to do this. This is intended to nurture bottom-up experimentation and innovation. In Chile, the government has taken a more top-down approach, encouraging and funding the creation of consortia of universities or nongovernmental organizations and clusters of schools to develop and implement interventions to support school improvement.

In Mexico, a number of nongovernmental organizations have developed innovative programs that are influencing and informing government interventions, such as the work of Enlaces, an organization committed to supporting the development of technological literacies, or of La Vaca Independiente, an organization promoting the development of empathy and critical thinking through appreciation of visual arts, or Via Educacion, an organization promoting youth leadership development through civic education.[8]

India has also implemented twenty-first-century learning through nongovernmental organizations, including Digantar, Lend a Hand India, Barefoot College, and Design for Change. Some of these contributed to conversations that led to the development of the new curricular goals, and others to the implementation of the same goals.

Frequently, such models have been generated as a result of policies specifically intended to support innovation. In China, some local jurisdictions have been granted freedom from the usual regulatory mandates as a way to enable innovation. Singapore relied on demonstration schools to pilot twenty-first-century pedagogies. In India, Mexico, and the United States, public-private partnerships have enabled nongovernmental organizations to design innovative pedagogies and teacher professional development programs. Such active participation of civil society in the design of educational innovation may express the growing awareness of the importance of education quality as discussed in the introduction, perhaps along with growing skepticism regarding the ability of the public sector to successfully meet this demand without additional support.

THE NEED FOR SYSTEMIC STRATEGIES TO SUPPORT TWENTY-FIRST-CENTURY LEARNING

The case studies included in this book demonstrate that clear goals are important to education reform, but goals are not self-executing. Attention to implementation requires a theory about how best to get teachers and school administrators to develop the kind of learning opportunities that provide students meaningful chances to gain the more ambitious set of competencies hoped for in the curricular reforms undertaken in all countries included in this study.

A systems theory needs to address how learning experiences are shaped by curriculum and pedagogy, answering such questions as 1) are subjects the appropriate means to develop those competencies?, and 2) what is the appropriate role and balance of didactic pedagogies, independent study, project-based learning, and outdoor education? With clear ideas about how learning opportunities should be structured in a coherent way, this systems theory could inform also the kind of school organization and management that can best support such opportunities, as well as the kinds of resources and structures that can make such organization and pedagogy feasible. Outside the institution of the school, the theory would address the role of participation on goal setting, system assessment, innovation management, resource generation, culture—including the basic grammar of schooling and the larger societal expectations for schools—and communication between schools and communities. It is as a result of the interplay of these various elements of a system of education that the culture of education, the day-to-day practice of learning and teaching in schools, is shaped.

Supporting the development of such a culture requires addressing those elements as a system, knowing that addressing any single one of them will affect the impact that the other elements have on instruction. For instance, new curricular goals require communication, frequent and repeated, at all levels of the system—a practice well exemplified in Singapore, to good effect in supporting execution of policy aspirations. But communication of goals alone is unlikely to make much dent in practice. Change in practice will require opportunities to develop new capacities for teachers and school leaders, as well as changes in the social context of school so that social expectations and values—of peers, supervisors, even students and parents—are supportive of the pedagogical changes in question. And changes in support and expectations need to be coupled with changes in assessment and in the mechanisms of accountability, so those reinforce the changes in question, rather than work at cross purposes with them. Finally, the strategy to guide systemic, mutually reinforcing changes in support of twenty-first-century learning, needs to be aligned with other strategies at play to achieve different or complementary objectives in school.

THE NEED TO BUILD A ROBUST TEACHING PROFESSION

Concomitant with the expansion of expected learning outcomes for students to thrive in the twenty-first century, a pedagogy that supports such learning requires an expanded set of competencies for teachers. Deep expertise in supporting twenty-first-century learning calls for a robust and coherent set of standards of practice and opportunities for professional development to sustain professional practice. Because of the multidimensional nature of twenty-first-century learning, it calls for greater professionalism among teachers, rather than training to develop narrow teaching skills. In addition to a powerful theory to guide the implementation of twenty-first-century education, leaders need to pay attention to the governance structures of education, so that schools are the kind of organization where intrinsically motivated people—students and teachers—engage in the kind of innovative practice and hard work that will be necessary to teach to a more ambitious set of standards. This will require achieving a fine balance between school autonomy and centralization. Clear standards and expectations—the expectation, for example, that *all students* means *all* when it comes to providing them the competencies for empowerment—are necessary. These standards need the supports that centralized efforts can provide, in the form of funding, for example, or opportunities to build capacity, or assessment of results. But those efforts need also to be coupled with the autonomy that provides room for professionalism, voice, and innovation where it most matters—in the classroom and in the school—and coupled as well with openness for rich and multiple forms of collaboration between schools, communities, and other organizations of civic society, all of which requires greater teacher professionalism.

Twenty-first-century education is only the next step in a global movement that began in 1945, when the right to education was included in the Universal Declaration of Human Rights. This global education movement, engaging societies and governments, national as well as supranational organizations, transformed humanity by providing the majority of the world's children the opportunity to go to school. In a relatively short period, that movement achieved great progress in providing access to all, and in creating the conditions to gain basic cognitive competencies. Standing on the shoulders of those achievements of the last seven decades, the bolder aspirations of twenty-first-century education require new thinking and new ways of doing, and those require everyone involved, particularly the adults working in schools and those who support them, to learn new ways. Figuring out how best to support the learning of those new ways is perhaps the single most important next step in the global movement to educate all children to build the future.

NOTES

INTRODUCTION

1. Colleen Walsh, "The Big Share," *Harvard Gazette* (Aug. 5, 2014), http://news.harvard.edu/gazette/story/2014/08/the-big-share.

2. Pew Research Center, *Emerging and Developing Economies Much More Optimistic About the Future* (Washington DC: Pew Research Center, Oct. 2014).

3. Gallup.com, "Confidence in Institutions. Historical Trends" (June 2–7, 2015), http://www.gallup.com/poll/1597/confidence-institutions.aspx.

4. Clayton M. Christensen and Derek van Bever, "The Capitalist Dilemma," *Harvard Business Review* (June 2014).

5. Fernando Reimers, "Educating the Children of the Poor: A Paradoxical Global Movement," in *Rethinking Education and Poverty*, ed. William G. Tierney (Baltimore: Johns Hopkins University Press, 2015).

6. Benjamin Bloom, *Taxonomy of Educational Objectives* (New York: Longmans, 1956).

7. Richard Murnane and Frank Levy, *Teaching the New Basic Skills: Principles for Educating Children to Thrive in a Changing Economy* (New York: Marking Kessler Books, Free Press, 1996).

David Autor and Brendan Price, *The Changing Task Composition of the US Labor Market: An Update of Autor, Levy and Murnane (2003)* (Cambridge, MA: MIT Mimeograph, 2013), http://economics.mit.edu/files/9758.

8. UNESCO had only once during its entire history published a report outlining a vision for education—the Faure Report, a milestone publication also known as *Learning to Be*, which argued for the necessity of lifelong education to develop capacities for effective functioning and participation in society and of a society committed to supporting lifelong learning.

9. UNESCO, *Learning: The Treasure Within: Report to UNESCO of the International Commission on Education for the Twenty-first Century* (Paris: UNESCO Publications, 1996).

10. Dominique Simone Rychen and Laura Hersh Salganek, eds., *Key Competencies for a Successful Life and a Well-functioning Society* (Gottingen: Hogrefe and Huber, 2003).

11. Cheryl Lemke, *enGauge. 21st Century Skills for 21st Century Learners* (Naperville, IL: North Central Regional Educational Lab, 2003).

12. World Economic Forum. 2014, http://www3.weforum.org/docs/WEFUSA _NewVisionforEducation_Report2015.pdf.

13. Lemke, *enGauge*, p. 3.

14. Johann Heinrich Pestalozzi, *Letters of Pestalozzi on the Education of Infancy* (Boston: Carter and Hendee, 1830), https://books.google.com/books/about/Letters_of _Pestalozzi_on_the_education_o.html?id=iYLtAAAAMAAJ.

15. Howard Gardner, *Frames of Mind: The Theory of Multiple Intelligences* (New York: Basic Books, 1983).

16. National Research Council, *Education for Life and Work: Developing Transferable Knowledge and Skills in the 21st Century*, ed. James Pellegrino and Margaret Hilton (Washington, DC: National Academies Press, 2012).

17. Pew Research Center, *Families May Differ, But They Share Common Values on Parenting* (Washington, DC: Pew Research Center, 2014), http://www.pewresearch.org /fact-tank/2014/09/18/families-may-differ-but-they-share-common-values-on-parenting/.

18. Pew Research Center, *The Skills Americans Say Kids Need to Succeed in Life* (Washington DC: Pew Research Center, 2015), http://www.pewresearch.org/fact-tank /2015/02/19/skills-for-success/.

19. Pew Research Center, *Americans Want More Pressure on Students, the Chinese Want Less* (Washington DC: Pew Research Center, 2011), http://www.pewglobal.org /2011/08/23/americans-want-more-pressure-on-students-the-chinese-want-less/.

20. A Report to the Secretary by the Equity and Excellence Commission of the US Department of Education, 2013, p. 12, http://www2.ed.gov/about/bdscomm/list/eec /equity-excellence-commission-report.pdf.

CHAPTER ONE

We would like to acknowledge the support and input of Mrs. Chua-Lim Yen Ching, deputy director-general of education (Professional Development) and executive director, Academy of Singapore Teachers; Professor Lee Sing Kong, vice president (Education Strategies), Nanyang Technological University; Ms. Eugenia Tan, deputy director, Curriculum Policy Office, Ministry of Education and her team; Ms. Tan Hwee Pin, principal, Kranji Secondary School and her team of teachers; and focus group discussion participants at the Singapore Global Education Innovation Initiative Symposium held at the National Institute of Education in March 2014. We would also like to thank our research team Dr. Lee Ling, Ms. Avila Ava Patricia Cabiguin, and Ms. Janey Ng Wee Leng, who helped in this or earlier versions of this draft.

1. Sing Kong Lee and Ee-Ling Low, "Conceptualising Teacher Preparation for Educational Innovation: Singapore's Approach," in *Educational Policy Innovations: Levelling up and Sustaining Educational Achievement*, ed. Sing Kong Lee, Wing On Lee, and Ee-Ling Low (Singapore: Springer, 2014), 49–53.

2. Marilyn Binkley et al., "Defining Twenty-First Century Skills," in *Assessment and Teaching of 21st Century Skills*, ed. Patrick Griffin, Barry McGaw, and Esther Care (Netherlands: Springer, 2012), 17–66.

3. National Research Council, *Education for Life and Work: Developing Transferable Knowledge and Skills in the 21st Century*, ed. James Pellegrino and Margaret Hilton (Washington DC: National Academies Press, 2012).

4. Lee and Low, "Conceptualising Teacher Preparation," 53.

5. Binkley et al., "Twenty-First Century Skills," 17–66.

6. International Monetary Fund, *World Economic Outlook Database, April 2015,* https://www.imf.org/external/pubs/ft/weo/2015/01/weodata/index.aspx.

7. S. Gopinathan, "Globalisation, the State and Education Policy in Singapore," *Asia Pacific Journal of Education* 16, no. 1 (1996): 74–87.

8. Cheng Yong Tan and Clive Dimmock, "How a 'Top-performing' Asian School System Formulates and Implements Policy: The Case of Singapore," *Educational Management Administration Leadership* 43, no. 15 (Sept. 2014): 743–763.

9. The Primary Six Leaving Examination (PSLE) is conducted in Singapore annually. It is a national examination which pupils sit at the end of their sixth and final year of primary school education, typically when they are twelve years old (Source: Singapore Examinations and Assessment Board, "SEAB," Retrieved from www.seab.gov.sg).

10. Tilak Abeysinghe, *Singapore: Economy* (Singapore: National University of Singapore, 2007), http://courses.nus.edu.sg/course/ecstabey/Singapore%20Economy-Tilak.pdf.

11. Gopinathan, "Globalisation," 74–87.

12. TSLN is a vision for a total learning environment including students, teachers, parents, workers, companies, and government. Schools are central to this vision as they must develop future generations of thinking and committed citizens, capable of making good decisions to keep Singapore vibrant and successful in the future. To achieve this, MOE undertook a fundamental review of curriculum and assessment systems spearheaded by the Education Review and Implementation Committees—PERI, SERI and JERI—for the Primary, Secondary, and Junior College levels, respectively. (Source: Ministry of Education, Government of Singapore, "Speech by Prime Minister Goh Chok Tong at the opening of the 7th International Conference on Thinking," retrieved from http://www.moe.gov.sg/media/speeches/1997/020697.htm.)

13. Heng Swee Keat, "Opening Address by Mr Heng Swee Keat, Minister for Education at the Ministry of Education (MOE) Work Plan Seminar 2011," retrieved from http://www.moe.gov.sg/media/speeches/2011/09/22/work-plan-seminar-2011.php.

14. Secondary Education places students in the Express, Normal (Academic), or Normal (Technical) stream according to how they perform at the PSLE. The different curricular emphases are designed to match their learning abilities and interests. (Source: http://www.moe.gov.sg/education/secondary/.)

15. Marc S. Tucker, *The Phoenix: Vocational education and training in Singapore* (Washington DC: National Center on Education and the Economy, 2012).

16. National Institute of Education, *TE21 Report: A teacher education model for the 21st century* (Singapore: National Institute of Education, 2009).

17. Sing Kong Lee, e-mail interview with author, 2014.

18. Ministry of Education, *Building a National Education System for the 21st century: The Singapore Experience* (Toronto: Ontario Ministry of Education, 2010).

19. Ministry of Education, *The Desired Outcomes of Education* (Singapore: Ministry of Education, 2009), http://www.moe.gov.sg/education/desired-outcomes.

20. The Desired Outcomes of Education (DOE) were first introduced in 1997 and the current version was published online on 1 Dec 2009 at http://www.moe.gov.sg /education/desired-outcomes.

21. Ibid.

22. The review was done by the Primary Education Review and Implementation Committee (PERI). This committee was set up by the MOE in October 2008 to look at ways to raise the quality of primary education in Singapore. Source: http://www.moe.gov .sg/media/press/2009/01/strong-fundamentals-for-future.php.

23. Ibid.

24. Ministry of Education, *MOE to Enhance Learning of 21st Century Competencies and Strengthen Art, Music and Physical Education* (Singapore: Ministry of Education, March 2010), http://www.moe.gov.sg/media/press/2010/03/moe-to-enhance-learning -of-21s.php.

25. Ibid.

26. Ministry of Education, *2014 Syllabus: Character and Citizenship Education Primary* (Singapore: Ministry of Education, 2014), http://www.moe.gov.sg/education /syllabuses/character-citizenship-education/files/2014-character-citizenship-education -eng.pdf.

27. National Research Council, *Education for Life and Work*.

28. Ibid.

29. Ministry of Education, *Updates on curriculum matters—sharing with NIE* (Singapore: Ministry of Education, 2014).

30. Ibid.

31. Ministry of Education, *Nurturing Our Young for the Future: Competencies for the 21st Century* (brochure published by the Ministry of Education, Singapore, March 2010).

32. Curriculum in our case study generally refers to the curriculum as enacted in schools based on the national curriculum framework.

33. Ministry of Education, *Teaching and Learning of 21st Century Competencies in Schools: NIE TE21 Summit, Presentation by Education Programmes Division/MOE* (Singapore: Ministry of Education, 2010).

34. CCE was rolled out in phases, staring with Primary One and Two, followed by Secondary One to Five, and then Primary Three to Six (from http://www.moe.gov.sg /media/press/2012/11/new-syllabus-and-textbook-titl.php).

35. Ministry of Education, *2014 Syllabus: Character and Citizenship Education*.

36. Aaron Koh, "Singapore Education in 'New Times': Global/local imperatives," *Discourse: Studies in the Cultural Politics of Education* 25, no. 3 (2004): 335–349; Leslie Sharpe and S. Gopinathan, "After Effectiveness: New Directions in the Singapore School System?" *Journal of Education Policy* 17, no. 2 (2002): 151–166.

37. Koh, "Singapore Education in 'New Times,'" 335–349.

38. Aaron Koh, "Towards a Critical Pedagogy: Creating 'Thinking Schools' in Singapore," *Journal of Curriculum Studies* 34, no. 3 (2002): 255–264; Allan Luke et al.,

"Towards research-based innovation and reform: Singapore schooling in transition," *Asia Pacific Journal of Education* 25, no. 1 (2005): 5–28.

39. Ministry of Education, *Project Work* (Singapore: Ministry of Education, 2005), http://www.moe.gov.sg/education/programmes/project-work.

40. Pak Tee Ng, "The Phases and Paradoxes of Educational Quality Assurance: The Case of the Singapore Education System," *Quality Assurance in Education: an International Perspective* 16, no. 2 (2008): 112–125.

41. Goh Chok Tong, "Shaping Our Future: Thinking Schools, Learning Nation," speech by Prime Minister Goh Chok Tong at the Opening of the 7th International Conference on Thinking, Singapore, 2 June 1997.

42. Ministry of Education, *Teaching and Learning,* 2010.

43. Clive Dimmock and Jonathan W. P. Goh, "Transformative Pedagogy, Leadership and School Organisation for the Twenty-First-Century Knowledge-Based Economy: The Case of Singapore," *School Leadership and Management* 31, no. 3 (2011): 215–234.

44. Koh, "Towards a critical pedagogy," 255–264; Jason Tan and S. Gopinathan, "Education Reform in Singapore: Towards Greater Creativity and Innovation?" *NIRA Review* (Summer 2000), http://www.nira.or.jp/past/publ/review/2000summer/tan.pdf.

45. Pak Tee Ng, "Quality Assurance in the Singapore Education System in an Era of Diversity and Innovation," *Educational Research for Policy and Practice* 6, no. 3 (Oct. 2007): 235–247.

46. Tan and Gopinathan, "Education Reform in Singapore."

47. Liew Wei Li, "Development of 21st Century Competencies in Singapore" (presentation at the OECD-CCE-MOE Educating for Innovation workshop, 15 Jan 2013), http://www.oecd.org/edu/ceri/02%20Wei%20Li%20Liew_Singapore.pdf.

48. Ng, "Quality Assurance," 235–247; Charlene Tan, "Globalisation, the Singapore State and Educational Reforms: Towards Performativity," *Education, Knowledge and Economy* 2, no. 2 (2008): 111–120.

49. Ibid.

50. Lee and Low, "Balancing between Theory and Practice: Singapore's Teacher Education Partnership Model," *Institute for Learning,* https://www.ifl.ac.uk/publications/in-tuition/intuition-16-spring-2014/opinion-balancing-between-theory-and-practice-singapore%E2%80%99s-teacher-education-partnership-model/.

51. Lee and Low, "Conceptualising Teacher Preparation."

52. National Institute of Education, *TE21 Report.*

53. Linda Darling-Hammond and Milbrey W. McLaughlin, "Policies that Support Professional Development in an Era of Reform," *Phi Delta Kappan* 76, no. 8 (1995): 597–604; Donald McIntyre, "Theory, theorizing and reflection in initial teacher education.," in *Conceptualizing Reflection in Teacher Development,* eds. James Calderhead and Peter Gates (Washington DC: Routledge, 1993), 39–52; May Britt Postholm, "Teachers Developing Practice: Reflection as Key Activity," *Teaching and Teacher Education* 24, no. 7 (Oct. 2008): 1717–1728.

54. Christopher Day, Bob Elliot, and Alison Kington, "Reform, Standards and Teacher Identity: Challenges of Sustaining Commitment," *Teaching and Teacher Education* 21, no. 5 (July 2005): 563–577; Christopher Day and Alison Kington, "Identity, Well-being and Effectiveness: the Emotional Contexts of Teaching," *Pedagogy, Culture and Society* 16, no. 1 (2008): 7–23; Christopher Day et al., "The Personal and Professional Selves of Teachers: Stable and Unstable Identities," *British Educational Research Journal* 32, no. 4 (2006): 601–616; Geoff Troman, "Primary Teacher Identity, Commitment and Career in Performative School Cultures," *British Educational Research Journal* 34, no. 5 (2008): 619–633.

55. Linda Darling-Hammond and Nikole Richardson, "Teacher learning: What matters?" *How Teachers Learn* 66, no. 5 (Feb. 2009): 46–53; Thomas H. Levine, "Tools for the Study and Design of Collaborative Teacher Learning: The Affordances of Different Conceptions of Teacher Community and Activity Theory," *Teacher Education Quarterly* 37, no. 1 (Winter 2010): 109–130; Judith Warren Little et al., "Looking at Student Work for Teacher Learning, Teacher Community, and School Reform," *Phi Delta Kappan* 85, no. 3 (Nov. 2003): 184–192.

56. Linda Darling-Hammond, "Constructing 21st-Century Teacher Education," *Journal of Teacher Education* 57, no. 3 (2006): 300–314; Sharon Feiman-Nemser, "From Preparation to Practice: Designing a Continuum to Strengthen and Sustain Teaching," *Teachers College Record* 103, no. 6 (Dec. 2001): 1013–1055; Tom Russell, Suzin McPherson and Andrea K. Martin, "Coherence and Collaboration in Teacher Education Reform," *Canadian Journal of Education* 26, no. 1 (2001): 37–55.

57. Elizabeth M. Curtis, "Embedding 'Philosophy in the Classroom' in Pre-Service Teacher Education," in *Teacher Education and Values Pedagogy: A Student Well-being Approach,* eds. Ron Toomey et al. (Terrigal, NSW, Australia: David Barlow, 2010), 108–120.

58. Terence Lovat, "Value Education and Teachers' Work: A Quality Teaching Perspective," *New Horizons in Education* 112, (2005): 1–14.

59. Lee and Low, "Conceptualising Teacher Preparation."

60. Ministry of Education, *Building a National Education System.*

61. OECD, *Teachers Matter: Attracting, Developing, and Retaining Effective Teachers* (Paris: OECD, 2005).

62. Tan and Dimmock, "How a 'Top-performing' Asian School System," 743–763.

63. S. Gopinathan, Benjamin Wong, and Nicholas Tang, "The Evolution of School Leadership Policy and Practice in Singapore: Responses to Changing Socio-economic and Political Contexts (Insurgents, Implementers, Innovators)," *Journal of Educational Administration and History* 40, no. 3 (Dec. 2008): 235–249.

64. Tan and Dimmock, "How a 'Top-performing' Asian School System," 743–763.

65. Ministry of Education, "MOE to Enhance Learning of 21st Century Competencies."

66. Academy of Singapore Teachers, *Presentation to NIE about AST* (2014).

67. Ministry of Education, *Greater Support for Teachers and School Leaders* (Singapore: Ministry of Education, 2005) http://www.moe.gov.sg/media/press/2005 /pr20050922b.htm.

68. Ministry of Education, *Flexible School Design Concepts to Support Teaching and Learning* (Singapore: Ministry of Education, 2005), http://www.moe.gov.sg/media/press /2005/pr20051229.htm.

69. Ministry of Education, *Building a National Education System.*

70. Ibid.

71. Pak Tee Ng, "Students' Perception of Change in the Singapore Education System," *Educational Research for Policy and Practice* 3 (2004): 77–92.

72. These issues were raised by participants at a public symposium held on 19 March 2014 at NIE, Singapore, as part of the GEI². The symposium was titled "Educating Students for the 21st Century."

73. Dimmock and Goh, "Transformative Pedagogy," 215–234.

74. OECD, "Singapore: Rapid improvement followed by strong performance," in *Strong performers and successful reformers in education: Lessons from PISA for the United States* (Paris: OECD, 2010).

75. Thomas J. Bellows, "Meritocracy and the Singapore Political System," *Asian Journal of Political Science* 17, no. 1 (2009): 24–44.

76. OECD, "Singapore: Rapid improvement."

77. Bellows, "Meritocracy," 24–44.

78. Blackbox, "You Know Anot? Private Tuition in Singapore: A Whitepaper Release," http://www.blackbox.com.sg/wp/wp-content/uploads/2012/09/Blackbox-You -Know-Anot-Whitepaper-Private-Tuition.pdf.

79. Pak Tee Ng, "Educational Reform in Singapore: From Quantity to Quality," *Educational Research for Policy and Practice* 7 (2008): 5–15.

80. Ibid.

81. Ng, "Students' Perception of Change," 77–92.

82. Leonel Lim, "Meritocracy, Elitism, and Egalitarianism: A Preliminary and Provisional Assessment of Singapore's Primary Education Review," *Asia Pacific Journal of Education* 33, no. 1 (2013): 1–14.

83. Ibid.

CHAPTER TWO

I would like to acknowledge the helpful input of Ms. Li Ming, director of division for curriculum and pedagogy, Department for Basic Education II, Ministry of Education. Thanks also to the interview informants, including Mr. Jiang Jiwei, deputy director-general, Chao Yang District Education Commission of Beijing, and Mr. Zang Tiejun, director-general, Beijing Education Examination Institute, for their contribution, and to Ms. Guo Xiaoying, who provided administrative support in the process of writing the chapter.

I would also like to thank my husband Cai Shiming and my son Cai Shuchen; without giving up many weekends and after-work time when I should have been with them, I would not have been able to finish the chapter.

1. Additional offshore territory, including territorial waters, special economic areas, and the continental shelf, totals over 3 million square kilometers, bringing China's overall territory to almost 13 million square kilometers.

2. National Bureau of Statistics, "Population Basic Profile," [(renkou jiben qingkuang], last modified 2014, http://data.stats.gov.cn/tablequery.htm?code=AD03.

3. Ministry of Education, *2012 National Education Development Statistics Bullet* (Beijing: 2014), http://www.moe.edu.cn/publicfiles/business/htmlfiles/moe/moe_633 /201308/155798.html.

4. Ministry of Education, "Number of Students of Formal Education by Type and Level," http://www.moe.edu.cn/publicfiles/business/htmlfiles/moe/s7567/201309 /156896.html.

5. Haifeng Liu, *Zhongguo keju wenhua* [China's Keju culture] (Shenyang, China: Liaoning Education Press, 2010).

6. Liu, *Zhongguo keju wenhua*; Kai-ming Cheng, "Shanghai: How a Big City in a Developing Country Leaped to the Head of the Class," in *Surpassing Shanghai: An Agenda for American Education Built on the World's Learning Systems,* ed. Marc S. Tucker (Cambridge, MA: Harvard Education Press, 2013), 21–50.

7. The Common Programme of the Chinese People's Political Consultative Conference [Zhongguo renmin zhengzhi xieshang huiyi gongtong gangling], *Xinhua News*, http://news.xinhuanet.com/ziliao/2004-12/07/content_2304465.htm.

8. Fang Xiaodong, Li Yufei, Bi Cheng, Song Jiange, Wang Hongyuan, *A Brief History of Education of the People's Republic of China [Zhonghua renmin gongheguo shigang]* (Haikou: Hainan Publishing House, 2002).

9. Qualification for entering the universities and colleges was largely based on political identity and recommendation by masses.

10. Qili Hu, "Zhonggong zhongyang guanyu jiaoyu tizhi gaige de jueding chutai qianhou" [Before and after promulgation of the CCPCC's decision on education structural reform], *Yan Huang Chun Qiu* 12 (2008).

11. *Gaige kaifang yilai de jiaoyu fazhan lishixing chengjiu he jiben jingyan yanjiu ketizu* [Historical achievement and essential lessons of education development since reform and opening up] (Beijing: Educational Science Publishing House, 2008).

12. Modernization of industry, agriculture, national defense, and science and technology.

13. *Gaige kaifang yilai*, 84–86.

14. CCP, State Council, *The Programme of Educational Reform and Development* [Zhongguo jiaoyu gaige he fazhan gangyao] (Beijing: 1993), http://www.moe.edu.cn /edoas/website18/34/info3334.htm.

15. *Gaige kaifang yilai*, 124–127.

16. CCP, State Council, *Decision on Deepening Education Reform and Fully Advancing Quality Education of the CCP and State Council* [Zhonggong zhongyang guowuyuan guanyu shenhua jiaoyu gaige yu quanmian tuijin suzhi jiaoyu de jueding] (Beijing: 1999), http://www.edu.cn/zong_he_870/20100719/t20100719_497966.shtml.

17. Other programs related to "cross-century teaching workforce," high-level creative talents, flagship universities (211 Initiative), distance education, university-industry cooperation, expansion of higher education, vocational and adult education, education funding, structural reform, and moral education in higher education institutions.

18. *Gaige kaifang yilai*, 84–86.

19. Author's experience with several major policy documents including *2001 Outline of Basic Education Curriculum Reform*.

20. The basic education curriculum standards were updated in 2011.

21. Ministry of Education, *Compulsory Education Mathematics Curriculum Standards* (Beijing: Beijing Normal University Publishing Group, 2011).

22. Ministry of Education, *Lower Secondary School Science Curriculum Standards* (Beijing: Beijing Normal University Publishing Group, 2011).

23. Ibid.

24. Zhong Qiquan, "One curriculum, multiple textbooks: pursuit for education democracy-review of textbook policies in China" [Yigang duoben: jiaoyu minzhu de suqiu-woguo jiaokeshu zhengce shuping], *Education Development Research* [Jiaoyu fazhan yanjiu] 4 (2009).

25. Such as love toward motherland, people, labor, science, and socialism; observe disciplines and obey laws, be honest and credible, concerned for the collective, maintain social morality; preserve the environment.

26. Andreas Schleicher and Yan Wang, "Reconciling Fairness with Efficiency: Reforming the Chinese Examination System," in *The World Leaders in Education: Lessons from the Successes and Drawbacks of Their Methods*, ed. Hani Morgan and Christopher Barry (New York: Peter Lang Publishing, forthcoming.)

CHAPTER THREE

We would like to thank Olga Espinoza who collaborated in the analysis of the Chilean curriculum. We also want to thank José J. Brunner, who read a previous version of this chapter, and Jacqueline Gysling for her comments and suggestions. This work was supported by the PIA-CONICYT Basal Funds for Centers of Excellence under Grant BF0003; and PIA-CONICYT ANILLO under Grant SOC-1104.

1. Cristián Cox, "Las políticas educacionales de Chile en las últimas décadas del siglo XX," in *Políticas educacionales en el cambio de siglo. La reforma del sistema escolar de Chile*, ed. Cristián Cox (Santiago: Editorial Universitaria, 2003).

2. National Research Council, *Education for Life and Work: Developing Transferable Knowledge and Skills in the 21st Century*, ed. James Pellegrino and Margaret Hilton (National Research Council, Washington DC: National Academies Press, 2012); Marilyn

Binkley et al., "Defining Twenty-first Century Skills," in *Assessment and Teaching of 21st Century Skills*, ed. Patrick Griffin, Barry McGaw, and Esther Care (Netherlands: Springer, 2012); Pacific Policy Research Center, *21st Century Skills for Students and Teachers* (Honolulu: Kamehameha Schools, Research and Evaluation Division, 2010); OECD, *The Definition and Selection of Key Competencies. Executive Summary* (OECD, DeSeCo Project, 2005).

3. Martin Carnoy, *Cuba's academic advantage: Why Students in Cuba Do Better in School* (Redwood City, CA: Stanford University Press, 2007).

4. Varun Gauri, *School Choice in Chile. Two Decades of Educational Reform* (Pittsburgh: University of Pittsburgh Press, 1998); Chang-Tai Hsieh and Miguel Urquiola, "The Effects of Generalized School Choice on Achievement and Stratification: Evidence from Chile's Voucher Program," *Journal of Public Economics* 90, no. 8 (2006): 1477–1503; Cristián Bellei, "The Private–Public School Controversy: The Case of Chile," in *School Choice International,* ed. Paul Peterson and Rajashri Chakrabarti (Cambridge, MA: MIT Press, 2009), 165–192.

5. Juan Pablo Valenzuela, Cristián Bellei, and Danae de los Ríos, "Socioeconomic School Segregation in a Market-oriented Educational System. The Case of Chile," *Journal of Education Policy* 29, no. 2 (2014): 217–241.

6. J. Edo Garcia-Huidobro and Cristián Cox, "La reforma educacional chilena 1990–1998. Visión de Conjunto," in *La Reforma educacional chilena* (Santiago: Editorial Popular, 1999); Isidora Mena and Cristián Bellei, "The New Challenge: Quality and Equity in Education," in *Chile in the Nineties*, ed. Cristian Toloza and Eugenio Lahera (Stanford: Stanford University Libraries, 2000), 349–391.

7. Cox, "Las políticas educacionales de Chile"; Francoise Delannoy, *Education Reforms in Chile, 1980–98. A Lesson in Pragmatism,* Country Studies, Education Reform and Management Publication Series (Washington, DC: Education Reform and Management Team, Human Development Network-Education, World Bank, 2000).

8. Cristián Bellei and Cristián Cabalin, "Chilean Student Movements: Sustained Struggle to Transform a Market-oriented Educational System," *Current Issues in Comparative Education* 15, no. 2 (2013): 108.

9. Viola Espínola and Juan Pablo Claro, "El Sistema Nacional de Aseguramiento de la Calidad: Una Reforma Basada en Estándares" in *Ecos de la revolución pingüina,* ed. Cristián Bellei, Daniel Contreras, and Juan Pablo Valenzuela (Santiago: Editorial Pehuén, 2010).

10. Cristián Bellei and Xavier Vanni, "The Evolution of Educational Policy in Chile, 1980–2014," in *Education in South America*, ed. Simon Schwartzman (New York: Bloomsbury, 2015).

11. ECLAC-UNESCO, *Conocimiento: Eje de la transformación productiva con equidad* (Santiago: 1992).

12. Fernando Fajnzylber, *Industrialization in Latin America: From the" Black box" to the "Empty box": A Comparison of Contemporary Industrialization Patterns* (Santiago: ECLAC, 1990).

13. ECLAC-UNESCO, *Conocimiento*, 157.

14. Ibid.

15. Jacqueline Gysling (academic at the Department of Pedagogical Studies at Universidad de Chile, coordinator of the social sciences area at the Ministry of Education during the high school curriculum reform (1996–2002), and coordinator of the curriculum area between 2006–2010), interview with author, 2014.

16. José Joaquin Brunner, *Informe de la Comisión Nacional para la modernización de la Educación: Los desafíos de la educación Chilena frente al siglo XXI* (Santiago: Editorial Universitaria, 1995.

17. Partnership for 21st Century Skills, *The Intellectual and Policy Foundations of the 21st Century Skills Framework*, 2007, http://youngspirit.org/docs/21stcentury.pdf.

18. Pacific Policy Research Center, *21st Century Skills.*

19. Binkley et al., *Defining Twenty-first Century Skills*; Pellegrino and Hilton, *Education for Life and Work.*

20. Brunner, *Informe de la Comisión Nacional.*

21. Richard J. Murnane and Frank Levy, *Teaching the New Basic Skills: Principles for Educating Children to Thrive in a Changing Economy* (New York: Free Press, 1996); R. Reich, *The work of nations* (New York: Knopf, 1991); European Commission, Directorate-General XXII, Training, and Youth, *Teaching and learning: towards the learning society*, vol. 42 (Office for Official Publications of the European Communities, 1996); OECD, *The curriculum redefined: Schooling for the 21st century* (Paris: OECD, 1994.

22. Cristián Cox, "Currículo escolar de Chile: génesis, implementación y desarrollo," *Revue International de Education de Sevres*, no. 56 (2011).

23. Leonor Cariola et al., *Educación media en el mundo: estructura y diseño curricular en diferentes países* (Santiago: Ministerio de Educación de Chile, Programa de Mejoramiento de la Calidad y Equidad de la Educación, 1994).

24. María José Lemaitre et al., "La reforma de la educación media," in *Políticas educacionales en el cambio de siglo. La reforma del sistema escolar de Chile*, ed. Cristián Cox (Santiago: Editorial Universitaria, 2003).

25. Chile, Ministerio de Educación, *Objetivos Fundamentales y Contenidos Mínimos Obligatorios de la Educación Media* (Santiago: 1998), 8.

26. Gysling, interview with author, 2014.

27. Ibid.; Chile, Ministerio de Educación,¿Cómo trabajar los Objetivos Fundamentales Transversales en el aula? Segundo Ciclo de Enseñanza Básica y Enseñanza Media (Santiago: 2003).

28. Cox, "Currículo escolar de Chile."

29. Pellegrino and Hilton, *Education for Life and Work.*

30. Chile, Ministerio de Educación, ¿Cómo trabajar los Objetivos Fundamentales?

31. José Pablo Arellano, *Reforma Educacional. Prioridad que se consolida* (Santiago: Los Andes, 2000); Sergio Bitar, *Educación. Nuestra Riqueza* (Santiago: El Mercurio / Aguilar, 2005).

32. Cristián Cox (Dean of the School of Education at Universidad Católica, director of the curriculum and evaluation unit of the Ministry of Education from 1998 to 2006), interview with author, 2014.

33. Martin Miranda, "Transformación de la educación media técnica profesional," in *Políticas educacionales en el cambio de siglo. La reforma del sistema escolar de Chile*, ed. Cristián Cox (Santiago: Editorial Universitaria, 2003).

34. Ibid., 386.

35. Ibid.

36. Binkley et al., *Defining Twenty-first Century Skills.*

37. Pellegrino and Hilton, *Education for Life and Work.*

38. UNESCO, *Global Citizenship Education. Preparing learners for the challenges of the 21st century* (Paris: UNESCO, 2014).

39. Martin Bascopé, Cristián Cox, and Robinson Lira, "Tipos de Ciudadanía en los Currículos del Autoritarismo y la Democracia," in *Aprendizaje de la ciudadanía. Contextos, Experiencias, Resultados*, ed. Cristián Cox and Juan Carlos Castillo, 245–282 (Santiago: Ediciones UC, 2015).

40. Cox, "Las políticas educacionales de Chile."

41. Jacqueline Gysling, "Reforma Curricular: Itinerario de una Transformación Cultural," in *Políticas Educacionales en el Cambio de Siglo. La Reforma del Sistema Escolar de Chile*, ed. Cristián Cox (Santiago: Editorial Universitaria, 2003).

42. Ibid.; Cox, "Currículo escolar de Chile."

43. Cox, "Las políticas educacionales de Chile."

44. Chile, Ministerio de Educación, *Formación ciudadana. Actividades de apoyo para el profesor* (Santiago: 2004).

45. Lemaitre et al., "La reforma de la educación media."

46. Fernando Reimers, "Civic education when democracy is in flux: The impact of empirical research on policy and practice in Latin America," *Citizenship and Teacher Education* 3, no. 2 (Dec. 2007).

47. Judith Torney-Purta and Jo-Ann Amadeo, *Strengthening Democracy in the Americas through Civic Education: An Empirical Analysis Highlighting the Views of Students and Teachers: Executive Summary* (Organization of American States, Social Development and Education Unit, 2004).

48. Raúl Zarzuri, "Jóvenes, participación y ciudadanía," in *Fortaleciendo la asesoría de los centros de alumnos y alumnas. Manual de apoyo* (Santiago: Ministerio de Educación de Chile, 2006).

49. Comisión Formación Ciudadana, *Informe Comisión Formación Ciudadana* (Santiago: Ministerio de educación de Chile, 2004).

50. This is still an issue in Chile: recently, a group of representatives proposed reintroducing a specific course on citizenship education in high school, as many countries do (Shultz 2009);
Chile, Ministerio de Educación, *Objetivos Fundamentales y contenidos Mínimos Obligatorios de la Educación Media y Media. Actualización 2009* (Santiago: 2009).

51. Cristián Cox and Carolina García, "Objetivos y contenidos de la formación ciudadana en Chile 1996–2013: tres curriculos comparados," in *Aprendizaje de la ciudadanía. Contextos, experiencias, resultados*, ed. Cristián Cox and Juan Carlos Castillo (Santiago: Ediciones UC, 2015), 283–320

52. Loreto Egaña et al., *Reforma Educativa y Objetivos Fundamentales Transversales. Los dilemas de la innovación* (Santiago: Programa interdisciplinario de Investigación en Educación, 2003).

53. Vásquez H. Cárcamo, "Importancia atribuida al desarrollo de la ciudadanía en la formación inicial docente," *Estudios Pedagógicos* 34, no. 2 (2008): 29–43; Carlos Muñoz and Bastián Torres, "La formación ciudadana en la escuela: Problemas y desafíos," *Revista Electrónica Educare* 18, no. 2 (mayo-agosto 2014): 233–245.

54. Ibid.

55. Egaña et al., *Reforma Educativa*; Muñoz and Torres, "La formación ciudadana."

56. Wolfram Shultz, *ICCS 2009 Latin American Report. Civic knowledge and attitudes among lower-secondary students in six Latin American countries* (Amsterdam: International Association for the Evaluation of Educational Achievement, 2011).

57. Bellei and Cabalin, "Chilean Student Movements."

58. Arellano, *Reforma Educacional*; Cristián Cox, "El Nuevo Currículum del Sistema Escolar," in *La educación en Chile, hoy*, ed. R. Hevia (Santiago: Ediciones Universidad Diego Portales, 2003), 117–135.

59. Lemaitre et al., "La reforma de la educación media," 357.

60. J. Edo García-Huidobro and Carmen Sotomayor, "La centralidad de la escuela en la política educativa chilena de los años noventa," in *Políticas educacionales en el cambio de siglo. La reforma del sistema escolar de Chile*, ed. C. Cox (Santiago: Editorial Universitaria, 2003); Lemaitre et al., "La reforma de la educación media," 357; Cristián Bellei, "¿Ha tenido impacto la Reforma Educativa Chilena?" in *Políticas educacionales en el cambio de siglo*, ed. C. Cox (Santiago: Editorial Universitaria, 2003), 125–209.

61. Mena and Bellei, "The New Challenge"; Bellei, "¿Ha tenido impacto la Reforma?"

62. Delannoy, *Education Reforms in Chile*; Carnoy, *Cuba's academic advantage*.

63. Gysling, interview with author, 2014.

64. Bárbara Eyzaguirre (Coordinator of Educational Studies and Standards from 2010 to 2014), interview with author, 2014; Bárbara Eyzaguirre and Loreto Fontaine, *El futuro en riesgo: nuestros textos escolares* (Santiago: Centro de Estudios Públicos, 1997).

65. Enlaces was a national program that introduced computers, software, and Internet, along with teachers' training, in almost all publicly funded schools. Pedro Hepp, "El programa de informática educativa de la reforma educacional chilena," in *Políticas educacionales en el cambio de siglo. La reforma del sistema escolar de Chile*, ed. C. Cox (Santiago: Editorial Universitaria, 2003).

66. Eyzaguirre, interview with author, 2014.

67. Gysling, interview with author, 2014.

68. Egaña et al., *Reforma Educativa*.

69. OECD, *Chile. Reviews of National Policies for Education* (Paris: OECD, 2004); Carnoy, *Cuba's academic advantage.*

70. Beatrice Ávalos, "La formación de profesores y su desarrollo profesional. Prácticas innovadoras en busca de políticas. El caso de Chile", in *Políticas educacionales en el cambio de siglo*, ed. C. Cox (Santiago: Editorial Universitaria, 2003); Beatrice Ávalos, "Formación inicial docente en Chile: calidad y políticas," in *Ecos de la revolución pingüina*, ed. Cristián Bellei, D. Contreras, and J. P. Valenzuela (Santiago: Editorial Pehuén, 2010).

71. Cox, "El Nuevo Currículum del Sistema Escolar."

72. Ávalos, "Formación inicial docente en Chile."

73. Cristián Bellei and Juan Pablo Valenzuela, "¿Están las condiciones para que la docencia sea una profesión de alto estatus en Chile?" in *Fin de Ciclo: Cambios en la Gobernanza del Sistema Educativo* (Santiago: Facultad de Educación, Pontificia Universidad Católica de Chile y Oficina Regional para América Latina y el Caribe UNESCO, 2010).

74. Jorge Manzi, "Programa INICIA: fundamentos y primeros avances," in *Ecos de la revolución pingüina*, ed. Cristián Bellei, D. Contreras, and J. P. Valenzuela (Santiago: Editorial Pehuén, 2010).

75. Lorena Meckes and Rafael Carrasco, "Two decades of SIMCE: an overview of the National Assessment System in Chile," *Assessment in Education: Principles, Policy and Practice* 17, no. 2 (2010): 233–248; Cox, interview with author, 2014.

76. Gysling, interview with author, 2014; Eyzaguirre, interview with author, 2014.

77. Bellei and Vanni, "The Evolution of Educational Policy;" Alejandro Carrasco, "Mecanismos performativos de la institucionalidad educativa en Chile: pasos hacia un nuevo sujeto cultural," *Observatorio Cultural*, 15, 2013.

78. Eyzaguirre, interview with author, 2014.

79. Cox, interview with author, 2014.

80. Bellei and Vanni, "The Evolution of Educational Policy."

81. Gysling, interview with author, 2014.

82. Cristián Bellei, "Supporting Instructional Improvement in Low-Performing Schools to Increase Students' Academic Achievement," *Journal of Educational Research* 106, no. 3 (2013): 235–248; Carmen Sotomayor, "Programas públicos de mejoramiento de la calidad de escuelas básicas en contextos urbanos vulnerables: evolución y aprendizajes de sus estrategias de intervención (1990–2005)," *Pensamiento Educativo* 39, no.2 (2006): 255–271.

83. Juan Cassasus, "Las Reformas Basadas en Estándares: un camino equivocado," in *Ecos de la revolución pingüina.* ed. Cristián Bellei, D. Contreras, and J. P. Valenzuela (Santiago: Editorial Pehuén, 2010); Espínola and Claro, "El Sistema Nacional;" Carrasco, "Mecanismos performativos."

84. Cox, interview with author, 2014.

85. Gysling, interview with author, 2014.

86. Juan Pablo Valenzuela et al., "¿Por qué los jóvenes chilenos mejoraron su competencia lectora en la prueba PISA?" in *Evidencias para Políticas Públicas en Educación* (Santiago: Ministerio de Educación de Chile, 2011), 265–311.

87. Eyzaguirre, interview with author, 2014.

88. Gysling, interview with author, 2014.

89. Eyzaguirre, interview with author, 2014.

90. José Joaquin Brunner (researcher at Universidad Diego Portales and UNESCO Chair for Comparative Higher Education Policies, former coordinator of the 1994 advisory committee of the Commission for the Modernization of the Education), interview with author, 2014.

91. Ibid.

92. Ibid.; Gysling, interview with author, 2014.

93. Eyzaguirre, interview with author, 2014.

94. Ibid.

95. Egaña et al., *Reforma Educativa*.

96. Eyzaguirre, interview with author, 2014.

97. Cristián Cox, "Políticas de reforma curricular en Chile," *Pensamiento Educativo* 29 (2001): 190.

98. Miranda, "Transformación de la educación."

99. Cox, interview with author, 2014.

100. Shultz, *ICCS 2009 Latin American Report*.

101. Bitar, *Educación. Nuestra Riqueza*.

102. Camila Pérez, "Promoción de ciudadanía en la escuela. Conceptualizaciones en textos escolares chilenos, 2005 y 2010" (Masters thesis in social sciences, University of Chile, 2013).

103. Shultz, *ICCS 2009 Latin American Report*.

CHAPTER FOUR

1. Parametría, "Carta Paramétrica," in *Encuesta Nacional en Vivienda*, 2013.

2. SEP, *Acuerdo número 592 por el que se establece la Articulación de la Educación Básica* (Mexico: Secretaría de Educación Pública, 2011).

3. As the former undersecretary for basic education declared, "The consultation resulted in the participation of nearly 7,428 citizens . . . and the inclusion of nearly 7,970 key ideas," Notimex, "Necesario que reforma educativa llegue a todos: Martínez Olivé," *El Economista*, June 12th, 2014, http://eleconomista.com.mx/sociedad/2014/06/12/necesario-que-reforma-educativa-llegue-todos-martinez-olive.

4. SEP, *Acuerdo número 592*.

5. Frida Díaz-Barriga, "Reformas curriculares y cambio sistémico: una articulación ausente pero necesaria para la innovación," *Revista Iberoamericana de Educación Superior*, 3, no. 7 (2012): 23–40.

6. SEP, *Acuerdo número 592*.

7. National Research Council, *Education for Life and Work: Developing Transferable Knowledge and Skills in the 21st Century*, ed. James Pellegrino and Margaret Hilton (Washington DC: The National Academies Press, 2012).

8. OECD, *21st Century Learning: Research, Innovation and Policy. Directions from recent OECD analyses* (Paris: Centre for Educational Research and Innovation, 2008).

9. National Research Council, *Education for Life and Work*.

10. Richard Elmore, *School Reform from the Inside Out: Policy, Practice, and Performance* (Cambridge, MA: Harvard Education Press, 2004).

11. Kiira Kärkkäinen, "Bringing About Curriculum Innovations: Implicit Approaches in the OECD Area (OECD Education Working Paper no. 82, OECD Publishing, 2012).

12. K. Ananiadou and M. Claro, *21st Century Competencies and Competences for New Millennium Learners in OECD Countries* (EDU working paper no. 41, OECD, 2009).

13. Martinic and Pardo, eds., *Economía Política de las reformas educativas en América Latina* (Santiago, Chile: CIDE-PREAL, 2001).

14. Instituto Nacional para la Evaluación de la Educación, *Panorama Educativo de México 2013: Indicadores del Sistema Educativo Nacional. Educación Básica y Media Superior* (México: INEE, 2014); OECD, *Education at a Glance 2013* (OECD, 2013); World Bank, *World Development Indicators*, 2015, http://data.worldbank.org/country/mexico.

15. Release of PISA results every three years since 2000 has raised concern among policy makers and NGOs, given that Mexico is constantly labeled as the OECD country with the worst performance, with a high concentration of examined students in the lowest performance levels (55% of students below or in level II for Reading, 46% of students concentrated in level I or less in the case of Science, and 53% of students in level I or less for Mathematics for 2012).

16. Centro de Investigación para el Desarrollo, A. C., *Encuesta de Competencias Profesionales 2014. ¿Qué buscan—y no encuentran—las empresas en los profesionistas jóvenes?* (México: CIDAC, 2014), http://www.cidac.org/esp/uploads/1/encuesta_competencias _profesionales_270214.pdf.

17. Secretaría de Desarrollo Económico Sustentable, *Estudio del Mercado Laboral en Guanajuato 2013. Identificación de Perfiles Laborales de los Sectores Automotriz, Metalmecánico y Plástico* (Mexico: SEDES, 2014).

18. Similar publications/projects were found in other states, like in the case of Nuevo León or Coahuila, although with a limited discussion about new competencies/skills to be promoted.

19. An additional effect related to the dissemination of PISA results is the public concern about whether high school graduates are acquiring relevant competencies for the labor market. Indeed, a curriculum reform has been implemented in the national high school system since 2008, defining goals related to developing eleven generic competencies, including some references to 21CC, like self-knowledge and metacognition, appreciation for arts, healthy lifestyle, effective communication, reflective thinking, teamwork, community participation, and respect for diversity. Although positive, recognizing the relevance of these competencies is still not enough to result in an enacted curriculum promoting the acquisition of new competencies, as data from the CIDAC study suggests, with 26% of surveyed business owners informed that open positions could not be filled despite having applications, due to the lack of knowledge and relevant competencies among applicants.

20. This sample (representative at the state level) was estimated with a two-stage probabilistic design (municipalities and schools), based on INEGI (2009), and it was administered with support from the Instituto de Financiamiento e Información para la Educación (EDUCAFIN). For more details, see Cárdenas, Arriaga, and Castrejón,"Evalución del programa de Uniformes Escolares" (unpublished paper, n.d.)

21. Tony Wagner, *The Global Achievement Gap: Why Even Our Best Schools Don't Teach the New Survival Competencies Our Children Need—and What We Can Do About It* (New York: Basic Books, 2008); Ananiadou and Claro, *21st Century Competencies*; National Research Council, *Education for Life and Work*; Mary Margaret Ruettgers, "A Content Analysis to Investigate the Evidence of 21st Century Knowledge and Competencies within Elementary Teacher Education Programs in the United States" (Ed.D. dissertation, Lindenwood University, 2013).

22. For example, see A. K. Lindell and E. Kidd, "Consumers favor 'Right Brain' training: The dangerous lure of neuromarketing," *Mind, Brain, and Education* 7, no. 1 (2013), 35–39.

23. This situation might be related as well to the use of different denominations for the same type of competencies, a problem documented and described by Pellegrino and Hilton (2012): The concept "21st century competencies" could be considered as an umbrella term, causing confusion among school actors about implications for the definition of learning goals.

24. R. Bolaños, "Orígenes de la educación pública en México", in *Historia de la Educación Pública en México*, ed. F. Solana, R. Cardiel, and R. Bolaños (México: Fondo de Cultura Económica, 1997), 11–40; Meneses, "El Saber Educativo," in *Un Siglo de Educación en México*, P. Latapí (México: Fondo de Cultura Económica-CONACULTA, 1998) 9–45; Miranda, "La reforma curricular de la Educación Básica," in *Los Grandes Problemas de México,* vol. 7, *Educación*, ed. Arnaut y Giorguli (México: El Colegio de México, 2010).

25. Diaz-Barriga, "Reformas curriculares y cambio sistémico: una articulación ausente pero necesaria para la innovación," *Revista Iberoamericana de Educación Superior* 3, no. 7 (2012): 23–40.

26. Ananiadou and Claro, *21st Century Competencies*.

27. SEP, *Acuerdo número 592.*

28. National Research Council, *Education for Life and Work.*

29. Ibid.

30. For the purpose of this study it will be conducted using only "documentary evidence" (Ariav, 1986), thus avoiding observation of practice or examination of how results are assessed. In addition, "curriculum" is considered for this study as the set of materials guiding instructional practices: textbooks, teachers´ handbooks ("Guías del maestro"), and study plans.

31. Cecilia Plaza et al., "Curriculum mapping in program assessment and evaluation," *American Journal of Pharmaceutical Education* 71, no. 2 (2007): 20; Richard T. Houang and William H. Schmidt, "TIMSS international curriculum analysis and

measuring educational opportunities" (paper presented at 3rd IEA International Research Conference, Taiwan Normal University, Taipei, 2008); Ruettgers, "A Content Analysis."

32. Kathleen Carley, "Coding choices for textual analysis: A comparison of content analysis and map analysis," in *Sociological methodology*, ed. P. Marsden (Oxford: Blackwell, 1993), 75–126.

33. Bruce L. Berg, *Qualitative research methods for the social sciences* (Boston: Allyn and Bacon, 2001).

34. Philip J. Stone et al., *The general inquirer: A computer approach to content analysis* (Cambridge, MA: MIT Press, 1966); Kimberly A. Neuendorf, *The Content Analysis Guidebook* (Thousand Oaks, CA: Sage Publications, 2002).

35. National Research Council, *Education for Life and Work*; The search for "message units" was implemented through a two-stage process. In the first stage, *"a priori"* coding was conducted (Stemler, 2001) defining *operational terms* from textbooks and teachers' reference materials, based on a review using the concepts included in the "clusters of closely related competencies," developed by Hilton and Pellegrino after conducting a content analysis of eight relevant reports (see Appendix B in Hilton and Pellegrino (2012)). Once several *operational terms* were identified (table 4.1), a thorough review of textbooks and teachers' reference materials for all six grades and subjects was conducted based on this list, to identify ELO related to 21st century skills within subjects and grades.

36. Although by design it is assumed teachers will integrate competencies across all subjects and grades, the review showed that two competencies are dominant across the textbooks (teamwork and use of ICT). For instance, students are constantly requested to collaborate during lessons with peers, to discuss and present findings about specific topics or search for information in websites designed by the Ministry of Education. However, little guidance is provided about how to *develop* the arguments to be discussed among peers, or how to *manage information* or *produce innovations* in the classroom. Furthermore, textbooks emphasize homogenous processes that might well pose additional challenges for teachers willing to adapt activities for students with different ethnic or cultural background, thus compromising respect for diversity.

37. Expected learning outcomes are concrete descriptions of goals to be achieved through instruction and classroom activities in each of the subjects to be taught in primary education level.

38. National Research Council, *Education for Life and Work*.

39. Based on Plaza et al., "Curriculum mapping," 20; also based on Andrew W. Porter and John L. Smithson, "From policy to practice: The evolution of one approach to describing and using curriculum data," in *Towards coherence between classroom assessment and accountability*, ed. M. Wilson (Chicago: National Society for the Study of Education, 2004).

40. Only in the case of Language for the 4th grade is a balanced distribution of ELO21 observed across the three domains identified by Pellegrino and Hilton (2012).

41. National Research Council, *Education for Life and Work*.

42. Regarding participation of public officials in public debates about contents and educational goals, incidental references to concepts related to 21CC are frequently observed in the media. For instance, in many occasions while explaining the orientation of the curriculum for basic education implemented since 2011, it was argued that Mexico was abandoning "root learning" for a "competencies based" curriculum that would provide "competencies necessary for a globalized environment." However, it is likely that ambiguous references to 21CC may be explained by the condition suggested by Ananiadou and Claro (2009), where clear definitions/classifications of 21CC were often absent among public officials.

43. Roger A. Hart, *Children's Participation: From Tokenism to Citizenship*, Innocenti Essay 4 (Florence: UNICEF Innocenti Research Center, 1992), http://www.unicef-irc.org/publications/pdf/childrens_participation.pdf.

44. National Research Council, *Education for Life and Work*.

45. F. Froy, S. Giguère, and M. Meghnagi , "Skills for Competitiveness: A Synthesis Report" (OECD Local Economic and Employment Development (LEED) Working Papers, 2012/09, OECD Publishing, 2012), http://dx.doi.org/10.1787/5k98xwskmvr6-en.

46. Andrew C. Porter and John L. Smithson, "Are content standards being implemented in the classroom? A methodology and some tentative answers," in *From the capitol to the classroom: Standards-based reform in the states. One hundredth yearbook of the National Society for the Study of Education, Part 2*, ed. S. H. Fuhrman (Chicago: University of Chicago Press, 2001), 60–80.

47. Diaz-Barriga, "Reformas curriculares y cambio sistémico." 23–40.

CHAPTER FIVE

We would like to thank Mr. Ajay Piramal, chairman of the Piramal Group, for supporting this research. We gratefully acknowledge all those we interviewed during our research for giving us their valuable input and insights. This includes officials of the government of India and of the Gujarat and Rajasthan state governments. We would like to specially mention the following people: Goverdhan Mehta, research scientist and professor, School of Chemistry, University of Hyderabad; Rohit Dhankar, dean of education, Azim Premji University; Atul D. Patel, chairman, Surat School Board; Hitesh J. Makheja, administrative officer, Surat School Board; Shyam S. Agrawal, Rajasthan state additional chief secretary, State School Education, Sanskrit Education, Higher Education and Technical Education; Hanuman Singh Bhati, Rajasthan state project director; Sarva Shiksha Abhiyan; Swami Swatmanand, director (West Zone) of All India Chinmaya Yuva Kendra Council, Chinmaya Mission; Reena Das, director, Digantar; Ramlal Gurjar, teacher, Digantar; Sunita, teacher, Digantar; Elizabeth Mehta, founder, Muktangan; Kiran Parab, teacher trainer, Socioemotional Development Department, Muktangan; Jayanthi Nayak, teacher trainer, science department, Muktangan; Purvi Vora, founding partner at Reniscience Education; Tamara Philip, teacher and coordinator, Avsara Leadership Fellows; Stephen Philip, math teacher, Avsara Leadership Fellows;

Rohit Kumar, manager, Service Learning Programme, Akanksha Foundation; Poorvi Shah, director of student enrichment, Akanksha Foundation; Usha Pandit, founder, Mindsprings; Rajesh Jain, founder and managing director, Netcore Solutions Pvt Ltd; Nirav Modi, founder, Nirav Modi Foundation; Vivek Sharma, program director, Piramal Foundation; Niraj Lele, program director, Piramal Foundation; Manmohan Singh, program director, Piramal Foundation; and Nandita Raval, program director, Piramal Foundation, for their contributions.

Additionally, our research tries to understand the concerted efforts of innumerable school teachers and education officials of India, who face the complex challenge of bringing school education to millions of children from diverse socioeconomic and cultural backgrounds in India. We thank them for their efforts and for informing and contributing toward this research.

We also thank Lopa Gandhi for supporting the research team. We give thanks also to staff and team members of the Piramal Foundation and our families for supporting us during our research work and travel.

1. National Council of Educational Research and Training, *National Curriculum Framework (NCF) 2005* (New Delhi: NCERT, 2005), http://www.ncert.nic.in/rightside /links/pdf/framework/english/nf2005.pdf.

2. National Research Council, *Education for Life and Work: Developing Transferable Knowledge and Skills in the 21st Century,* ed. James Pellegrino and Margaret Hilton (Washington, DC: National Academies Press, 2012).

3. Michael Fullan, *Change Theory: A Force for School Improvement* (Victoria: Centre for Strategic Education, 2006).

4. Ministry of Human Resource Development, *National Policy on Education 1968* (New Delhi: MHRD 1968), http://mhrd.gov.in/sites/upload_files/mhrd/files/ document-reports/NPE-1968.pdf.

5. Government of India, *The Right of Children to Free and Compulsory Education (RTE) Act, 2009* (New Delhi: 2009), http://ssa.nic.in/rte-docs/free%20and%20compulsory.pdf.

6. These practitioners are education professionals who have been practicing a definite pedagogy, teaching-learning process, in their classrooms and have also been through a process of self-change required in a teaching professional for 21st century learning.

7. One of the policy makers has been a critical contributor to the making of NCF2005, the second policy maker has been a significant contributor to many committees initiated by the Central Government for secondary and higher education.

8. The business leaders are entrepreneurs who have grown their businesses on scale and are critical recruiters of professionals; their perspectives on human capabilities required in the current work world in the country provided a direction in locating "work-centered" education in NCF2005.

9. All the government leaders were officials at the state level, their understanding of the curricular goals and their responsibilities towards 21st century learning contributed

to our understanding of the complexities of decision making involved in their roles and responsibilities.

10. Education Leadership development is a new area in the Indian Education System. Some education professionals have turned to initiating change in student learning outcomes via education leadership development. Their perspectives helped us locate the gaps in the system. It helped us articulate that the Indian legislature provides for progressive policies, but implementation is dependent on mind-sets that are trained in the traditional system.

11. Previous revisions to the National Curriculum Framework took place in 1975, 1988, and 2000.

12. "Disadvantaged and weaker sections of society" includes those who come from the lower and backward castes, tribes, and economically weaker classes.

13. India has 29 states and 7 Union Territories and follows a federal system, where the national policy guides states; however different state governments are free to design their own policy formulations as per their local requirements and contexts, in line with the larger national policy guidelines.

14. Caste-based segregation / Untouchability: This was an ancient Indian practice, endorsed by Hindu religion wherein those belonging to the lower castes were treated as impure, segregated, and not touched to maintain purity. Those belonging to the lower castes were restricted to ghettos usually outside the main village. Menial scavenging work and labor was the main source of livelihood for those from lower castes.

15. The Hindu community was divided according to nature of work: the upper castes were the Brahmins who were associated with intellectual work of spiritual and religious nature, the Kshatriyas were associated with the warrior class, the Vaishyas belonged to the trading and business community, and the Shudras formed the lowest rung of the society. Gradually the caste system became pervasive in the Indian society.

16. The National Policy on Education Programme of Action 1992 gives emphasis to work-related education and emphasizes training youth for self-employment. The same is also recommended by the National Focus Group members in the Position Paper of Work and Education. MHRD, *National Policy on Education 1986: Programme of Action 1992* (New Delhi: 1992), 12, 17, http://rajshiksha.gov.in/Education_Policy_1992.pdf; NCERT, *Position Paper: National Focus Group on Work and Education* (New Delhi: 2007), 13, http://www.ncert.nic.in/new_ncert/ncert/rightside/links/pdf/focus_group/workeducation.pdf.

17. The National Policy on Education (NPE) is a policy formulated by the Government of India to guide the states and union territories in their education policy; the first NPE was drafted in 1968, the second in 1986; the most recent one, in 1992, is called the Programme of Action (POA) of NPE.

18. MHRD, *National Policy on Education 1986* (New Delhi: 1986).

19. Planning Commission, *Eighth Five Year Plan (1992–1997)*, vol. 2 (New Delhi), http://planningcommission.nic.in/plans/planrel/fiveyr/8th/vol2/8v2ch11.htm.

20. The period after the introduction of India's new economic policy of 1991 is referred to as the post-liberalized era.

21. MHRD, *Programme of Action 1992*

22. Ibid., 6.

23. NCERT, *Work and Education*, 2.

24. National University of Education and Planning and Administration, *School Education in India 2013–14 Statistics Report* (New Delhi), http://www.dise.in/.

25. NCERT, *NCF2005*; Rohit Dhankar, personal communication, August 2014.

26. NCERT, *Work and Education*.

27. Ibid., 2–3, 113.

28. Ibid., 44. This example is about the children of the Adharshila School at Village Saakad, near Sendhwa, Distt. Badwani, Madhya Pradesh, where children learn from being actively engaged in community life.

29. NCF position paper Work and Education pg. 39 cites the example of a municipal school in Karad in Satara District (Maharashtra) where teachers invited local artisans including Seetaram the carpenter as teacher to teach basic geometry and maths to children

30. NCERT, *Work and Education*, 39.

31. NCERT, *Position Paper: National Focus Group on Teaching of Mathematics* (New Delhi: 2006), http://www.ncert.nic.in/new_ncert/ncert/rightside/links/pdf/focus_group/math.pdf; NCERT, *Standard 3 Mathematics Textbook* (New Delhi), 43, http://www.ncert.nic.in/NCERTS/textbook/textbook.htm?cemh1=0-14.

32. National Council for Education Research and Training published textbooks that are aligned to the NCF2005. The current examples are taken from the NCERT, *Standard 5 Environment Studies Textbook* (New Delhi), ch. 6, http://www.ncert.nic.in/ncerts/textbook/textbook.htm?eeap1=0-22 and NCERT, *Standard 4 Environment Studies Textbook* (New Delhi), ch. 16, http://www.ncert.nic.in/ncerts/textbook/textbook.htm?deap1=0-27.

33. Bal-Sabha is a children's conference usually held in school wherein children get together for discussions, games, activities, etc.

34. Bal-Sansad: Many state governments in India have made formation of the children's parliament or the Bal-Sansad compulsory for all schools so that it promotes a child-friendly environment in the schools.

35. NCERT, *Position Paper: National Focus Group on Teaching of Indian Languages* (New Delhi: 2006), 7, 16, 20, 25, 31–2, http://www.ncert.nic.in/new_ncert/ncert/rightside/links/pdf/focus_group/Indian_Languages.pdf.

36. A school run in Uttarakhand by an organization called Society for Integrated Development of Himalayas uses this method to teach children using local knowledge systems of the community.

37. NCERT, *Position Paper: National Focus Group on Education for Peace* (New Delhi: 2006), 5, http://www.ncert.nic.in/new_ncert/ncert/rightside/links/pdf/focus_group/education_for_peace.pdf.

38. Ibid., 4–6.

39. Based on analysis of information about poor students learning outcomes from 1. Annual Status of Education Reports (ASER reports), 2. Students learning outcomes data from Education Initiatives conducted across various schools.

40. Rohit Dhankar, personal communication, August 2014.

41. The NCF2005 specifies recommended pedagogy and curricular content; it does not provide mandatory guidelines. As a result many state board and private publishing companies publish textbooks that are not fully aligned to NCF2005 vision.

42. NCERT, *NCF2005*, 9.

43. Digantar, http://www.digantar.org/.

44. Ibid.

45. Ibid.

46. NCERT, *Work and Education*.

47. Lend-a-Hand India, http://www.lend-a-hand-india.org/.

48. Ibid.

49. "Multimedia Archives eServcies," UNESCO, http://www.unesco.org/archives /multimedia/.

50. NCERT, *NCF2005*; Barefoot College, www.barefootcollege.org; Center for Education Innovations, http://educationinnovations.org/.

51. Barefoot College, www.barefootcollege.org; Center for Education Innovations, http://educationinnovations.org/.

52. Ibid.

53. NCERT, *NCF2005*; Design for Change, http://www.dfcworld.com/.

54. Design for Change, http://www.dfcworld.com/.

55. "Review of Social Studies Textbooks," Asha for Education, http://www.ashanet .org/projects/project-view.php?p=483.

56. National Council of Educational Research and Training (NCERT) is an autonomous organization set up in 1961 by the Government of India to assist and advise the Central and State Governments on policies and programmes for qualitative improvement in school education: http://aises.nic.in/aboutncert.

57. Vatsala Shrangi, "NCERT to Review Books for Gender Inclusion," *Sunday Guardian*, Sept. 20, 2014, http://www.sunday-guardian.com/news/ncert-to-review -textbooks-for-gender-inclusion.

58. National Council for Teacher Education (NCTE), "Guidelines for Conducting Teacher Eligibilty Test (TET), Under the Right of Children to Free and Compulsory Education Act (RTE), 2009," Government circular to education officials, Feb. 11, 2011, http://www.ncte-india.org/RTE-TET-guidelines[1]%20(latest).pdf.

59. The National Policy on Education (NPE), 1986, and the Programme of Action thereunder, envisaged a National Council for Teacher Education with statutory status and necessary resources as a first step for overhauling the system of teacher education.

60. Ibid.

61. Vyjayanthi Shankar and Ritesh Mishra, "Executive Summary," in *A Status Report on Teacher Assessments, Especially in the Context of Nalanda Bihar* (New Delhi: USAID, 2011), http://www.teindia.nic.in/e9-tm/Files/Status-of-Teacher-Assessments-Exec -Summary-high_Bihar.pdf.

62. NCTE, "Background" and "Context, Concerns, and Challenges of Teacher Education," in *Curriculum Framework on Teacher Education* (New Delhi), http://www.ncte -india.org/curriculumframework/curriculum.htm.

63. *Status of District Institutes of Education and Training: A Brief Report on the State of DIETs* (Azim Premji Foundation, 2010), http://www.azimpremjifoundation.org/pdf /Status%20Report%20on%20DIET.pdf.

64. Shankar and Mishra, "Executive Summary."

65. *State of DIETS*, http://www.azimpremjifoundation.org/pdf/Status%20Report %20on%20DIET.pdf.

66. Prema Clarke, "Culture and Classroom Reform: The Case of the District Primary Education Project, India," *Comparative Education* 39, no. 1 (2003): 36–40.

67. NCERT, *NCF2005*.

68. N. V. Varghese, "A Note on State Institute of Education Management and Training (SIEMAT)" (paper presented at a Seminar on State, School and Community—Role of Educational Management and Training in a Changing Perspective, Bihar, Patna, March 20–21, 1999), http://www.educationforallinindia.com/page109.html.

69. Ibid.

70. Fullan, *Change Theory*, 10.

71. Joanne Robinson, "Dynamic Leadership: The Key to 21st Century Graduates," *Queensland Principal* 41, no.1 (March 2014): 13–16, http://www.chicagomanualofstyle .org.ezp-prod1.hul.harvard.edu/16/ch14/ch14_sec180.html; Joanne Robinson, "Mentoring and Coaching School Leaders: A Qualitiative Study of Adapative Expertise for School Administrators," http://www.principals.ca/documents/Mentoring_and_Coaching_School _Leaders-Joanne%20Robinson-OPC_Register_Vol.13_No.2.pdf; Ontario Principals Council, *Preparing Principals and Developing School Leadership Associations for the 21st Century: Lessons from Around the World*, http://www.principals.ca/documents/International %20Symposium%20White%20Paper%20-%20OPC%202014.pdf; Nandita Raval, Niraj Lele, Vivek Sharma, and Manmohan Singh, personal communication, December 2014.

72. Ibid, 14.

73. Fullan, *Change Theory*, 8.

74. Ibid., 10.

75. Ibid., 9.

76. Ibid., 4.

77. Robinson, *Instructional Leadership*, 9.

78. NCTE, National Curriculum Framework for Teacher Education 2009, (New Delhi: 2009), http://www.azimpremjifoundation.org/pdf/NCFTE-2010.pdf.

CHAPTER SIX

We would like to thank the Jacobs Foundation for funding this research. We also would like to thank the following people for sharing their insights for this chapter: Mitchell Chester, Cliff Chuang, Eric Conti, Paul Dakin, Nick Donahue, David Driscoll, Ken Kay, Patrick Larkin, Linda Noonan, Paul Reville, Shailah Stewart, Paul Toner, and Keith Westrich.

1. James P. Comer and Henry Louis Gates, *Leave No Child Behind : Preparing Today's Youth for Tomorrow's World* (New Haven, CT: Yale University Press, 2004).

2. National Research Council, *Education for Life and Work: Developing Transferable Knowledge and Skills in the 21st Century,* ed. James Pellegrino and Margaret Hilton (Washington, DC: National Academies Press, 2012).

3. Allison Henward and Jeanne Marie Iorio, "What's Teaching and Learning got to do with it?: Bills, Competitions, and Neoliberalism in the Name of Reform," *Teachers College Record* 16159 (Aug. 25, 2011).

4. US Department of Education, "Policy," ED.gov, http://www2.ed.gov/policy/landing.jhtml?src=pn.

5. Department of Education Organization Act. Public Law 96-88.

6. One only needs to review the history of the Boston busing crisis that took place in response to the Massachusetts 1965 Racial Imbalance Act, which ordered public schools in the state to desegregate, to see an example (Lukas, 1986).

7. Massachusetts, and the United States as a whole, has encouraged community participation and educational innovation through a number of additional programs. One is a program that allows the creation of publicly funded and privately managed schools that are exempt from some of the regulatory requirements of public schools, with the goal of allowing innovation and of providing parents' choice about the educational institution their children would attend. The creation of charter schools in Massachusetts followed the national Charter School Movement, in allowing qualified private groups or organizations to apply for a charter for a limited period that would allow them to receive public education funds, provided they met some regulations and achieved some predetermined educational outcomes. The Massachusetts Department of Education extended the freedoms of charter schools to some district-managed schools, embedding all of them in an Innovations School Initiative. To date, charters and innovation schools have been evaluated primarily with respect to their capacity to support students in learning in the domains of language and mathematics, and they have not been seen as primary instruments to innovate in delivering a 21st century skill curriculum, or in terms of the ambitious definition of college and career readiness recently adopted by the Departments of Elementary and Secondary Education and of Higher Education.

8. Comer and Gates, *Leave No Child Behind.*

9. Robert F. Butts, *Public education in the United States : From revolution to reform* (New York: Holt, Rinehart and Winston, 1978).

10. Chara H. Bohan and Wesley J. Null, "Gender and the evolution of normal school education: A historical analysis of teacher education institutions," *Journal of Educational Foundations* 21, no. 3 (2007): 3–26.

11. C. D. Wright, Sir William Mather, E. Swaysland, and C. F. Warner. *Report of the Commission on Industrial and Technical Education: Submitted in accordance with resolve approved May 24, 1905* (Boston: Wright and Potter Print. Co., state printers, 1906).

12. Diane Ravitch, *Left Back : A Century of Failed School Reforms* (New York: Simon and Schuster, 2000).

13. United States Congress Senate Committee on Labor and Public Welfare, *The National Defense Education Act of 1958; A Summary and Analysis of the Act* (Washington, DC: U.S. Govt. Print. Off, 1958).

14. Joel Klein and Condoleezza Rice, *US Education Reform and National Security* (Washington DC: Council on Foreign Relations, 2012), 3.

15. National Commission on Excellence in Education, *A Nation at Risk : The Imperative for Educational Reform: A Report to the Nation and the Secretary of Education, United States Department of Education* (Washington, DC: National Commission on Excellence in Education, 1983).

16. Ernest L. Boyer and Carnegie Foundation for the Advancement of Teaching, *High school : A report on secondary education in America* (New York: Harper and Row, 1983).

17. Committee for Economic Development Research and Policy Committee, *Investing in our children: Business and the public schools* (Washington, DC: Committee for Economic Development, 1985).

18. *PBS's Frontline*, "Standards—Are We There Yet?" http://www.pbs.org/wgbh/pages /frontline/shows/schools/standards/bp.html.

19. Ibid.

20. New York State Archives, http://nysa32.nysed.gov/edpolicy/research/res_essay _johnson_cole.shtml.

21. In 2012, the state of Massachusetts had a total elementary and secondary student population of 955,739 in 408 school districts. There are a total number of 70,489 teachers, making the student to teacher ratio 13.6 to 1. Combining all types of public schools together, the total number reaches 1,860 schools. In addition, Massachusetts has 81 charter schools. In 2012, the total expenditure of the state Department of Education was $13.3 billion, which comes to $13,636 per student spending.

22. Massachusetts Department of Elementary and Secondary Education, "Massachusetts Students Score among World Leaders in Assessment of Reading, Mathematics, and Science Literacy," http://www.doe.mass.edu/news/news.aspx?id=7886.

23. National Center for Education Statistics, *Program for International Student Assessment*

(PISA)—Overview, Institute of Education Sciences, http://nces.ed.gov/surveys/pisa/.

24. Paul Dakin, Superintendent of Revere Public Schools (2013 MA superintendent of the year), interview with authors, 2014.

25. Ibid.

26. *Massachusetts Statement Against High-Stakes Testing*, http://matestingstatement
.wordpress.com/statement/.

27. *Washington Post*, http://www.washingtonpost.com/blogs/answer-sheet/wp/2013
/02/22/massachusetts-professors-protest-high-stakes-standardized-tests/.

28. Michael Hout and Stewart Eliott, eds., *Incentives and Test-based Accountability in
Education* (Washington, DC: National Academies Press, 2011).

29. *A Nation at Risk*, Ed.gov (archived), 1985, https://www2.ed.gov/pubs/NatAtRisk
/risk.html.

30. US Department of Education, *Overview and Mission Statement*, ED.gov, 2014,
http://www2.ed.gov/about/landing.jhtml?src=ft.

31. In 2010, Governor Patrick signed into law the Achievement Gap Act, which requires the state's lowest performing schools—called Level 4 schools—to include strategies
for addressing the nonacademic needs of students as part of their school redesign plans,
http://archives.lib.state.ma.us/bitstream/handle/2452/125361/ocn795183245-2010-01
-18.PDF?sequence=1.

32. National Research Council, *Education for Life and Work*, 3.

33. At the time this organization began working with Massachusetts, they were
known as Partnership for 21st Century Skills; currently (2015), they are known as Partnership for 21st Century Learning. We will use the name Partnership for 21st Century
Learning in this chapter.

34. A result of the 1993 Reform Act, the Massachusetts Curriculum Frameworks
have been, along with the Massachusetts Comprehensive Assessment System, the most explicit policy instruments to define the knowledge and skills students should gain during
their compulsory education, from kindergarten to high school. The frameworks consist of
descriptions of objectives of knowledge and skills students should gain, but they are not a
detailed curriculum and do not outline specific pedagogies that can help gain such knowledge; rather, they provide guidance, by subject and by grade, detailing the expectations of
the content to be covered in instruction. Based on these standards, school districts, departments within schools, and teachers are expected to plan their curriculum and lesson
plans, and to decide on which instructional materials and textbooks to use.

35. Massachusetts Department of Elementary and Secondary Education, *Massachusetts Curriculum Framework for Mathematics: Grades pre-Kindergarten to 12, Incorporating
the Common Core State Standards for Mathematics* (MA Department of Elementary and
Secondary Education, 2011).

36. Massachusetts Department of Elementary and Secondary Education, *Massachusetts History and Social Studies Curriculum Framework* (MA Department of Elementary
and Secondary Education, 2003), 54.

37. For more explanation about Bloom's Taxonomy, see for example: https://cft
.vanderbilt.edu/guides-sub-pages/blooms-taxonomy/.

38. See for example, the curriculum that Expeditionary Learning developed for New
York State, based on the Common Core: https://www.engageny.org/.

39. *Massachusetts Curriculum Framework for Mathematics*, 90.

40. *Massachusetts History and Social Studies Curriculum Framework*, 89.

41. William Mathis, *Research-based options for education policymaking* (Boulder, CO: National Education Policy Center, 2013).

42. US Department of Education, *For each and every child: A strategy for education equity and excellence* (Washington, DC: US Department of Education, 2013).

43. Hout and Eliott, eds, *Incentives and test-based accountability*, S-4.

44. Michael Barber and Simon Day, *The new opportunity to lead: A vision for education in Massachusetts in the next 20 years* (Massachusetts Business Alliance for Education, 2014).

45. Ibid, 2–3.

46. Ibid., 2.

47. Massachusetts Department of Elementary and Secondary Education, *Task Force Recommends Integration of 21st Century Skills* (2008), http://www.doe.mass.edu/news /news.aspx?id=4429.

48. Ibid.

49. Massachusetts Department of Elementary and Secondary Education, *Statement of Secretary of Education, Paul Reville, on the Report of the Task Force on 21st Century Skills*, http://www.doe.mass.edu/news/news.aspx?id=4434.

50. Massachusetts Department of Elementary and Secondary Education, *Task Force Recommends Integration of 21st Century Skills Throughout K12 System*, http://www.doe .mass.edu/news/news.aspx?id=4429.

51. MA Department of Elementary and Secondary Education, *Integration of 21st Century Skills*, 23.

52. Pioneer Institute, *Our Mission*, http://pioneerinstitute.org/pioneers-mission.

53. Pioneer Institute, *A Step Backwards: An Analysis of the 21st Century Skills Task Force Report*, *Policy Brief* (Boston: Pioneer Institute, 2009), http://pioneerinstitute.org /download/a-step-backwards-an-analysis-of-the-21st-century-skills-task-force-report/.

54. Ibid., 1.

55. Ibid., 2.

56. US Department of Education, *President Obama, US Secretary of Education Duncan Announce National Competition to Advance School Reform*, ED.gov (archived), 2009, http://www2.ed.gov/news/pressreleases/2009/07/07242009.html.

57. US Department of Education, *Nine States and District of Columbia Win Second Round Race to the Top Grants*, ED.gov (archived), 2010, http://www.ed.gov/news/press -releases/nine-states-and-district-columbia-win-second-round-race-top-grants.

58. Paul Reville (former Secretary of Education for the Commonwealth of Massachusetts), interview with authors.

59. Massachusetts Department of Elementary and Secondary Education, *From Cradle to Career: Educating our Student for Lifelong Success*, 5, Mass.gov, www.doe.mass.edu /ccr/ccrta/2012-06BESEReport.docx .

60. Ibid.

61. Massachusetts Department of Elementary and Secondary Education, *Connecting Activities—Massachusetts School to Career*, Mass.gov, http://www.doe.mass.edu /connect/; Keith Westrich (Connecting Activities Director at the Massachusetts Department of Elementary and Secondary Education), interview with authors, 2014; Shailah Stewart (Coordinator of Connecting Activities at Massachusetts Department of Elementary and Secondary Education), interview with authors, 2014.

62. http://www.doe.mass.edu/ccr/.

63. Ken Kay (former president of 21 Partnerships for Learning and current leader of Edleader21), interview with authors, 2014.

64. Paul Reville, personal communication, July 10, 2014.

65. Paul Dakin, interview with authors, 2014.

66. Ibid.

CONCLUSION

1. William Mathis, *Research-based options for education policymaking* (Boulder, CO: National Education Policy Center, 2013).

2. US Department of Education, *For each and every child: A strategy for education equity and excellence* (Washington, DC: US Department of Education, 2013).

3. Albert Bandura, *Self-Efficacy : The Exercise of Self-Control* (New York : W.H. Freeman, 1997); Albert Bandura, "Social Cognitive Theory: An Agentic Perspective," *Annual Review of Psychology* (2001): 1.

4. Howard Gardner, *Frames of mind: the theory of multiple intelligences* (New York: Basic Books, 1983).

5. Carol Dweck, *Mindset* (London : Robinson, 2012).

6. Angela Duckworth, "Significance of self-control," *Proceedings of the National Academy of Sciences of the United States of America* 108, no. 7 (2011): 2639–2640; Angela Duckworth, Eli Tsukayama, and Teri Kirby, "Is It Really Self-Control? Examining the Predictive Power of the Delay of Gratification Task," *Personality and Social Psychology Bulletin* 39, no. 7 (2013): 843–855.

7. Roberta Ness, *Genius Unmasked* (New York : Oxford University Press, 2013); Ken Robinson, *Out of Our Minds: Learning to be Creative* (New York : John Wiley, 2001).

8. Claudia Madrazo, "The *dia* Program: The Development of Intelligence through Art," in *International Perspectives on the Goals of Universal Basic and Secondary Education*, ed. Joel Cohen and Martin Malin (New York : Routledge, 2009); Fernando Reimers, Maria Elena Ortega, Mariali Cardenas, Armando Estrada, and Emanuel Garza, "Empowering Teaching for Participatory Citizenship. Evaluating Alternative Civic Education Pedagogies in Secondary School in Mexico," *Journal of Social Science Education* 13, no. 4 (Winter 2014), http://www.jsse.org/index.php/jsse/article/view/1357/1452.

ACKNOWLEDGMENTS

Based at the Harvard Graduate School of Education, the Global Education Innovation Initiative is a collaborative of researchers and practitioners from six institutions in Chile, China, India, Mexico, Singapore, and the United States. A complex and ambitious international research collaborative like this one requires support from many people and we are very appreciative not only of the material support we have received from many colleagues, but especially for their trust in the potential of a cross-national collaborative to advance our understanding of the ways in which schools can prepare students to gain the competencies they need to thrive throughout their lives.

We are grateful to our founding partners who enthusiastically responded to our invitation to collaborate with us to plan and execute this ambitious research project: Cristián Bellei and Liliana Morawietz from the Center for Advanced Research in Education, at the University of Chile; Yan Wang from the National Institute of Education Sciences in China; Monal Jayaram and Aditya Natraj from the Piramal Foundation in India; Sergio Cárdenas from the Center for Economics Research and Teaching (CIDE) in Mexico; and Ee-Ling Low and Oon-Seng Tan from the National Institute of Education in Singapore. The learning journey we have traveled together has been immensely rewarding and we look forward to the continuation of this collaboration.

We are also grateful to the members of our advisory board who provided advice as we conceptualized this research collaborative and got it off the ground: Jim Champy, Arjun Gupta, Charito Kruvant, Luther Luedtke, Charles MacCormack, Leonard Schlesinger, and David Weinstein. Their enthusiastic support at the outset of this initiative was critical to helping us launch it.

We received financial support for this project from a number of sources. We would like to thank the former dean of the Harvard Graduate School of Education, Kathleen McCartney, for providing the seed funding for this initiative, and the current dean, Jim Ryan, for his continuing support. We would also like to thank the Jacobs Foundation and Simon Sommer, our project officer, for their generous support of our research and for their dedicated commitment to the overall purpose of our initiative. Thanks are due as well to M. Charito Kruvant for her generous stewardship and support, and to the David Rockefeller Center for Latin American Studies at Harvard University for their financial support.

At our institutional home, the Harvard Graduate School of Education, we are grateful to many good colleagues whose trust in the value of this work enabled us to launch the Global Education Innovation Initiative. In particular, we want to thank those colleagues in the leadership team who assisted us in various ways and rooted for us when we needed it: Jack Jennings, Keith Collar, and Daphne Layton for their overall support of the initiative. We are indebted to Douglas Clayton and his colleagues Christopher Leonesio, Laura Cutone, and Christina DeYoung at Harvard Education Publishing for a wonderful partnership in publishing this book. We look forward to many more. We thank Allie Ai, Gino Benjamino, Janet Cascarano, Jason Dewaard, and William Wisser, from HGSE's Informational Technology Department for helping us with our website and communications technologies so that the knowledge we are gaining is useful to those whose work constructs educational opportunity around the world. We also want to thank Helen Page and Rane Bracey-Westbrook from the sponsored research team at HGSE, and Rafael Horta, Kymberly Henry, and Eliza Xenakis from the HGSE finance office, for their support in keeping track of our accounts. We met in various locations around the world to facilitate our discussions about our research, and we want to thank those who facilitated the logistics for these meetings, including Jessica Hallam from the dean's office at DePaul University, Edna Gomez-Fernandez from CIDE, and the staff of the NIE.

We wish to thank our editorial assistants Ashim Shanker and Anastasia Aguiar as well as HEP's copyeditor, David Pritchard, for their valuable work getting the chapters in the necessary form for publication.

There are so many colleagues who have been helpful that we might have missed some in this acknowledgement. To those who played a role in supporting this initiative, we thank you and ask for forgiveness if we forgot to include your name here.

FERNANDO M. REIMERS is the Ford Foundation Professor of Practice in International Education at the Harvard Graduate School of Education. He is also the director of HGSE's Global Education Innovation Initiative and of the International Education Policy Masters Program, a program that prepares global education leaders committed to advancing educational opportunity. His research focuses on the effects of pedagogy, curriculum, and leadership in helping students develop autonomy, agency, and cognitive skills. He has studied the effects of civic education and entrepreneurship education programs in Latin America and the Middle East, and conducted extensive education policy research in the developing world. He leads and teaches in a number of executive leadership education programs at the Harvard Graduate School of Education and has designed global education curricula for the K–12 level. He has authored, coauthored, and edited twelve books and sixty articles and chapters, including *Informed Dialogue: Using Research to Shape Education Policy Around the World* (with Noel McGinn), and *Unequal Schools, Unequal Chances* (as editor).

He is a Fellow of the International Academy of Education, and in 2015 was distinguished with the appointment as the CJ Koh Visiting Professor of Education at the National Institute of Education in Singapore. In 2009 he received an honorary degree from Emerson College for his work promoting human rights and the right to education around the world.

He keeps active engagements in the practice of international education policy and has consulted for many international development organizations, governments, and education organizations, working in many different countries and continents. He is a member of the Massachusetts Board of Higher Education, the vice chair of the board of LASPAU, a member of the Council of Foreign Relations, and a member of the US Commission for UNESCO. In 2015 he was appointed to the steering committee of the Education in Conflict and Crisis group of the United States Agency for International Development, and working with a task force of ministers of education of the Americas, he supported the development of an education strategy to advance the Inter-American Education Agenda agreed at the last Summit of Presidents of the Americas convened by the Organization of American States.

CONNIE K. CHUNG is the research director for the Global Education Innovation Initiative at the Harvard Graduate School of Education. Her field of research is in civic and global citizenship education, and she was involved in a multi-year, multi-site study of education reform and community organizing in the United States, the results of which are published in the book *A Match on Dry Grass: Community Organizing as a Catalyst for School Reform* (Oxford University Press, 2011). She has worked with various nonprofit educational organizations involved in human rights and civic education. She currently serves on the board of two nonprofits, including Aaron's Presents, an organization that offers grants to students in grades 8 and below to encourage positive development in themselves and in their community.

A former public high school English teacher, she was nominated by her students for various teaching awards. She has taught on the topics of nonprofit management and multicultural education and also was a curriculum consultant in the development of a K–12 global education curriculum.

Dr. Chung received her BA in English Literature from Harvard College and her master's degrees in Teaching and Curriculum (1999) and in International Education Policy (2007) from the Harvard Graduate School of Education. Her doctorate is also from the Harvard Graduate School of Education.

PAYAL AGRAWAL is the program co-manager and an assistant faculty member at Piramal Foundation, an Indian organization that offers leadership development training to the principals and teachers from 1,300 government schools in Rajasthan, Gujarat, and Maharashtra. She has co-created and designed the Principal Leadership Development Programme's curriculum for school change and has developed teaching and learning processes and support materials for effective education leadership in various formats. Currently she leads a team working towards identifying teacher competencies required to enable better student learning outcomes. She has worked with fellows and principals, supervising their field work in the program in Gujarat. Ms. Agrawal has received her social work training from the Tata Institute of Social Sciences in India.

CRISTIÁN BELLEI is an associate researcher of the Center for Advanced Research in Education and an assistant professor in the Department of Sociology, both at the University of Chile. He previously worked at the Chilean Ministry of Education and for UNICEF in Chile. His main research areas are educational policy, school effectiveness, and school improvement. He has published extensively about quality and equity in Chilean education. His last two books are *The Great Experiment: Market and Privatization of the Chilean Education* (2015) and *I Learned It at School: How Are School Improvement Processes Achieved?* (2014). Dr. Bellei received his doctorate in education from the Harvard Graduate School of Education.

SERGIO CÁRDENAS is a professor in the Department of Public Administration at the Center for Economics Research and Teaching (CIDE) in Mexico. He has been a lead researcher in several major research projects, including the evaluation of technology-based school interventions, a national study on distance education initiatives, an evaluation of the impact of school uniforms programs, as well as the first large-scale evaluation in Mexico of an early childhood care program for rural and indigenous populations. He is also part of a network comprised of public officials and scholars promoting the use of evidence in the design and implementation of education programs in local education systems in Mexico. Dr. Cárdenas received his doctorate in education from the Harvard Graduate School of Education.

JAHNAVI CONTRACTOR is the program co-manager and assistant faculty member at the Piramal Foundation, an organization that offers leadership development training to the principals and teachers from 1,300 government schools in Rajasthan, Gujarat, and Maharashtra. She has co-created and designed the Principal Leadership Development Programme's curriculum for school change and has developed teaching and learning processes and support materials for effective education leadership in various audiovisual and written formats. Her work has also included identifying places to align education leadership curriculum to student learning outcomes and textbooks. Currently she leads a team working to identify teacher competencies required to enable nonacademic student learning outcomes aligned with the aims of education for the 21st century as enumerated in the National Curriculum Framework of India 2005. Ms. Contractor has a master's degree in elementary education from Tata Institute of Social Sciences.

MONAL JAYARAM is the program director and faculty member at the Piramal Foundation, a leading institute in India that specializes in researching and providing leadership development programs for nation building. She leads a team of professionals who train, research, and develop learning materials for both the three-year Principal Leadership Development Program that offers leadership development to principals in public Indian schools to turn around failing schools and improve student outcomes, as well as the two-year full-time Gandhi Fellowship program that trains young people in leading social change, through which over five hundred fellows from India's best colleges have gone on to nation-building roles. Previously she trained and taught at Pratham Gujarat and at universities in India. She has also published over two hundred articles in a daily newspaper in India. Ms. Jayaram is trained as an art historian and has been practicing in the field of education for twenty years.

EE-LING LOW is an associate professor and the head of strategic planning and academic quality at the National Institute of Education, Singapore. She was the associate dean of teacher education from 2009 to 2013. Together with the NIE senior management team, she helped conceptualize the NIE Strategic Roadmap: Towards 2017 and the Teacher Education for the 21st Century model. She won the Fulbright Advanced Research Scholarship in 2008 through which she was able to spend a year at the Lynch School of Education at Boston College. In 2012 she was awarded the Public Administration Medal (Bronze) by the president of the Republic of Singapore for her dedication and commitment toward furthering the cause of education in Singapore. Dr. Low obtained her PhD in linguistics (acoustic phonetics) from the University of Cambridge, UK, under the university's Overseas Graduate Scholarship award.

LILIANA MORAWIETZ is an assistant researcher at the Center for Advanced Research in Education at the University of Chile and a part-time lecturer in the Department of Anthropology at Alberto Hurtado University. She has performed research on school effectiveness, school improvement, and educational policy; indigenous and intercultural bilingual education issues; and sociocultural issues that help explain students' performance on standardized evaluations. Ms. Morawietz holds a master's degree in oral history from Columbia University.

ADITYA NATRAJ is the founder and director of Piramal Foundation, an institution specializing in leadership development program for nation building in India. Previously he was the director of Pratham in Gujrat for five years, vice president of business development at ProXchange for two years, and a consultant at KPMG for five years. Mr. Natraj is an Ashoka Fellow and an Echoing Green Fellow. He is a qualified chartered accountant, and has a master's degree in economics and an MBA from INSEAD.

OON-SENG TAN is a professor and the director of the National Institute of Education in Singapore. He was previously dean of teacher education at NIE, where he spearheaded the Teacher Education for the 21st Century initiative as a major milestone innovation for teacher education both nationally and internationally. Professor Tan was president of the Asia-Pacific Educational Research Association (2008–2010) and the vice president (Asia and Pacific Rim) of the International Association for Cognitive Education and Psychology (2008–2011). He is currently editor-in-chief of the *Educational Research for Policy and Practice* journal and lead editor of the *Asia Pacific Journal of Education*. Professor Tan was a winner of The Enterprise Challenge (TEC) Innovator Award in Singapore for co-pioneering a project on innovation for the knowledge-based economy. In 2014, he was conferred the Public Administration Medal (Silver) by the president of the Republic of Singapore for his dedication and achievement in the field of education.

YAN WANG is senior specialist and director of the Department for International Exchange at the National Institute of Education Sciences of China. She is concurrently the APEC education network coordinator. Her research focuses on education policy, education reform, and the sociology of education and international studies. She has authored, coauthored, and edited numerous articles, reports, journals, and books on various educational topics. Prior to joining the NIES she was a consultant at the World Bank, and a curriculum specialist and coordinator of international programs at Beijing Education Research Institute. She holds a PhD in education policy, administration, and social sciences from the University of Hong Kong, a master's of educational economics and administration, and a first degree in English literature.

INDEX